MORE THAN A
GAME

DEDICATION

To Dave, Jack and Joe

MORE THAN A
GAME
WHEN SPORT AND HISTORY COLLIDE

JAN STRADLING

CONTENTS

INTRODUCTION

We're bombarded daily by sport in every shape and form, but occasionally a sporting event comes along that has the power to halt a nation in its tracks. These are the heart-stopping moments when the game taking place becomes a symbol of something much greater. Racial injustice, political grandstanding, ancient rivalries, national pride, sexual equality and the aim to win at any cost are just some of the ingredients that make these stories resonate with even the most non-sporting among us.

For many, racial conflict was the defining issue of the twentieth century. When African-American athlete Jesse Owens won four gold medals at what became known as 'Hitler's Olympics', it symbolised a blow to the Third Reich, debunking Hitler's myth of Aryan supremacy. Athletes such as Owens were reluctant heroes, but others used their position to radically change the status quo. None was more active in this sphere than Muhammad Ali, who challenged the American establishment on just about every front, including race, faith and its policy on Vietnam. African-American sprinters Tommie Smith and John Carlos also made good use of their time in the spotlight. Their protest for human rights at the 1968 Olympics is seen by many as a seminal moment in Olympic history. The image of the two men, each raising a black-gloved fist, was a watershed for the civil rights movement and is considered one of the iconic photographs of the twentieth century.

Tennis player Billie Jean King was another pioneer who campaigned for social change. In the 1970s she led the quest for equal prize money for women players at the US Open. Ex-champion and self-proclaimed chauvinist Bobby Riggs believed that women were inferior players and so deserved less money, and challenged her to a match. Sensationally billed as the 'Battle of the Sexes', this was never merely a tennis match. Had she lost, Billie Jean and her contemporaries had no doubt it would have set the women's movement back 50 years and been a worldwide blow to women's self-esteem.

For decades, sport has been used as a tool for political leverage. When South Africa's rugby team, the Springboks, toured New Zealand in 1981, their visit resulted in an unprecedented period of civil unrest. By hosting the Springboks,

OPPOSITE: Argentinian captain Diego Maradona holds aloft the 1986 World Cup trophy. He claimed one of his two goals was scored by the 'hand of god'.

7

many New Zealanders believed they would be seen to be supporting the South African apartheid system. The almost worldwide sporting boycott of South Africa was viewed by many as the single most potent weapon against apartheid. Years later, at the 1995 Rugby World Cup final in South Africa, Nelson Mandela demonstrated this understanding of the power of sport when he stunned spectators by donning a Springboks jersey, one of the most hated symbols of apartheid. In doing so, he shared his dreams for a unified South Africa. The shocked silence, followed by rapturous applause, was powerful proof that sport can erase in a moment a long history of hatred.

The Olympics might officially be a politics-free zone, but is in fact one of the most politically charged arenas in the world. For years, the Soviet Union and America used sport as a weapon of the Cold War as they fought to top the Olympic medal tally. The triumph of an inexperienced US ice hockey team over the much-favoured Russians during the 1980 Winter Olympics had far-reaching effects. The win restored American national pride and was seen as a victory over the communist system.

Ancient rivalries and national pride can invoke some deep-seated hostilities. To represent your country in sport is one of the greatest honours, but on many occasions the skirmish waged on the field is indicative of a larger and bloodier battle. George Orwell famously said, 'Serious sport is war minus the shooting.' In the world of cricket, the bodyline series almost destroyed diplomatic relations between England and Australia. When the English introduced a new style of bowling in which the ball targeted the batsman's body, there was more at stake than bad sportsmanship. It was a reflection of the complexity of colonial relationships as the mother country tried to reassert control over a renegade colony.

Athletes representing their country have often felt the 'call to duty'. In the 1986 FIFA World Cup, Argentinian player Diego Maradona scored off an illegal handball against England and swore that 'the hand of God' had intervened. It was no coincidence that this was the first time the two countries had faced each other since going to war over the Falkland Islands. For the Argentineans this victory restored a piece of national pride, but for the English, it was a bitter pill to swallow.

A fair playing field is a crucial part of any sporting event. When the game falls into disrepute and rules are broken, spectators may question what there is left to trust. When a gambling syndicate enticed eight baseball players from the

Chicago White Sox to throw the World Series against the Cincinnati Reds, the scandal was seen to represent the breakdown of the 'all-American' way of life, and the loss of traditional values. Similar questions are being asked today as drug scandals have become a regular occurrence and outstanding individual sporting achievements are often tainted by suspicion.

As the twenty-first century unfolds, new social and political battles will find their way into sporting arenas. Heroes will emerge, epic journeys will be taken and fresh ground will be broken as sport and the zeitgeist become one and the same. These hair-raising, spine-tingling moments are part of our history; the moments when, together, we witness something much more than a game.

WARNING: Aboriginal and Torres Strait Islander readers are warned that *More Than a Game* contains images of deceased persons in Chapter 1, 'The First Eleven'.

Pride and Prejudice

BACKGROUND:	British Empire exercising its might over the Dominions
EVENT:	Australian Aboriginal cricket team in England, 1868
OPPONENTS:	Australia v England
ARENA:	The cricket pitches of England

The First Eleven

ENGLAND, 1868

Nothing of interest comes from Australia except gold nuggets and black cricketers. — *DAILY TELEGRAPH,* LONDON

PREVIOUS PAGE: Jesse Owens winning the 100 metres at the 1936 Berlin Olympics. He won four gold medals at the Games, destroying Hitler's myth of Aryan supremacy.

OPPOSITE: Aboriginal cricketers alongside the Melbourne Cricket Ground Pavilion, c.1867.

In 1868 Australia's first international cricket team, comprising 13 Aboriginal players, set off for England. They departed without ceremony—the men had to be smuggled aboard a ship to escape the jurisdiction of the Central Board for Protection of Aborigines, which controlled the movement of Aboriginal people within the state of Victoria. After four long months at sea, the team landed in an unfamiliar country and took on the mighty colonial power in the quintessentially English game of cricket. Their gruelling schedule of 47 two-day games meant that they played on 100 of the 150 days they were in the country. After each match, the Aboriginal players entertained the English crowds with athletic demonstrations, including distance throwing using cricket balls, a 100-yard backwards sprint and boomerang- and spear-throwing. Despite being relative novices in the sport, the Australian team won an impressive 14 games, drew 19 and lost only 14. Of the 14 players, two were sent home with serious illnesses and another died tragically on the tour. One player stood out above all the others—Johnny Mullagh bowled 1877 overs, 831 of which were maidens. He took 245 wickets at an average of ten runs each, and made 1698 runs himself, proving to be one of the greatest cricketing talents of the time.

State of the Nation

Since its colonisation in 1788, Australia had been rife with racial tensions. Thousands of Aborigines had been massacred as the Europeans stole their land to set up farms and towns. Others were removed from their families and placed in institutions and missions where they were 'converted' to Christianity. When gold was discovered near Ballarat, Victoria, in 1851, the transportation of convicts ceased and, instead, free travel was given to potential gold miners. The resulting gold rush resulted in an influx of Chinese immigrants and an outbreak of race-related attacks. In northern Queensland the practice of 'blackbirding' became common, whereby Polynesian and Melanesian people were abducted from islands in the South Pacific and forced to work on the sugar-cane farms. In addition, anti-Irish sentiment reached an all-time high following the attempted assassination of Prince Alfred, Duke of Edinburgh, in 1868 in Sydney by Irishman Henry James O'Farrell. It was the first time a member of the Royal Family had visited Australia, and the event caused great embarrassment for the colonists. It was during this year that the Aboriginal cricket team toured England.

Start of Play

An English cricket tour of Australia in 1861–62 led to the formation of cricket clubs across the country, and in the state of Victoria it became common for Aboriginal stockmen to play against the white station owners. One of these stations was Pine Hill, situated between Edenhope and Harrow in the state's Western District. When the local team of Aborigines displayed particular skill on the cricket field, the town of Edenhope decided to sponsor them and employed Thomas W. Wills, one of Australia's top players, as their coach.

Before long the team received an invitation to play at the Melbourne Cricket Club in a match scheduled for Boxing Day, 1867. The event attracted a crowd of 8000 spectators, but the Aboriginal players were so nervous that they lost the match by lunchtime of the second day. However, two of them, Johnny Mullagh and Johnny Cuzens, impressed the state selectors enough to be picked to represent Victoria against New South Wales, becoming the first Aborigines to win representative selection. Johnny Mullagh had received lessons on how to bowl round-arm, and was already exhibiting extraordinary skills which attracted widespread attention.

In the crowd sat a self-styled entrepreneur, Captain William Gurnett, who came up with the idea of taking the team on a tour to Sydney and subsequently raising enough funds to take them much further afield, on a tour of England. Gurnett promised bonuses for all the players and a profit for Wills and team manager William Hayman, and his proposal was accepted. However, he turned out to be a conman and, after putting the players through an exhausting schedule of matches throughout New South Wales, he embezzled part of the funds and left the team stranded in Sydney.

Charles Lawrence, an English cricketer who had stayed in Australia as a coach after the 1861–62 tour, stepped in to help pay for the players' return journey. The tour of England was cancelled, and Wills and Hayman managed to get the team back to Victoria. However, in the unfamiliar urban environment some of the players had picked up diseases introduced by white society. By the time they reached home, four players had died and three others were seriously ill. Edenhope lost its faith in Thomas Wills, partly due to reports of his heavy drinking on tour, and Lawrence took over as coach of the remaining players.

The idea of the team touring England still held great appeal. Three months later, Lawrence found financial backing from Sydney cricket coach and former mayor George Smith and one W. G. Graham, and a second attempt was made. A tour by Aboriginal players suited the agendas of both the Australian colonists and their mother country. The idea of exhibiting evidence of 'newly civilised' indigenous people appealed to these Victorian-era Anglo-Saxon societies looking to justify their colonial actions. As the *Ballarat Star* said in 1867, 'The order of civilization in the Christian sense seems to be first to make savages men, and then to make them Christians ...To convert the savage into sheep shearers was something, but it seems more to make him into a smart cricketer.'

Smuggled to England

Lawrence chose his team and gave the players Anglicised names to make it easier for the English crowd. Johnny Mullagh, Johnny Cuzens, Harry Bullocky, Charley Dumas, Peter, Dick-a-Dick, Jimmy Mosquito, Jim Crow, Twopenny, King Cole,

Sundown, Tiger and Tommy Red Cap made up a thirteen-member squad which played some matches throughout Victoria in preparation for the crossing to England. Dressed in red Garibaldi shirts with diagonal blue sashes, white flannel trousers and individually coloured caps to help the English identify them, these men who had never before left Australian shores now set off for the country responsible for destroying their culture and robbing them of their land.

However, just before the team was due to leave for England, the Victorian government (through its recently established Central Board for the Protection of Aborigines) stepped in and attempted to stop the tour. The idea of three white men taking 14 Aborigines overseas on a moneymaking venture rang alarm bells. Lawrence decided to sidestep the board. While the team was in Victoria they were duty bound to abide by the board's wishes, but moving over the state border into New South Wales would take them out of the board's jurisdiction. On 8 February 1868, under the pretence of a fishing trip, the team was smuggled out of Australia from Sydney on a ship called the *Parramatta*. Three months later, on 13 May, the ship docked in Gravesend, England.

Bats and Boomerangs

Attitudes towards the team varied, yet players possessed curiosity value for the English who flocked to see them play. The first match was on 25–26 May against Surrey at The Oval in London, and it attracted 20,000 spectators. Australia's first international eleven lost the match by an innings and seven runs, but judging by local press at the time people hadn't come merely to watch the cricketing contest. The *Times* reported that 'Their hair and beards are long and wiry, their skins vary in shades of blackness, and most of them have broadly expanded nostrils ... they are perfectly civilized and are quite familiar with the English language.'

The *Daily Telegraph* remarked, 'It is highly interesting and curious, to see mixed in a friendly game on the most historically Saxon part of our island, representatives of two races so far removed from each other as the modern Englishman and the Aboriginal Australian. Although several of them are native bushmen, and all are as black as night, these Indian fellows are to all intents and purposes, clothed and in their right minds.'

Despite the newspapers' preoccupation with their appearance, the British public could not help being impressed by the team's athletic ability. It wasn't long before the skills of Mullagh were singled out. 'I have never bowled to a better batsman,' said English fast bowler George Tarrant.

The *Manchester Chronicle* reported on the way the Aborigines entertained the crowd after the match, saying they gave 'a highly interesting exhibition of skill and dexterity in the use of the boomerang and throwing spears. The eccentric aerial flights of the boomerang and its manipulation by the blacks, created unlimited curiosity and wonderment to the beholders.'

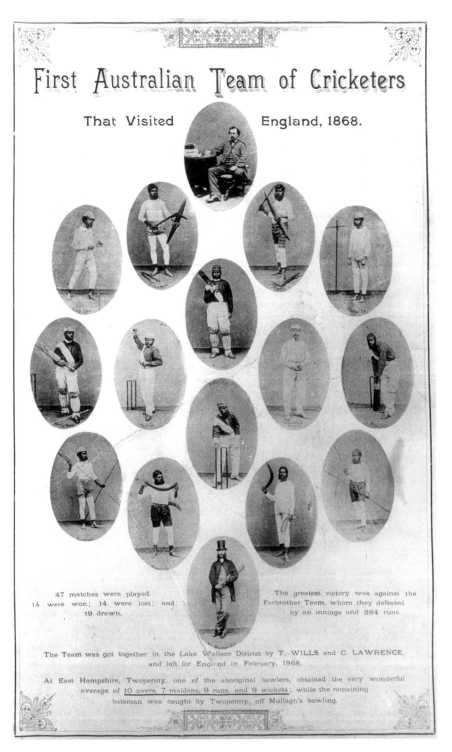

First Australian Team of Cricketers

That Visited England, 1868.

47 matches were played. 14 were won; 14 were lost; and 19 drawn.

The greatest victory was against the Farbrother Team, whom they defeated by an innings and 284 runs.

The Team was got together in the Lake Wallace District by T. WILLS and C. LAWRENCE, and left for England in February, 1868.

At East Hampshire, Twopenny, one of the aboriginal bowlers, obtained the very wonderful average of 10 overs, 7 maidens, 9 runs, and 9 wickets; while the remaining batsman was caught by Twopenny, off Mullagh's bowling.

LEFT: The Aboriginal team of 1868 was the first Australian cricket side to visit England.

LEFT: The Aboriginal team
in England in 1868, is with
C. Lawrence who chose the
players and managed the team.

Dick-a-Dick proved particularly popular when he invited spectators to pay a shilling to try to hit him with a cricket ball. Volunteers would stand ten paces away and pelt him with balls, which he deflected with a parrying shield. Rarely did one find its mark.

The Australians versus the Aristocracy

The Marylebone Cricket Club, which selects and manages the England national team, initially banned the visitors from playing at Lords, the home of cricket. However, the decision was later reversed and a match rich in incongruity ensued. On 12 June 1868, the Australian First Eleven took the field in a two-day game against the British aristocracy. The MCC batted first, and Mullagh bowled the Earl of Coventry, knocking out his off stump. England's topscorer in a team which included Viscount Downe and Lieutenant-Colonel F. H. Bathurst was Robert Fitzgerald, who managed 50 runs. At the close of the first innings, England had scored 164, with Mullagh taking 5 for 82 off 45 overs. Proving that they could bat as well as bowl, the First Eleven outscored the English with a first innings total of 185, in which Mullagh topscored with 75.

The next day Johnny Cuzens delighted the spectators with a bowling performance of 6 for 65 in the MCC second innings—but it wasn't enough to secure the match and the MCC won by 55 runs. While the British public applauded the visitors, the *Times*, a bastion of conservative England, referred to the occasion as 'a travestie upon cricketing at Lord's', and described the players as 'the conquered natives of a convict colony'.

Unfortunately, the bad weather and the inevitable stresses and strains of the trip proved too much for one player. On 24 June, King Cole died from tuberculosis, no doubt weakened by the gruelling schedule. His body was not taken home to Australia, instead being buried in Bethnal Green Cemetery, with a single eucalyptus tree marking his grave. Two other players, Sundown and Jim Crow, became seriously ill and were forced to return to Australia, leaving the remaining players to carry on the tour.

By the end of the tour, two of the players had taken over 350 wickets and scored over 3000 runs between them. Cuzens made 1364 runs at a very respectable average for those days of 18.94; he also took 113 wickets at an average of 11.38. Johnny Mullagh had shown himself to be the equal of any of the English players.

The team left with the English press singing their praises. *Sporting Life* spoke for them all when it remarked that 'No eleven has in one season ever played so many matches so successfully—never playing less than two matches in each week, and frequently three, bearing an amount of fatigue that now seems incredible.'

The *Sheffield Telegraph* called the tour 'the event of the century', and *Reynolds News* described the games as marking 'a new epoch in the history of cricket'.

A Glitch in Time

For the Aboriginal players, however, that new epoch never arrived. The tour had taken place during a window of opportunity which would not present itself again for another century. Having been applauded by English audiences, the team returned to Australia without fanfare, and the men resumed their status as non-citizens. By the time the team arrived back in Sydney in February 1869, official policy regarding Aboriginal people was changing. By November of that year, the Victorian government had passed legislation giving the state greater power over where and how Aborigines lived. There was a social consensus that Aboriginal people were dying out, and many were moved onto reserves by way of 'protection'. It was now illegal to move Aborigines from Victoria without the board's authority. Despite the First Eleven's achievements, these developments brought a sad end to their cricketing career. To add insult to injury, the players were not paid, nor did they receive the bonus they had been promised.

However, many of the cricketers themselves appeared to think they had been fairly treated and were happy to have had the opportunity of an experience they would never forget. Cuzens and Mullagh went on to play for the Melbourne Cricket Club in the 1869–70 season, but then returned to western Victoria. Cuzens died from dysentery in 1871, aged only 26. Mullagh, undoubtedly one of the greatest players of his day, died in 1891 and was laid to rest in a cemetery overlooking the Harrow cricket ground, along with his favourite cricket bat and cricket stumps. Dick-a-Dick also moved back to the Western District to work as a drover. He disliked his name and later changed it to Kennedy.

Most of the players died young, or simply disappeared from public record, displaced by a white society which failed to recognise their cultural identity in the push to introduce them to 'civilisation'. By the early 1900s many Aboriginal people had lost their traditional way of life and were dependent on the settlers, who considered them an inconvenience. At the time of Australia's Federation in 1901, Aboriginal people were denied citizenship, and Australians adopted an assimilation policy—Aboriginals were expected to fit into white society.

It is thought that the First Eleven's tour of England did much to develop the game of cricket in Australia, particularly in bowling. Before the tour, most Australian bowlers used an underarm action. In England, Mullagh and Cuzens started to use a new windmill-type bowling technique employed by English fast bowlers such as George Tarrant. When they returned, they influenced the game by introducing the new style of overarm, which has become standard today.

However, it would be another 120 years before an Aboriginal team would tour England again, and 130 years before a player of Aboriginal heritage (Jason Gillespie) would be selected to represent Australia. The First Eleven remain an inspiration to many Aborigines, and their extraordinary achievements in the English summer of 1868 are a source of pride for all Australians.

FOR THE RECORD

▶ Jemmy Tarpot could run the 100-yard backwards sprint in 14 seconds.

▶ In 1835, a player called Shiney became the first Aboriginal cricketer on record. He played for Hobart Town, Tasmania.

▶ Tom Wills is credited with being one of the founders and inventors of Australian Rules Football.

▶ Several Aboriginal players attempted to follow in the footsteps of the First Eleven. Alec Henry represented Queensland in 1901 and was tipped to play for Australia against a touring English team. When an umpire judged that his bowling action was illegal due to throwing, Henry complained and was forcibly relocated from Brisbane, charged with 'defying authority'. Bowler Eddie Gilbert also played for Queensland and was renowned for bowling Donald Bradman for a duck in 1931. When the Australian public demanded that he be selected for a test against South Africa, Gilbert was also no-balled for an illegal bowling action.

BACKGROUND:	White v black
EVENT:	World heavyweight boxing championship
OPPONENTS:	Jim Jeffries v Jack Johnson
ARENA:	Reno, Nevada

The Great White Hope v The Black Menace

RENO, USA, 1910

I am going in to this fight for the sole purpose of proving that a white man is better than a Negro. **— JIM JEFFRIES**

OPPOSITE: Jack Johnson (right) takes on Jim Jeffries, the 'Great White Hope', in Reno in 1910.

THE YEAR WAS 1910

▶ George V became king of the United Kingdom after the death of his father, Edward VII.

▶ The British pound was phased out in Australia when the national treasury was given authority to issue currency.

▶ The Earth passed through the tail of Halley's Comet.

▶ Japan annexed Korea.

▶ Collingwood beat Carlton in an ill-tempered grand final to win Australia's Victorian Football League Premiership.

▶ In rugby union, France joined the Home Nations Championship, marking the birth of the Five Nations.

▶ The Newtown Jets won a closely fought New South Wales Rugby League Premiership in only the third season since the League was formed.

▶ Kent continued to dominate the English County Cricket Championship, winning the title for the second successive year.

On 26 December 1908, white society around the globe went into shock upon hearing the news that the African-American boxer Jack Johnson had defeated the Canadian boxer Tommy Burns to become the first black heavyweight champion of the world. A cry went up for the ex-world heavyweight champion James Jeffries to come out of retirement and teach 'the black menace' a lesson. Whites of all political and religious persuasions were appalled by Johnson. Not only did he claim to be the strongest man in the world, he was also breaking taboos by flaunting his relationships with white women. At a time when racial segregation was still deeply ingrained in American culture and public life, the Jeffries v Johnson fight would have far-reaching consequences, resulting in race riots and deaths throughout the United States. But it wasn't only about race; this was a fight about power, and one man's struggle for the freedom to live as he wished.

State of the Nation

In 1865, the Thirteenth Amendment to the US Constitution had officially abolished slavery. However, the federal government's attempts to ensure civil rights for all were unsuccessful and many African-Americans found themselves in limbo, neither slaves nor free. Most lived in Southern states, where a combination of intimidation and literacy requirements kept them disenfranchised. After 1865, many states enacted 'Jim Crow' laws which required segregation of the races in public places.

The social Darwinism of the nineteenth century had conditioned whites to believe that their position of dominance in world affairs meant they belonged to an inherently superior race. In the South of the United States, this had been used as a moral justification for the retention of slavery up until the end of the Civil War in 1865. The abolition of slavery saw this perceived superiority manifest itself in other ways. White America was fearful of African-American success in sporting or social ventures, as that would invalidate their assigned position in the racial hierarchy.

This fearfulness was particularly prevalent in white attitudes to interracial sexual relations. Between 1901 and 1908, 754 African-Americans met their deaths through lynching, and the reason most commonly given was that they had 'forgotten their place' and attempted the 'rape' of white women—revealing the depth of abhorrence that many white males had for the notion of an African-American man sleeping with a white woman.

The Galveston Giant

Jack Johnson was born John Arthur Johnson in Galveston, Texas, in 1878, the second of six children of Henry and Tiny Johnson. His parents had been slaves but in later years his father became a school janitor and his mother worked as a laundress to help support the family. Desperate to escape the underpaid grind of cotton-picking, Johnson saw boxing as his way out.

He was a natural boxer who got into the sport by way of 'battles royal'— exploitative spectacles in which three or more young African-Americans, often blindfolded, would entertain white crowds by punching each other until the last youth standing collected some small change from the onlookers. Johnson graduated from these bouts and started travelling around the country to take on other fighters for increasing amounts of money. His height—he was six foot one—soon earned him the nickname 'the Galveston Giant', but that didn't stop him from suffering his first loss by a knockout, handed to him in his home town in February 1901 by experienced Jewish heavyweight Joe Choynski. Boxing was still illegal in Texas at the time, and the two fighters were arrested after the bout and ended up sharing a jail cell for a month. Choynski used the time to tutor Johnson in the many tricks of the trade that he had picked up, and he helped the young fighter add a valuable new dimension to his strategy.

Johnson adopted a different style of boxing when he came out of prison. It was based on soaking up the pressure and waiting patiently for his opponent to make a mistake, then going in for a lethal strike. He became known for his counterpunches and his ability to absorb heavy punishment. The method won him fights; he was fast on his feet and had incredible strength. There were no rules being broken, but this defensive style was attacked in the white press (already highly suspicious of African-American athletes) for being lazy, cowardly and 'devious'. Interestingly, back in the mid-1890s, the same watchful, patient style had earned white heavyweight champion 'Gentleman' Jim Corbett the admiration of those very newspapers.

Although African-Americans were allowed to box, and some held titles in lighter divisions, they had never competed for the heavyweight title, as whites simply refused to fight them. For years Johnson chased the world heavyweight champion Jim Jeffries, trying to get a shot at his crown, but Jeffries continually refused. In 1905 the champion retired, saying there were no more worthy opponents to fight.

When Tommy Burns became champion in 1906, Johnson gave him the same treatment and followed him all over the world, demanding a title fight. By this time, it was impossible not to notice Johnson's boxing skills and public pressure started to mount. King Edward VII, a keen student of boxing, was said to have dismissed Burns as a mere bluffer because he wouldn't fight Johnson. Many commentators hinted that Burns did not deserve to be champion, because he had won the title without having to face Jim Jeffries.

When an Australian promoter offered US$30,000 for Burns to fight Johnson in New South Wales, Burns had run out of excuses. On 26 December 1908, Johnson defeated Burns at the old Sydney Stadium in Rushcutters Bay, Sydney.

SEGREGATION LAWS

The name 'Jim Crow' comes from a character of uncertain origin who was a parody of African-Americans. The Supreme Court ruled in *Plessy v Ferguson* (1896) that it was constitutional to enforce 'separate but equal' segregated facilities. This ruling upheld the Jim Crow laws, legalising racial discrimination in the United States and standing for over 60 years until overturned by the Civil Rights Act of 1964.

MORE ON JOHNSON

▶ Johnson was romantically linked with many prominent white women, including the alleged spy Mata Hari.

▶ In 1920 Johnson opened a nightclub in Harlem that would eventually become the Cotton Club.

▶ In 2009 Senator John McCain moved for a presidential pardon for Jack Johnson.

It was a humiliating fight in which Johnson was clearly the better fighter. He smiled and taunted Burns throughout every round. In the fourteenth, the police stepped in to stop the fight as a knockout was imminent and they did not want such a moment to be caught on film. As Burns slumped to the canvas, Johnson had achieved his dream and was the first African-American to become the heavyweight champion of the world.

While a resounding victory for his race, Johnson's title win was only the first round in a continuing struggle. On his return to America he met with almost universal hostility, even in black quarters. The prejudice against interracial couplings was strong on both sides of the colour bar, and many African-Americans felt that Johnson's flashy and provocative behaviour was not helping their cause. However, Johnson didn't care about public opinion. He continued to bed white women, drive fast cars and live life to the full.

The Search for the Great White Hope

In the international boxing establishment, the search began in earnest for a white champion who could reaffirm the superiority of the Caucasian race. It became known as the quest for the 'Great White Hope', but a suitable candidate did not immediately emerge. Johnson successfully defended his title against white boxers five times in as many months in 1909, and all eyes turned to Jim Jeffries to come out of retirement. Johnson wanted to fight Jeffries to prove that he was the true champion, but after six quiet years tucked away on his alfalfa farm Jeffries was reluctant. He had fought African-American boxers in the past, before winning his title, but he knew that an interracial title bout in America would generate a lot of unwelcome controversy.

Johnson wasn't someone to give up easily. He courted the mounting press campaign to force Jeffries out of hiding. With the pressure building, in stepped promoter George Lewis 'Tex' Rickard, a man who was said to be capable of persuading a Scotsman to part with his life savings to watch a game of marbles. Rickard finally persuaded Jeffries to accept the challenge by offering him a share in a previously unheard-of prize purse of US$101,000, plus movie rights.

In his prime, Jeffries was considered the fastest man of his size in boxing history. He had a powerful left and had never lost a fight. But when Jeffries accepted Rickard's invitation to fight Johnson, he had an uphill battle ahead of him. Having been out of the ring for six years, he was 100 pounds (45 kg) over his former fighting weight of 200 pounds, and he had to prepare for a gruelling contest for which 45 rounds of 3 minutes each had been scheduled.

At first the fight was booked to take place in San Francisco, but two weeks prior to the event the Governor of California cancelled it. Under pressure from anti-boxing campaigners, he said it would be 'demoralising to the youth of our state'.

Desert Heat

Reno, Nevada was finally decided upon as the fight venue. It had excellent access by rail but there was just one thing missing—a stadium. This was no impediment to Rickard, who was by this time billing the fight as 'the Battle of the Century' and was determined to build a stadium appropriate for the upcoming gladiatorial showdown. For the first time in history, a stadium was built for a single sporting event. The fight was scheduled for Independence Day, 4 July 1910. An invitation went out to the President of the United States, William Howard Taft, to referee the match. But this event was too much of a political hot potato for the President and he turned the offer down. The *Chicago Tribune* described the upcoming bout as 'a contest between the white man's hope and the black peril'.

While the stadium was being built both boxers arrived in Reno to acclimatise and prepare for the fight. Jeffries had an all-star squad of trainers—including 'Gentleman' Jim Corbett, Johnson's former prison cellmate Joe Choynski, and former wrestling champion William Muldoon—who had all arrived to do their bit for the white race. The former champion arrived in Reno on 23 June and got to work. Neither boxer had previously fought more than 25 rounds. At one stage, Jeffries's training regime was so harsh that he nearly pulled out.

The only person in Reno who seemed calm was Johnson. During his training he flaunted his relationship with his white Brooklyn society girlfriend Etta Duryea, sending a clear message that he would live as he wished. Commenting on the boxer's relaxed attitude, the *Chicago Tribune* reached its own conclusions: 'As essentially African, Johnson feels no deeper than the moment, sees no further than his nose and is incapable of anticipation.'

Ringside in Reno

Fight day, Monday 4 July 1910, was no ordinary Independence Day holiday. The country was at fever pitch. Over 15,000 paying spectators gathered in the new stadium for the fight, along with many gatecrashers. Telegraph offices all across the nation were inundated with people trying to get news of the fight. In Chicago, spectators paid to watch electronic figures on a large screen act out movements relayed by telegraph operators and in London on 5 July, crowds gathered around newspaper offices in Fleet Street to hear the earliest reports—as many as 3000 people in one area at a time.

In Reno itself, the racial tension at the stadium was coming to boiling point under the hot desert sun. By midday it was nearly 40° Celsius (101° Fahrenheit) and the fight promoters were appealing to the predominantly white crowd's baser instincts. The ringside band started playing 'All Coons Look Alike to Me' and the spectators were incited to take up a chant of 'Kill the nigger!'

Johnson stepped into the ring first, to the jeers of the crowd.

ABOVE: Johnson (right) knocks Jeffries down in the fifteenth round, not long before being declared the winner. Following Johnson's victory, anti-black violence broke out across the country.

More than 25,000 people gathered to watch the fight and as I looked about me and scanned the sea of white faces I felt the auspiciousness of the occasion. Few men of my own race were among the spectators. I realised my victory in the event meant more than on any previous occasion. The honour of my race was at stake.

Jeffries stepped into the ring and his supporters went wild. Like Johnson, he carried the weight of his race on his shoulders and the retired boxer was feeling the full burden of that collective expectation.

After a delay of over an hour to allow the huge crowd to find their way into the stadium, the fight commenced at 2.45 pm with Tex Rickard officiating as referee. Jeffries set the tone by refusing to shake hands. Johnson held his ground as Jeffries tried to push and shove him around the ring. For several rounds, Jeffries tried to force Johnson to make a move but the Galveston Giant maintained the defensive style for which he was famous. Johnson was just too good. His hands were fast, he was swift on his feet and he was much sharper than the retired boxer. Throughout the contest Johnson taunted Jeffries with 'Mr Jeffries, where is your punch?' By the twelfth round, Corbett, who had been screaming insults at

Johnson from Jeffries's corner in an attempt to rattle him, was almost apoplectic. By the end of the fourteenth round, Jeffries had a broken nose and his challenge was falling apart.

Finally, in the fifteenth round, after an hour of fighting, Johnson took charge of the action and knocked Jeffries down onto the bottom rope. Jeffries made an attempt to get back to his feet as referee Rickard tried to hold Johnson back, but the champion knocked Jeffries down a second time, pushing him through the ropes of the ring. Trainers and spectators rushed in to haul Jeffries back up to face Johnson, only to see him be battered across the ring and hit the ground for a third time. The crowd's earlier shouts of encouragement had now changed to pity and fear: 'Don't let the negro knock him out!'

A towel was thrown in which the referee didn't see, and it was only when one of Jeffries's seconds stepped into the ring that the count stopped at seven and Johnson was declared the winner. As Johnson raised his arms in victory, the crowd was already silently filing out of the stadium. Jeffries had lost for the first time in his career and Johnson was the undisputed champion.

Johnson took home a prize bag of over US$100,000 and silenced the press. Jeffries claimed to have got only $10,000 from the fight, saying, 'It was a small return for trying to recover the honour of the Nordic race', but had actually received over $70,000. At one point, he also claimed that he had been doped but later relented, saying, 'I could never have whipped Jack Johnson at my best. I couldn't have hit him. No, I couldn't have reached him in a thousand years.'

**My Lord,
What a Morning
O my Lord
What a morning,
O my Lord,
What a feeling,
When Jack
Johnson
Turned Jim
Jeffries'
Snow-white face
to the ceiling.**

– WILLIAM WARING CUNEY

Out for the Count

The press had made the fight into a race war and the American public reacted accordingly. While African-Americans all over America dared to party, whites were looking to teach them a lesson. Riots broke out that night in 50 cities across 25 states, with every Southern state reporting disturbances. In Roanoke, Virginia, white mobs roamed the streets victimising any African-American person they came across. In Houston, Texas, Charles Williams was another black victim—he was celebrating the outcome of the fight when a white man slashed his throat from ear to ear.

There was a gun battle in Uvaldia, Georgia. In Atlanta, Georgia, police had to call mounted officers to prevent race riots turning to civil war.

African-Americans were the perpetrators of violence too, for example when preventing whites from entering African-American communities. In Tyler, Texas, one African-American was killed and three injured when two African-American groups attacked each other, one accusing the other of supporting Jeffries. In Kentucky, a white newsboy was attacked for shouting 'Extra! All about the nigger's victory.'

The North was also affected. There were riots in Washington, Boston, Kansas and St Louis. The *New York Herald* reported: 'In Eighth Avenue between 37th and 39th Streets more than 3,000 whites gathered and all the Negroes that appeared were kicked and beaten.' And according to the *New York Times*, 'Between 9th and 11th Streets a wounded negro was taken to the West 37th Street police station on an average of one every 15 minutes.' The number of fatalities which occurred across America on that Independence Day evening is still unknown.

The white press went to town, with most reports blaming Johnson for the violence. The *Texas El Paso Times* stated that 'the conduct of the negro is becoming more intolerable'. Other papers characterised the whole event as a catastrophe, with journalist Rex Beach proclaiming 'Today saw a tragedy. A remarkable, crushing, anticlimax has happened and we are dazed.' It was viewed as 'a calamity worse to this country than the San Francisco earthquake'. The *Washington Times* directed some of the blame at Jeffries for getting into the fight and African-American leaders were reserved in their comments, saying that Johnson's involvement was always going to provoke violence.

Many states banned footage of the fight. Congress went further, outlawing the interstate transfer of boxing films to make sure that no-one outside Nevada got to see the ignominy of a white man lying at an African-American man's feet. The ban angered African-American journalists—the *Washington Bee* wrote, 'The white man cannot expect always to be in the front rank without competition.'

Johnson's pre-bout notoriety ensured that the finger of blame for the carnage was often pointed squarely at him, and commentators accused him of being a public menace for his part in provoking the riots. In a way, the violence marked the beginning of the end of his career. His white conservative enemies found they could use his flamboyant lifestyle to knock him out of the ring more effectively than any of his opponents ever had. In 1913 he was accused of violating the White-Slave Traffic Act of 1910 (known as the Mann Act), which had been passed to prevent the transportation of women over state or national borders 'for the purpose of prostitution, debauchery, or for any other immoral purpose'. Despite the women in question being his fiancé, he was convicted by an all-white jury and sentenced to a year and a day in prison.

While on bail, Johnson fled the country and spent several years as a fugitive in Europe. Overall, he successfully defended his title in four more bouts, three of them fought while he was in exile from the United States. In 1914 he lost his title to Jess Willard in Cuba. He returned to the US in 1920, surrendered to authorities and served his time in prison. In 1946, Johnson died in a car crash. It was said that he had been refused service at a segregated lunch counter and had driven away furious at the racist slur. His obituary in the *New York Times* called him 'one of the craftiest boxers known to the ring, recognized by many as one of the five outstanding heavyweight champions of all time'.

'Ghost in the house!'

Until the thirties the boxing world was dominated by white champions such as Jack Dempsey. In 1937, African-American boxer Joe Louis became only the second African-American heavyweight champion when he thrashed Jim Braddock for the title. Louis was the first African-American athlete to be accepted by white society, a man who was seen as being capable of 'acting white' and who publicly declared that he would 'never disgrace the race'. Subsequently, upcoming athletes were warned not to boast the way Jack Johnson had done, and to always 'act white'. Johnson himself was furious at the subservience implied in this approach. He also took offence at the Louis camp's attempts to distance itself from him and from his reputation, and he even offered to help train Braddock for his title bout with Louis (though the offer was not taken up).

Many years later, a similarly outspoken African-American boxer emerged on the scene, one who also fought for the freedom to be an individual. Muhammad Ali often referred to Johnson, and held him up as a role model. 'I grew to love the Jack Johnson image,' he said. 'I wanted to be rough, tough, arrogant, the nigger white folks didn't like.' During a number of Ali's major fights, his cornerman Drew 'Bundini' Brown was heard to urge him on by shouting to him, 'Ghost in the house! Jack Johnson's here! Ghost in the house!'

FOR THE RECORD

Jack Johnson's
boxing record

Bouts:	123
Won:	77
Lost:	13
Drew:	14
No decisions:	19
Knockouts:	48

BACKGROUND:	Against fascism
EVENT:	To destroy Nazi claims of Aryan superiority
OPPONENTS:	Jesse Owens v Adolf Hitler
ARENA:	1936 Summer Olympics, Berlin

A Demonstration of Aryan Supremacy

BERLIN, GERMANY, 1936

If I could just win those gold medals, I said to myself, the Hitlers of the world would have no more meaning for me. For anyone, maybe. — **JESSE OWENS**

OPPOSITE: Jesse Owens makes his winning long jump, winning his second gold medal for the US and setting an Olympic record that would stand for 20 years.

THE YEAR WAS 1936

▶ The Spanish Civil War began after General Franco's troops rose up against the legal Republic.

▶ Germany allied with Japan by signing the Anti-Comintern Pact.

▶ Edward VIII succeeded his father, George V, as King of the United Kingdom before abdicating the throne. His brother Albert became King George VI.

▶ Construction of the Hoover Dam was completed on the Colorado River.

▶ 'The Phantom', the first superhero to wear a skin-tight costume and mask, made his first appearance in US newspapers.

▶ The British Broadcasting Corporation launched the first regular high-definition television service.

▶ Stress was first recognised as a medical condition.

▶ An Adelaide to Brisbane air race was held to celebrate South Australia's centenary.

▶ The first edition of *Life* magazine was published.

As fascism spread throughout Europe, the political spotlight fell on the 1936 Berlin Olympics. Adolf Hitler, the leader of Germany's Third Reich, was keen to promote the myth of Aryan superiority, and used Olympic propaganda to promote the ideal 'master race' as blonde and blue-eyed, with chiselled features and athletic prowess. As German anti-Semitism forced Jews out of the public arena and racism took hold, the United States and other countries questioned the validity of holding the games in a country whose core values represented the antithesis of the Olympic spirit. Despite early threats to boycott the Olympics, the US eventually recanted and sent a team of 312 athletes; among them, 19 black athletes and five Jews.

The Third Reich viewed the black athletes as 'sub-humans' and when on the first day of competition Hitler refused to shake the hands of African-American high-jumpers Dave Albritton and Cornelius Johnson, it was seen as an aggressively racist statement by the Nazi regime. Consequently, when one African-American athlete started to dominate the games, the symbolism of his success became impossible to ignore. Jesse Owens, the son of a poor sharecropper from Alabama, abruptly smashed all claims of Nazi superiority by becoming the first athlete to have ever received four gold medals in a single Games. In 1950, the Associated Press voted Owens the greatest track and field star of the first half of the twentieth century.

State of the Nation

Europe was in a state of flux. Spain was erupting in a bloody civil war, Mussolini's Fascist movement was spreading throughout Europe, and Italy had occupied Ethiopia. In Germany laws had been passed which allowed the sterilisation of blacks, gypsies and the disabled, and criminalised homosexuality. Hitler and the Nazis were becoming a growing concern as they promoted an ideology that believed in racial superiority, ethnic persecution, imperialist expansion and genocide.

In America, Jim Crow laws barred African-Americans from sharing public places such as restaurants with whites and encouraged policies of segregation based on ethnicity. World politics had turned ugly, with racism taking centre stage. People around the world questioned the morality of supporting an Olympic games—traditionally a bastion of international peace and co-operation—on the home ground of Adolf Hitler, the international champion of racism and fascism.

The Nazi Olympics

Anti-semitic public policies were openly removing Jews from the German way of life. Jewish athletes were no exception and had been banned from all sports facilities. Hitler further implemented an 'Aryans only' policy on the German

Olympic team. This resulted in huge controversy throughout the world, being seen as a violation of the Olympic code of equality and fair play.

As the Committee for Fair Play stated in November 1935:

Sport is prostituted when sport loses its independent and democratic character and becomes a political institution ... Nazi Germany is endeavouring to use the Eleventh Olympiad to serve the necessities and interests of the Nazi Regime rather than the Olympic ideals.

Countries all over the world began to talk about boycotting the Games. American participation was hotly debated, with many people having serious concerns for the safety of African-American athletes if they were sent to Nazi Germany. The Head of the American Olympic Committee, Avery Brundage, had at first supported the boycott. When the Nazis invited Brundage to Germany to see the situation for himself, he did an about-face and returned to the US favourably impressed with Germany's Olympic preparation. On 26 September 1934, the American Olympic Committee officially accepted Germany's invitation to compete at what the press were calling the 'Nazi Olympics'.

The stage was set for one of the most elaborately choreographed Games of all time. It had taken the propaganda Minister, Joseph Goebbels, some effort to persuade Hitler of the value of the Games. Hitler was aware of the possible repercussions of mixing Aryan and non-Aryan athletes and conscious that the fastest men in the world were African-American. However, this was offset by the opportunity to showcase the new Germany to the rest of the world. Forty-two million Reichsmarks were spent on building an impressive Olympic Sports complex, the centrepiece being the world's biggest Olympic Stadium. The streets of Berlin were cleaned up and the commonplace 'Jews Not Welcome' signs were removed from shop windows.

The Starter's Gun

The opening ceremony of the Games of the XI Olympiad took place on 1 August 1936. Hitler, his entourage and the Olympic officials staged their entrance perfectly as the crowd gave a rousing rendition of 'Deutschland über Alles', the German national anthem. As the ceremony unfolded against cloudy skies, every angle was covered by filmmaker Leni Riefenstahl, who produced a groundbreaking film of the event, called *Olympia*.

Famous for their pageantry and meticulous attention to detail, the Nazis were determined to outdo all other Olympic ceremonies. The *Hindenburg* airship hovered over the stadium, dangling the Olympic flag, as over 5000 athletes marched below. However, it wasn't quite as perfect as Hitler would have liked. Many countries were confused as to what was expected as they

PIONEER OF FILM

Leni Riefenstahl was chosen by Hitler to direct *Olympia*. Using 30 different camera operators, Riefenstahl shot over a million feet of film. She was the first person to put a camera on rails–to film the crowds in the stadium as well as the movement of the athletes–and the first director to shoot sport as an art form. To this day it is still one of the most celebrated sports documentaries ever made.

THE RACE THAT MIGHT HAVE BEEN

Despite going on to have a very successful career as a sportscaster, relay runner Marty Glickman never got over his disappointment at being pulled from the race. In 1985, he returned to the Olympic Stadium in Berlin and later spoke of how he felt. 'As I walked into the stadium, I began to get so angry ... It shocked the hell out of me that this thing of forty-nine years ago could still evoke this anger ... Not about the German Nazis ... that was a given. But the anger at Avery Brundage and Dean Cromwell for not allowing an eighteen-year-old kid to compete in the Olympic Games just because he was Jewish.'

paraded past his viewing stand. Some gave the Olympic salute, others gave the Nazi salute, and the Belgians surprised everyone by goose-stepping. The US upset organisers by refusing to dip their flag as they passed Hitler, as tradition decreed that the American flag should only be dipped for the President of the United States.

The Nazi wheels of propaganda were now turning at full speed. Germany had skilfully promoted the Olympics with a media campaign well ahead of its time. For the first time, a lone runner entered the stadium holding aloft the Olympic torch, which had been carried all the way from Athens. This was an inspired stunt, as in the eyes of the German public it furthered the connection between the civilisations of Germany and ancient Greece, reinforcing German claims on the origins of Aryan culture.

Controversy Erupts

The competition started well, with Hitler magnanimously congratulating the first winners of the day, a German and a Finn. However, things quickly soured when it became apparent that two African-Americans, Cornelius Johnson and Dave Albritton, were about to claim the gold and silver medals respectively for the high jump. Rather than shake the hand of a black athlete, Hitler chose to leave the stadium. Immediately the International Olympics Committee complained, insisting Hitler should greet each and every medallist or none at all. In a clear statement, he was absent from all further medal presentations for the remainder of the Games. The German press referred to the African-American athletes as 'black auxiliaries', never accepting them as true members of the US team. The German State Secretary, Baldur von Schirach, reported that Hitler had made it clear where he stood.

> The Americans should be ashamed of themselves, letting Negroes win their medals for them. I shall not shake hands with this Negro ... do you really think that I will allow myself to be photographed shaking hands with a Negro?

As 23-year-old Jesse Owens crouched at the starting line of the 100-metre sprint, he was aware the eyes of the world were on him. Having broken three world records and tied another in the space of 45 minutes the preceding year, Owens was recognised as a serious Olympic contender, but no-one could have anticipated that this descendant of slaves was about to become a symbol of freedom and equality.

Flying in the face of red and black swastikas, Jesse Owens powered down a muddy track, winning the gold medal for the 100 metres in 10.3 seconds, edging out African-American team mate Ralph Metcalfe. To Hitler's dismay, Owens quickly became a favourite with the Berlin crowd.

Jesse Owens
glides over
the track with
the grace of
a streamlined
express flying
over the open
prairie.

– ARTHUR DALEY

LEFT: The last torch carrier arrives in the Lustgarten in Berlin to light the Olympic flame and officially start the Games.

An Unlikely Ally

As Owens warmed up for the qualifying rounds of the broad jump (now known as the long jump), a symbolic drama started to unfold. Each athlete was allowed three jumps to qualify for the event. Thinking that he was merely having a practice jump, Owens was shocked to be told that he had already used up one attempt. Shaken, he then fouled the next jump and was left with only one more attempt to qualify. 'I fought,' he said, 'I fought harder ... but one cell at a time, panic crept into my body, taking me over.'

The atmosphere in the stadium was tense. As Owens sat dejectedly considering his next jump, he was approached by top German athlete Luz Long, a blond, blue-eyed German athlete who was considered to be Hitler's favourite and who had already set an Olympic record in the preliminary heats.

To everyone's surprise Long offered Owens some advice. If he aimed to jump a little before the take-off board, he would hopefully avoid a foul. Owens judged that Long could be trusted, and the advice got him through to the next round.

Later that day, the two men met once more, going head to head in the Olympic final. In his fifth jump, Long managed to match the leading distance set by Owens of 7.87 metres. On his next jump, Owens stretched to 8 metres. As the competition intensified, Owens focused all his thoughts on the final jump. 'I decided I wasn't going to come down. I was going to fly. I was going to stay up in the air forever.'

He performed a huge final jump of 8.05 metres, winning his second gold medal for the US and setting an Olympic record that wouldn't be broken for 20 years. Luz Long, the ultimate symbol of Aryan purity, congratulated Owens and the two men retired from the field arm in arm.

It took a lot of courage for him to befriend me in front of Hitler. You can melt down all the medals and cups I have and they wouldn't be a plating on the 24-carat friendship I felt for Luz Long at that moment. Hitler must have gone crazy watching us embrace. The sad part of the story is I never saw Long again. He was killed in World War II.

The next day Owens amazed the world with his performance in the 200-metre dash when, despite running into a headwind, he won a third Olympic gold medal in a record time of 20.7 seconds. He was an Olympic sensation and the German fans loved him, chasing him for autographs and chanting his name whenever he entered the stadium. The Games, being filmed by Riefenstahl as a Nazi propaganda piece, now had an African-American as its leading man. There was more controversy to come.

Passing the Baton

Two Jewish athletes, Marty Glickman and Sam Stoller, were scheduled to run for the US in the relay race. However, on the morning of the race they were removed from the team and replaced by Owens and Metcalfe. It was rumoured that at the last minute the Nazis had requested they be removed from the team. Black athletes had already publicly beaten the Germans and it was thought that Hitler was determined not to be further humiliated. Avery Brundage acquiesced.

SLAVERY AVERY

When the track and field competition was over and the Games were still going, Owens and his team mates were forced to travel around Europe, attending race meets in front of large crowds and raising money on behalf of the Amateur Athletics Union and the American Olympic Community. Exhausted by the gruelling schedule, Owens finally snapped and demanded that he be allowed to go home. Avery Brundage reacted by suspending Owens indefinitely from Amateur Athletics. Known to be a racist and pro-Nazi, Brundage had already earned himself the nickname 'Slavery Avery'.

Glickman later told of how Owens asked not to run, saying 'Coach, I have won my three gold medals; I have won the races I set out to win.' But the coach was adamant.

Yet again, Owens was in the spotlight. He led the 4 x 400 metres relay team, which went on to win by 4.572 metres in a record time of 39.8 seconds. It was a fourth gold medal for Owens and again the record would stand for 20 years. Owens and his fellow African-Americans had won 14 of the 56 US medals and he himself had undoubtedly become the champion of the Berlin Olympics. His record of four track and field gold medals in a single Games wouldn't be equalled until the 1980 Olympics with Carl Lewis.

As the Games came to a close, they were heralded as the most organised and successful to date. But it was no more than a façade. Those present at the closing ceremony were unaware that it would be another 12 years before the next Olympics would take place, as Hitler had more ambitious plans ahead, which would culminate in World War II. Owens and his team mates reported hearing the rattle of machine guns start up behind them as they left the Olympic Village in Berlin, as the village reverted to a military training camp.

Riding the Freight Elevator

Owens returned to America. Reflecting on his Olympic performance, he wrote a letter to the *Pittsburg Courier*.

> *I am proud that I am an American. I see the sun breaking through the clouds when I realise the millions of Americans will recognize that what I and the boys of my race are trying to do is attempted for the glory of our country and our countrymen. Maybe more people will now realize that the Negro is trying to do his part as an American citizen.*

The symbolic role of Jesse Owens's part in the 1936 Olympics transcends all others. In the summer of 1936, he not only successfully smashed Olympic records, but also destroyed Hitler's myth of Aryan supremacy. Yet for Owens, and most African-Americans, the experience also highlighted racism in the US.

> *When I came back to my native country, after all the stories about Hitler, I couldn't ride in the front of the bus. I had to go to the back door. I couldn't live where I wanted. I wasn't invited to shake hands with Hitler, but I wasn't invited to the White House to shake hands with the President, either.*

Initially Owens was treated like a hero, a tickertape parade being held in New York in his honour, along with a reception at the Waldorf-Astoria Hotel. However, he was made to ride in the freight elevator to his own

LEFT: Owens (centre) prepares to accept the gold medal for the 100 metres, the first of four gold medals he would win during the Games.

reception, because the lobby elevator was only for whites. Because he was black, he received no endorsement deals and was forced to sell himself as a racing runner for hire—he would challenge people, horses, dogs and even motorbikes.

This was a demoralising situation for a man in his early twenties who had returned from the Games with such high expectations. 'People said it was degrading for an Olympic champion to run against a horse, but what was I supposed to do?' Owens said. 'I had four gold medals, but you can't eat four gold medals.'

By the 1950s Americans felt a certain nostalgia towards Owens. At the height of the Cold War, he himself became a propaganda tool of sorts when the American government appointed him as an ambassador of sport for the United States. Owens travelled the world, speaking up for American values and ideals as well as telling his own inspirational story. Black militant groups of the time were angered that Owens didn't use his platform for more aggressive change, but Owens didn't believe in militancy. When John Carlos and Tommie Smith were planning to stage a protest at the 1968 Olympics, it was Jesse Owens who was sent to dissuade them. However, by the 1970s Owens had a different point of view, no doubt having grown weary of the way he had been treated. He said, 'I realized now that militancy in the *best* sense of the word was the *only* answer where the black man was concerned, that any black man who wasn't a militant in 1970 was either blind or a coward.'

To a sprinter, the hundred-yard dash is over in three seconds, not nine or ten. The first 'second' is when you come out of the blocks. The next is when you look up and take your first few strides to attain gain position. By that time the race is actually about half over. The final 'second'—the longest slice of time in the world for an athlete—is that last half of the race, when you really bear down and see what you're made of. It seems to take an eternity, yet is all over before you can think what's happening. – JESSE OWENS

It was 40 years before American society had changed enough for the White House to recognise this great athlete. In 1976, Owens was awarded the highest honour a civilian of the United States can receive when President Gerald R. Ford awarded him the Medal of Freedom. In 1990, ten years after his death, Jesse Owens was awarded the Congressional Medal of Honour for his achievements at the Berlin Olympics, with US President George Bush calling them 'a triumph for all humanity'. In Berlin, a street was named after him—proving that Germans and Americans alike will never forget what one man achieved in the summer of 1936.

BACKGROUND:	Against fascism
EVENT:	World heavyweight boxing championship
OPPONENTS:	Joe Louis v Max Schmeling
ARENA:	Yankee Stadium, New York

The Reluctant Nazi Warrior

NEW YORK, USA, 1938

Every defeat has its good side. A victory over Joe Louis would perhaps have made me into the toast of the Third Reich.

— MAX SCHMELING

OPPOSITE: The German heavyweight boxing champion Max Schmeling in 1936. By this time, he was no longer at his peak.

The famous Joe Louis v Max Schmeling fights of 1936 and 1938 were contests of epic proportions, fought out against the backdrop of a looming world war against fascism. When they first met in 1936, Schmeling shocked the boxing world by knocking out the young and upcoming Louis, and Hitler embraced Schmeling as the perfect icon for his white supremacist ideology. Two years later, the two boxers met again. This time, Louis was the world heavyweight boxing champion and the fight had another layer of meaning. It was no longer just a fight to prove who was the strongest man in the world. Instead, it was Joe Louis, black American hero, versus Max Schmeling, reluctant warrior of Hitler's Nazi regime. For the first time ever, black and white Americans joined together in supporting Joe Louis, believing that a victory in the ring could signify a victory on the battlefields in the war that threatened.

State of the Nation

Hitler's persecution of the Jews began when the Nazi Party came to power in Germany in 1933. In 1938 Germany annexed Austria and was poised to invade Czechoslovakia and Poland. The world was heading towards a war from which few countries would be exempt and Hitler was using all available means of propaganda to spread the ideology of the Third Reich. In the United States, racial discrimination was an everyday experience for African-Americans, one that included segregation and even lynchings. The country was still recovering from the devastating effects of the Great Depression, and now the prospect of a war against Germany and fascism loomed on the horizon. In such uncertain times, Americans clung together and a new wave of patriotism swept the country.

The Brown Bomber

By 1936, Joe Louis, known as 'the Brown Bomber', was carving his way through the heavyweight division, with an undefeated record of 27 fights for 27 wins (including 23 knockouts) in just 18 months. He had beaten former world champions Primo Carnera and Max Baer and was on track for the world heavyweight boxing title. Joe Louis thought of himself as invincible. He certainly didn't envisage that changing when previous titleholder Max Schmeling of Germany was brought in as an opponent. The fight would be no different from all his other wins, Louis believed, especially as his German opponent was a has-been.

Max Schmeling had become world heavyweight boxing champion in 1928, after then-titleholder Gene Tunney retired and left the title vacant. The next bout to decide the title was held on 13 June 1930, and Schmeling won it when his opponent, Jack Sharkey, was disqualified for a foul blow in the fourth round. Schmeling managed one successful defence of the title, then lost it to Sharkey when they met in a rematch in 1932. By 1936 his time at the top was a distant memory, though he was an experienced boxer and a good puncher. But Schmeling wasn't finished yet. Indeed, he would have a lasting impact on Louis' career.

At that time, the 1936 Berlin Olympics were approaching. Hitler had appointed Schmeling as an emissary for the Games. In an attempt to ward off the impending boycotts from countries already opposed to the rise of fascism in Germany, and its treatment of Jews, Schmeling would personally deliver a letter to the US Olympic Committee, promising that all US athletes would be protected during their time in Germany. But when Schmeling set off for New York to take on Joe Louis, he did so without the support of the German government. Hitler was worried that Schmeling was risking the reputation of the Nazis by fighting a black man over whom the chances of victory were slim. Louis was said to have a right cross as devastating as his left hook. His punches were so powerful that some estimated he could knock a man out with a punch that travelled just 15 centimetres. Schmeling assured Hitler that he was confident of victory, and set sail for America.

A Chink in the Armour

During his preparation for the fight, Schmeling had been watching film footage of Louis in action. He believed that he had spotted a chink in Louis' armour—he kept boasting to the press that he had 'seen something'. Not that anyone took the German champion seriously. Most people believed it would be another easy win for Louis. On 19 June 1936, the day of the fight, Yankee Stadium was only half full. Heavy rain had delayed the fight by a day, and Jewish spectators boycotted the game in protest at Hitler's Nuremberg Laws, which had stripped German Jews of their civil rights.

Schmeling entered the ring as the 10–1 underdog, but he left having caused one of the biggest upsets in sporting history. For he had indeed seen something while watching the footage of his opponent. After Louis jabbed, he let his left hand drop instead of keeping it high to protect his face. That meant he left himself wide open to a counter-right.

In the fourth round, Schmeling's overhand right hit Louis hard on the chin, and he followed this up with a flurry of punches that dropped the shocked favourite to the mat. Louis managed to struggle back to his feet mid-count and start fighting again. But Schmeling just kept right on, delivering relentless right crosses to Louis' face at every chance. This went on until the twelfth round, when the German followed a powerful left to Louis' face with three quick rights to his jaw. Louis hit the canvas for the second time in the fight. This time, he didn't get up. For the first time in his professional career, Joe Louis was counted out.

It was a massive blow to Louis, and to the entire African-American community. Harlem rioted. Louis cried in his dressing room, punch-drunk and confused. Meanwhile, Hitler dispatched a telegram to Schmeling in New York—

The whole damned country was depending on me.

– JOE LOUIS

ABOVE: Joe Louis rains blows on Schmeling, who tries vainly to defend himself. It took Louis just two minutes and four seconds to win by technical knock-out.

'Most cordial congratulations on your victory'—and claimed the win for Germany. Propaganda Minister Josef Goebbels added, 'I know you fought for Germany; that it was a German victory. We are proud of you. Heil Hitler! Regards.'

After his win, the *Hindenburg* airship carried Schmeling back to Germany, where he received a hero's welcome. The German press quoted him as saying 'The black man will always be afraid of me—he is inferior', a statement Schmeling always denied making. He dined with Hitler and together they watched the film of the fight, with Hitler slapping Schmeling's thigh every time Louis took a punch. However, as Schmeling was to say later, 'What can you do if your president invites you to tea? Of course you must accept.' The film was released in cinemas throughout the country, showcasing Schmeling as an Aryan masterpiece.

Louis out for Revenge!

After this, Schmeling believed that his victory over Louis entitled him to a world championship bout against the then-titleholder, the American Jimmy Braddock, also known as the Cinderella Man. However, anti-German feeling was so high in the United States that the fight never took place. Instead, on 22 June 1937 it was Joe Louis who took on Braddock and succeeded in knocking him out in the eighth round. Louis became the first African-American heavyweight boxing champion since the great Jack Johnson, and the entire black community celebrated. As Alistair Cooke wrote, 'For one night, in all the darktowns of America, the black man was king.'

But Louis hadn't forgotten his bitter defeat by Schmeling and downplayed his title, saying, 'I don't want to be called champ until I lick Max Schmeling.'

Finally, two years later, he got his chance when the highly anticipated rematch was organised. But this time the stakes were higher. Both men had been forced into becoming champions of causes with which neither felt comfortable.

Take Your Corners

By 1938, the international political climate had changed. The threat of fascism made the likelihood of a world war imminent. The fight was deeply politicised. In one corner stood Max Schmeling, inadvertent representative of Hitler and Nazism, a reluctant symbol of the 'Aryan master race'. In the other corner stood Joe Louis, the new face of freedom, democracy and everything that the United States stood for. While the boxers had their minds firmly on the heavyweight title, their respective governments were exploiting the fight for its propaganda value and casting the men as national warriors. In truth, neither man fitted his country's stereotype.

Despite pressure from Hitler, Schmeling refused on several occasions to join the Nazi Party and to publicise its propaganda. Instead, he publicly supported the Jews by refusing Goebbels's direct request that he sack his Jewish manager in America, Joe Jacobs. However, it was impossible for such a popular and public figure to entirely avoid the politics. Before the fight, he received messages from Hitler warning him that the reputation of the Third Reich was at stake. One good-luck telegram from Hitler even went so far as to address him as 'the new heavyweight champion of the world'.

Meanwhile, 24-year-old Louis found himself under similar pressure. For Americans, a Louis victory had become symbolic, too. They believed that if he could beat Schmeling, there was a chance they could beat Hitler. He was invited to the White House and had his biceps felt by President Roosevelt, who said, 'Joe, we need muscles like yours to beat Germany'. Louis later recalled how fired up he felt about the contest after meeting the President. 'Let me tell you, that was a thrill. Now, even more, I knew I had to get Schmeling good.'

In later years, however, he spoke of the hypocrisy of many white Americans. The Ku Klux Klan was still active, and racism and segregation were daily facts of life for African-Americans. Indeed, many conservative Americans had applauded Hitler's snub of black athlete Cornelius Johnson at the Berlin Games in 1936.

Joe Louis was used to fighting for a greater cause than himself. As Chester Higgins wrote in *Ebony* magazine:

He gave inspiration to downtrodden and despised people. When Joe Louis fought, blacks in ghettos across the land were indoors glued to their radios, and when Louis won, as he nearly always did, they hit the streets whooping and hollering in celebration. For Joe's victory was their victory, a means of striking back at an oppressive and hateful environment. Louis was the black Atlas on whose broad shoulders blacks were lifted, for in those days, there were few authentic black heroes.

But Joe Louis wasn't used to white Americans being in his camp. Now, for the first time ever, a black athlete was being supported by a large part of the white community as all Americans joined together against a common enemy.

The two boxers tried to keep their minds on the fight. Schmeling wanted to prove his worth in the heavyweight division, while Louis wanted to prove he was the best boxer in the world and get his revenge on Schmeling for his 1936 defeat. On the afternoon before the fight, he was brimming with confidence, saying, 'I'm scared ... I'm scared I might kill Schmeling tonight'.

'Two Minutes and Four Seconds of Murder'

As the day of the rematch, 22 June 1938, approached, both fighters were well prepared. Louis had proved himself in an epic title defence against Welshman Tommy Farr and in two other wins against Americans Nathan Mann and Harry Thomas. Schmeling had also won his last three fights. But the punters were giving solid backing to the Brown Bomber, with the odds at 9–5 on a Louis victory. Schmeling, aged 32, weighed in at 193 pounds (87.5 kilograms). Louis, 24, was the heavier boxer, weighing in at 198 ¾ pounds (90 kilograms).

This time 70,000 people poured into Yankee Stadium to watch the fight of the century. And over 100 million people worldwide—the biggest radio audience of its time—tuned in to listen.

Schmeling stepped into the ring first. The crowd vented their hatred of Hitler by throwing objects and jeering. When the bell rang, Joe Louis immediately put in two straight lefts, hitting Schmeling hard in the face. He followed with a combination of left hooks and right crosses. Schmeling missed with a right and Louis moved in to attack his opponent's body, then followed up with a combination to the head. Schmeling found himself tangled on the ropes and unable to stand straight. Louis continued to rain blow after blow onto Schmeling, who tried to turn away from the onslaught. As a huge sledgehammer of a right smashed into his back, the German let out a piercing scream that could be heard above the crowd's roar. Louis had broken one of Schmeling's spinal vertebrae.

OPPOSITE: Announcer Harry Balogh holds Louis' hand high as he declares him the world heavyweight title holder, having beaten Schmeling in a single round.

> Usually the champion rides on the shoulder of the nation and its people. But in this case, the nation rode on the shoulders of its hero.
>
> – REVEREND JESSE JACKSON

The referee pushed Louis back to the neutral corner and started the count. As the referee reached 'three', Schmeling staggered towards Louis and walked straight into a single right to the jaw. He staggered to his feet again, only to receive a five-punch combination ending with a final devastating right to the jaw. As Schmeling hit the canvas for a third time, his trainer, Max Machon, threw a white towel into the ring to signify that Schmeling was too hurt for the fight to go on. But because this practice wasn't recognised in the United States the referee, Arthur Donovan, threw the towel back out of the ring and let the fight continue. Realising that Schmeling couldn't take any more, Machon stepped into the ring to put a stop to the carnage, leaving the referee with no alternative but to end the fight.

The win was the second-shortest title fight in history, referred to by one columnist as 'two minutes and four seconds of murder'. It left Louis in no doubt as to his claim on the title. 'You can call me champ now,' he said.

Streets in Harlem were closed for celebrations as Americans, black and white, congratulated each other on what felt like a victory over the Nazis. In Germany some listeners were left uncertain about the final result. There were reports that Goebbels ordered the radio feed to be pulled after Schmeling's first standing count.

In the *New York Times*, John Kieran reported:

Well, of all things! It's on and it's over. Just as Joe promised. He stepped in and started a lightning attack. Lefts and rights—bang! Bang! Bang! Schmeling reeled into the ropes on the first-base side of the ring and clung like a shipwrecked soldier to a lifeline … Swaying on the ropes, Max peered out in a bewildered manner. He pushed himself off and Louis struck like dark lightning again. A ripping left and a smashing right. The right was the crusher. Schmeling went down. He was up again and then, under another fusillade, down again. Once more, and barely able to stand, and then down for the third and final time.

Life time Friends

Joe Louis was one of the best heavyweight boxing champions of all time. Over the next 12 years he successfully defended his title 25 times, earning himself a place in American history as one of the most celebrated champions ever. He enlisted in the army in 1942 and fought almost a hundred exhibition fights, twice donating his prize purse to support the military. His hero status remained intact. He appealed to the American psyche by telling journalists that America would win the war because 'we're on God's side'.

There was no such hero's welcome for Schmeling. He was reprimanded for losing to a black man and continually befriending Jews. He was dropped from favour, which didn't trouble him unduly. Then Hitler punished him for continually refusing to become a member of the Nazi Party by conscripting him into the paratroopers. In 1941, Schmeling landed badly after a jump from a plane and further aggravated the back injury he had sustained during the 1938 fight.

But when the war came to an end, Schmeling bought a Coca-Cola franchise and was appointed chief executive of the Coca-Cola Corporation in Germany. He made a huge financial profit. His 1933 marriage to a beautiful Czech film actress lasted until her death in 1987, and financially he grew ever more successful.

Louis' lifetime prize winnings totalled US$4,626,721. In his 1938 fight against Schmeling, he had earned $349,288.40, which worked out at $2,832 per second. Unfortunately, he got into debt with the taxation department and was forced back into the ring. He finally retired for good after Rocky Marciano knocked him out in the eighth round of their 1951 fight. He spent time advising Muhammad Ali, but the two were to fall out over politics. His financial problems continued, and were eventually such that he was forced into professional wrestling before becoming a public relations 'greeter' at Caesar's Palace in Las Vegas. In later years he became addicted to cocaine and suffered heavily from depression.

In 1954, 16 years after their famous fight, Schmeling visited Joe Louis in the United States and the two men became close friends. In 1977 Louis suffered a heart attack and a stroke and was confined to a wheelchair. On several occasions, Schmeling sent his old foe money to pay his hospital bills.

On 12 April 1981, Joe Louis died at the age of 66, having received a standing ovation the night before at Caesar's Palace, where he watched Larry Holmes retain his world heavyweight title by beating Trevor Berbick. With President Reagan's permission he was buried in Arlington National Cemetery. Frank Sinatra, Muhammad Ali, Larry Holmes and Caesar's Palace president Harry Ward were all pallbearers. The list of honorary pallbearers read like a boxing hall of fame—Jack Dempsey, Sugar Ray Robinson, Gene Tunney, Lou Nova and Floyd Patterson all paid their respects. Max Schmeling was not only an honorary pallbearer—it was reported that he also paid for much of the funeral.

Schmeling died on 2 February 2005, aged 99. Asked what he valued most in life, he replied, 'Tolerance, then tolerance again and finally, tolerance'.

FOR THE RECORD

Max Schmeling

Height: 185 cm (6 feet 1 inch)

Reach: 76 cm (30 inches)

Won: 56 (KO: 40)

Lost: 10 (KO: 4)

Drawn: 4

Joe Louis

Height: 188 cm (6 feet 2 inches)

Reach: 76 cm (30 inches)

Won: 69 (KO: 55)

Lost: 3 (KO: 2)

Drawn: 0

BACKGROUND:	For human rights and racial equality
EVENT:	Medal presentation for the men's 200 metres final
OPPONENTS:	Tommie Smith and John Carlos v The Establishment
ARENA:	1968 Summer Olympics, Mexico City

A Salute to Black Power

MEXICO CITY, MEXICO, 1968

When we spoke, it caused a commotion everywhere.
So now, we ran fast so that we could be heard.
— TOMMIE SMITH

OPPOSITE: American sprinters Tommie Smith (centre) and John Carlos (right) give the black power salute at the 1968 Olympics. Peter Norman of Australia wore a badge promoting human rights in support.

At the 1968 Olympics, African-American sprinters Tommie Smith and John Carlos stunned the world by staging a protest for human rights and racial equality when they took to the podium to receive their medals for the 200 metres. As evening fell across Mexico City and 'The Star Spangled Banner' started to play, Smith bowed his head and raised his black-gloved right hand in a fist to represent black power, while Carlos raised his black-gloved left fist to symbolise black unity. The third medal winner, Peter Norman from Australia, showed solidarity by wearing an Olympic Project for Human Rights badge. The protest caused a furore. The International Olympic Committee (IOC) accused the athletes of contravening the Olympic spirit by mixing sports with politics. Both Smith and Carlos were given 48 hours to leave the Olympic village, and they were banned from all subsequent Olympic competition. The photograph of the salute is one of the most famous ever taken, so much so that *Life* magazine declared it one of the 20 most influential images of the twentieth century.

State of the Nation

The year 1968 was a tumultuous one for the United States. On 4 April 1968, the black civil rights activist Martin Luther King, Jr was assassinated, just when the movement for equal rights for African Americans was at its height. Two months later, Robert F. Kennedy was also assassinated while campaigning to become the Democratic presidential candidate. Muhammad Ali had been stripped of his world heavyweight boxing title after he refused to fight in Vietnam, claiming conscientious objector status on religious grounds. The United States was witnessing the growth of a black separatist movement called the Black Panthers, one of the first organisations to condone violence in order to free ethnic minorities and the working class from poverty and inequality. The citizens of the United States were questioning the very meaning of democracy in a country run by the white, privileged class.

On 2 October 1968, just ten days before the Olympics were due to start in Mexico City, more than 300 students from Mexico City University were killed by army troops when a peaceful protest developed into a full-scale riot. The massacre shook the world. However, the IOC stuck to its belief that sport and politics should never mix and the XIX Olympiad went ahead as planned.

The African Olympics

In the late 1960s San Jose State College had two of the greatest sprinters in the world: Tommie Smith, the holder of the 200 metres world record, and John Carlos, ranked slightly lower. This was a time when many of the US sporting bodies were exclusively white and university campuses such as San Jose State allowed only white students access to housing on campus, whereas black

students were forced into rental accommodation, often miles from their place of study. Black students at white-dominated colleges started to campaign for more black coaches and better conditions and facilities.

ABOVE: Tommie Smith crosses the line jubilantly to win gold in the 200 metres, while John Carlos (to his left in the photo) won bronze. Carlos later claimed that he had let Smith win.

Then Dr Harry Edwards, a lecturer in sociology at the College, set up an organisation called the Olympic Project for Human Rights (OPHR). Both Smith and Carlos were friends of Edwards, and Smith in particular became a key member of the organisation. In 1967, with the Mexico City Olympic Games approaching, the OPHR put out a call to all black athletes to boycott the Games. One of the intentions was to highlight the racist treatment of African-Americans in the United States, but the OPHR's specific concern was Avery Brundage, President of the IOC, and the fact that he was in favour of allowing South Africa to compete in the Games. With the apartheid system entrenched and unchanging in South Africa, many international sporting bodies were starting to ban the South Africans from competing. Now pressure was mounting on the IOC to do the same. The OPHR put forward a list of requests: the restoration of Muhammad Ali's title, the removal of Avery Brundage from the IOC and the exclusion of South Africa from competition.

The OPHR also issued a press statement threatening to 'establish a second set of games preferably to be held in an African Nation during the late summer so that Black people and students may participate without interrupting their educational careers'. It stated:

We must no longer allow the sports world to pat itself on the back as a citadel of racial justice when the racial injustices of the sports world are infamously legendary ... any black person who allows himself to be used in the above manner is a traitor because he allows racist whites the luxury of resting assured that those black people in the ghettos are there because that is where they want to be. So we ask why should we run in Mexico only to crawl home?

The IOC reversed its decision on South Africa—that country was not invited to compete. This was a huge victory for the OPHR. Its initiative had motivated African-Americans to unite for the first time with other black nations in the fight for equality. But the IOC maintained that the threatened boycott had nothing to do with its decision, saying the decision was made out of concern for the safety of South African athletes in Mexico. Neither did the IOC give way on the other two issues.

Rumours of a boycott persisted, but it never materialised. Many of the athletes did not want to jeopardise their future careers, which they felt were riding on their Olympic performances. So instead, the athletes were asked to do whatever they, individually, felt comfortable with in the fight for equality. John Carlos would have gone with the boycott.

We first tried to have a boycott [of the Games] but not everyone was down with that plan. A lot of athletes thought that winning medals would supersede or protect them from racism. But even if you won the medal, it ain't going to save your momma. It ain't going to save your sister or children. It might give you 15 minutes of fame, but what about the rest of your life? I'm not saying that they didn't have the right to follow their dreams, but to me the medal was nothing but the carrot on a stick.

Faster and Louder

With the boycott called off, pressure mounted on the top athletes, who were probably assured a place on the winners' podium. The movement was picking up more and more support from black athletes around the world. Smith and his team mates had quickly realised that success on the track gave them an opportunity to promote their cause. At a time when they were being watched keenly by the world media, every race brought with it the possibility of a new world record and a horde of journalists keen for interviews.

For Smith in particular, winning the gold medal became a crucial pathway to achieving the goals he was setting himself off the track as a human rights activist.

The Olympic Games was part of a platform that I was able to use because of what I had accomplished, to make people realize what's going on in this country. You can't not use it ... But in order to use that platform, I had to win the race. There was no way I could lose; if I had lost, I would have lost everything.

The Race

On 16 October 1968, Smith and Carlos lined up for the 200 metres final. Smith was lucky to have made it. He had sustained a thigh injury in the semi-finals earlier in the day, and for a while it had looked doubtful that he would be able to run. As Smith waited for the race to begin, he could hear the commentator speculating on his form. 'And Tommie Smith has a pulled muscle; he's getting in his blocks now; we'll see how this race goes; I'm not sure if he'll be able to run.' Smith couldn't help being distracted. 'I heard him and wanted to say—Man, why don't you just shut up and let me run my race?'

The eight sprinters waited in their starting blocks. Both Carlos and Smith had received numerous death threats leading up to the race and, crouched there in front of thousands of people, both feared that they could be taken down at any moment.

Smith was in lane 3, Carlos in lane 4. With the lanes staggered across the track, Carlos was ahead of Smith, which suited Smith perfectly. He knew Carlos was the man to beat, and as a runner, Smith preferred to have his competition in his sights. The crack of the starter's gun echoed around the stadium and the fastest men on the planet blasted from the blocks.

Carlos was leading the field with Tommie Smith following closely. As they came out of the turn, Carlos was 3 metres ahead of Smith when Smith's reserve tank kicked in. 'I suddenly opened up at full throttle,' he said. 'I was conscious that I was gaining on people because their bodies got bigger, which means either they're coming back to you or you're going towards them.' Smith was quickly almost on top of Carlos. 'I was coming towards him at such a rapid pace that the attack, I think, was a surprise to him and I don't think he could recover from the initial blow of someone going by him that fast.' Smith's change of gear left everyone for dead as he flew up the finishing straight. With 10 metres still to go, Smith raised his hands to celebrate victory, a move that may have cost him valuable split seconds but didn't stop him winning gold and setting a world record of 19.83 seconds.

Meanwhile, Peter Norman of Australia was eating up the track. He had passed Frenchman Roger Bambuck 50 metres out, then he caught Carlos right on the tape, earning himself the silver with a time of 20.06 seconds. Carlos won the bronze, running at 20.1 seconds. It was the fastest 200 metres ever run at that time and Smith's new world record lasted 11 years.

Although the race was clearly a magnificent result for Smith, Carlos claimed that he had let Smith win, knowing how important the gold was to him.

I led the race for the first 130 metres to allow everyone to know that I had the ability to win the race if I wanted to do so. But I chose not to. I shut down my jets to autopilot around the 140 metre mark. I looked to my left to see if I could see Tommy coming. I did but it seemed like he was struggling … I looked back and yelled, 'Come on, Tommy, and quit bullshitting if you want to win this race.'

When asked at the time why he had looked to the side so close to the finish line, Carlos had said, 'The upper part of my calves were pulling pretty hard. I wanted to see where Tommie was and if he could win it. If I thought he couldn't have won it, I would have tried harder to take it.' Smith maintains that there was no chance of Carlos ever beating him.

The Unforgettable Protest

There had been lots of rumours that a demonstration was being planned. Both the IOC and the US track and field coaches had tried to dissuade Carlos and Smith from doing anything that might be against the spirit of the Games. Controversial as ever, Avery Brundage had even sent gold medallist Jesse Owens to talk 'sense' into all the African-American athletes. Owens was an American hero, the African-American athlete who had won four gold medals at the 1936 Berlin Olympics, symbolising a defeat of Hitler and his ideas of white racial superiority. Owens came from another time and could only see the actions of the black athletes as an embarrassment. The athletes listened with respect, but clearly told Owens where they stood.

No doubt anticipating trouble, Brundage left the Games for the day, taking a trip to Acapulco. Anti-Brundage sentiment was growing. Many of the black athletes were saying they didn't want their medals to be presented by the IOC President, whom Smith referred to as their very own Hitler and 'just another racist white man'. Even athletes who weren't militant agreed, for example American long jumper Ralph Boston, who said, 'You gotta be black to understand it. Brundage made those statements about the Negro problems in South Africa being only political and not an Olympic concern.'

Late in the evening of 16 October, 60,000 spectators filled the main stadium, waiting for the floodlit medal presentation ceremony to begin. One by one, the three athletes climbed the podium to receive their medals. Tommie Smith wore a black glove on his right hand and a black scarf around his neck to receive his gold. John Carlos wore a black glove on his left hand and beads around his neck. Both men wore black socks on their shoeless feet and carried a track shoe. Peter Norman wore an OPHR badge, just as Smith and Carlos did.

As the American flag ascended the flagpole and the sounds of 'The Star Spangled Banner' filled the stadium, Carlos and Smith bowed their heads and raised their gloved fists in the air. The crowd booed and jeered. John Carlos later said he had his head slightly raised, on the lookout for would-be assassins, and Smith expressed the same fear. A battery of photographers aimed their cameras, and one got the photo of the century.

Just as they disagreed over the race and how it had been run, Smith and Carlos had different versions of the origins of the protest. As the three winners waited for almost two hours for the medal ceremony to begin, they were still undecided on what the most powerful action would be. Smith said that he had the gloves with him and had decided to raise both hands up, as he did in church, and bow his head. Carlos said that the gloves were his and that it was his idea. Norman, probably the most unbiased witness, said that Carlos had forgotten his gloves and that he had suggested they wear one each of Smith's. However it came about, the protest became indelibly etched on public consciousness and created one of the most controversial moments in Olympic history.

Black America Will Understand

A press conference followed, at which no IOC members were present. It was here that Carlos and Smith attempted to explain the motives and the meaning behind their protest.

> *My raised right hand stood for power in black America. Carlos's left hand stood for the unity of black America. Together, they formed an arch of unity and power. The scarf around my neck stood for black pride. The black socks with no shoes stood for black poverty in racist America. The totality of our effort was the regaining of black dignity.*

In the aftermath of their dramatic gestures, Smith explained why he and Carlos had taken such a stand. 'If I win, I am an American, not a black American,' he said. 'But if I did something bad, then they would say I am a Negro. We are black and we are proud of being black. Black America will understand what we did tonight.' He added, 'It is very discouraging to be in a team with white athletes. On the track you are Tommie Smith, the fastest man in the world, but once you are in the dressing rooms you are nothing more than a dirty Negro.'

In an interview 35 years later, Carlos would explain:

> *We wanted the world to know that in Mississippi, Alabama, Tennessee, South Central Los Angeles, Chicago, that people were still walking back and forth in poverty without even the necessary clothes to live ... The beads were for those individuals that were lynched or killed that no one said a prayer for, that were hung and tarred. It was for those thrown off the side of the boats in the middle passage ... We were trying to wake the country up and wake the world up too.*

The United States is not united, because not all citizens are treated in the same manner. We do not represent the United States, but the black population of the United States. We want to be close to all the blacks worldwide. If, between now and Munich, certain problems are not dealt with, there will be a boycott by black athletes.

– CARLOS AND SMITH

At the grilling by the press in 1968, Smith highlighted the attitude towards black athletes. 'People recognise me as a fast nigger but that still means I'm a nigger.' Carlos added, 'We are great American athletes for 19.8 seconds; then we are animals so far as our country is concerned.' At the end of the press conference, Carlos threw his medal to his wife, saying, 'Here, honey, this is yours. I don't want it.'

Contrary to Olympic Spirit

Only hours later, the IOC deemed the protest to be 'a deliberate and violent breach of the fundamental principles of the Olympic spirit'. Determined that the Olympics and politics should remain separate, the IOC demanded the suspension of the two athletes and warned that any more protests would result in severe penalties. When the US Olympic Committee refused, the IOC threatened to ban all US athletes. Carlos and Smith had no choice but to leave. The Olympic village was divided, with remaining athletes hotly debating the protest and its ramifications.

On their return to the United States, thousands came out to greet the athletes in Washington and telegrams flooded in supporting their actions. However, for years Smith and Carlos were ostracised by the US sporting establishment and lampooned by the press, who accused the men of making a Nazi salute.

Death threats were common and the pressure took a great toll on the men's personal relationships, especially for Carlos, whose wife committed suicide. Both men followed similar career paths, playing American football and coaching track athletes. Neither man ever regretted his actions, although Smith in particular spoke of how he often wondered what might have been had he been allowed to continue competing. Not only was it a huge earnings loss but, more importantly, Smith lamented, he never had the opportunity to reach his potential. 'No one has ever broken 19 seconds in the 200, but I know I could have done it back then had I continued to run.'

Peter Norman also suffered for his actions. He was ostracised by the Australian media and, despite showing good form at the national trials, was overlooked for the 1972 Olympics. When the 2000 Olympics took place in Sydney, in Norman's home country, he was again overlooked and not invited to attend the Games. When Americans heard of the slight, they invited him to attend the Sydney Olympics as their guest. Norman donned an American shirt and took his place beside the US athletes.

On 17 October 2005, 37 years after their silent protest, Tommie Smith and John Carlos returned to what was now San Jose State University for the unveiling of a statue dedicated to the moment that had forever altered their lives. Dr Harry Edwards was there, as was Peter Norman, who introduced the men to the crowd, saying, 'These two men gave away that Olympic glory in 1968. San Jose State University, you're giving them back that glory today, and I'd like to thank you for that.'

The Australian wasn't part of the statue but his support for the cause was never forgotten. He died a year later and both Carlos and Smith were pallbearers at his funeral, honouring his support on that day. Carlos said:

Not every young white individual would have the gumption, the nerve, the backbone, to stand there. We knew that what we were going to do was far greater than any athletic feat. He said, 'I'll stand with you.' ... [When the crowd reacted] Peter never flinched. He never turned his eyes, he never turned his head. He never said so much as 'ouch'.

When Norman died in 2006, he still held the Australian 200 metres record after almost 40 years.

Both Carlos and Smith have taken their place in history as men who stood up for the human right to be treated as an equal. Their protest still resonates around the world today. As Smith said, 'It's not something I can lay on my shelf and forget about. My heart and soul are still on that team, and I still believe in everything we were trying to fight for in 1968. [It] has not been resolved and will be part of our future.'

OTHER PROTESTS

When African-American athletes Bob Beamon and Ralph Boston stood on the victory podium to receive the gold and bronze medals respectively for the men's long jump, they were shoeless and wearing long black socks in protest at the way Carlos and Smith had been treated. The Cuban men's and women's 400-metre relay teams dedicated their silver medals to Harry Edwards and the OPHR.

After winning the 400 metres at the 1994 Commonwealth Games in Canada, the Australian Aboriginal runner Cathy Freeman did a lap of honour with the Aboriginal flag and the Australian flag held aloft. She was criticised by the head of the Australian Commonwealth team and told not to do it again. But Freeman then won the 200 metres and again carried both flags around the track, defying team officials. The Australian public loved it, with three out of four agreeing with her action. When she won gold in the 400 metres at the Sydney 2000 Olympics and ran her victory lap in front of her home crowd with the two flags streaming out behind her, there was no controversy— even though the use of non-national flags at the Olympics is officially forbidden.

BACKGROUND:	Arab–Israeli conflict over Palestine
EVENT:	Against terrorism
OPPONENTS:	Black September guerillas v Israeli athletes
ARENA:	1972, Summer Olympics, Munich

Munich Massacre

MUNICH, GERMANY, 1972

The Games must go on! — **AVERY BRUNDAGE, PRESIDENT OF THE INTERNATIONAL OLYMPIC COMMITTEE**

OPPOSITE: An IOC official speaks with one of the Black September guerillas who invaded the Olympic Village at the 1972 Munich Olympics. Eleven members of the Israeli Olympic team were abducted and later killed.

On the morning of 5 September 1972, tragedy hit the Summer Olympics in the West German city of Munich when Arab terrorists belonging to the group Black September scaled the fences surrounding the village and stormed the building housing the Israeli contingent. For 24 hours the terrorists held nine people hostage as they demanded the release of 200 Palestinian prisoners. By the next day 17 people were dead, including 11 Israeli athletes and officials. The German insistence that the Games should be 'the happiest yet' had resulted in poor security and little foresight. The Munich Massacre was a turning point in the evolution of anti-terrorism measures. Organisers were no longer able to ignore the ongoing threat to the Olympics, and security is now of paramount concern for any host country. The 2008 Olympics saw China spend US$6.5 billion on surveillance equipment alone.

State of the Nation

Germany was still divided. East Germany maintained its alliances with the Soviet Union and throughout the fifties it gradually emerged as the most advanced country in the Warsaw Pact. However, like the Soviet Union it had an authoritarian government, which caused its citizens to look to West Germany for political freedom and prosperity—so much so that in 1961 the Berlin Wall was built to prevent East Germans from crossing over. By the 1970s relationships between East and West Germany were cordial but the Wall stood as a constant reminder that the Cold War still existed.

West Germany saw the 1972 Summer Olympics as a chance to eradicate the image of Hitler's 1936 Olympics. It was an opportunity to dismiss the long shadows cast by Nazi storm-troopers and to present to the world a new Germany full of positivity, optimism and democracy. As the Games approached, the German government made a decision to stay clear of any exhibits of military strength, which could act as a reminder of World War II. The death camp of Dachau was 16 kilometres (10 miles) outside Munich, but by hosting a successful Olympic games it was hoped that the city could be remembered for something other than the Jewish holocaust and that the Games would signify a rebirth for West Germany. Desperate to reposition itself on the world stage, West Germany made some crucial errors.

'The Happy Games'

Determined that the Munich Games should be controversy free, the German president Gustav Heinemann welcomed the Olympics as 'a milestone on the road to a new way of life with the aim of realising peaceful coexistence among peoples'.

Nicknamed 'the Happy Games', the Munich Olympics got underway on 26 August 1972. The Germans added to the light-heartedness of the event by introducing the very first named mascot, a dachshund called Waldi. They were the largest games to date, with 7173 athletes from 121 nations competing. And for the first ten days, everything went according to plan. Mark Spitz won an unprecedented seven gold medals in swimming for the United States and Russian gymnast Olga Korbut captured hearts around the world with her incredible skill and charisma.

Keen to promote an almost carnival atmosphere, security at the Olympic Village was particularly relaxed as security guards laughed and chatted with the athletes, who were coming as going as they pleased. A large fence surrounded the village, which many would scale late at night rather than bothering to to through the main gates.

However, to many people, particularly the team managers, the lack of security was of great concern. The head of the Israeli Olympic delegation, Shmuel Lalkin, was one who aired his worries only to be told, 'As manager of the Israeli Olympic team it would be advisable for you to concentrate on sports.' However on the morning of 5 September, the humorous spirit of the friendly security guards was dashed as Lalkin's concerns proved well founded.

Black September

On 5 September at 4.30 am, five Palestinian guerillas climbed the fence dressed in tracksuits and carrying gym bags. Despite giving the appearance of athletes, these men were members of the Black September group of Fatah, one of the most feared arms of the Palestinian Liberation Movement. Instead of exercise equipment, their bags concealed AK-47 assault rifles. In the early morning they made their way to Building 31, which housed 42 members of the Israeli team. They then joined forces with another three men who had been employed for the duration of the Games as kitchen staff.

The terrorists made their way through to one of the apartments where members of the Israeli team were fast asleep: Amitzur Shapira, track coach; Kehat Shorr, shooting coach; Andre Spitzer, fencing coach; Tuvia Sokolovsky, weightlifting trainer; Yacov Springer, weightlifting judge; Moshe Weinberg, wrestling coach; and wrestling referee Yossef Gutfreund.

Hearing a disturbance at the door, Gutfreund tried to block the terrorists' entry by putting his shoulder to the doors and shouting to the rest of the athletes in the apartment, 'Boys, get out!' This gave his room-mate Tuvia Sokolovsky time to smash a window and flee the apartment. 'I heard a burst of machine gun fire as I dived out of the window. They must have shot Gutfreund through the door. Now there are eight Israelis left inside. I heard someone crying behind me.'

Storming into another bedroom, the terrorists were confronted by wrestling coach Moshe Weinberg, who tried to attack them with a fruit knife. The terrorists wounded him and forced him to show them where the rest of the athletes were housed.

1972 OLYMPIC ATHLETES

Mark Spitz
Following the initial taking of the Israeli hostages, Jewish American swimming hero Mark Spitz, who had won seven medals in eight days, gave his last press conference, surrounded by Olympic guards and soldiers. 'As a human being and as a Jew, I am shocked and saddened by the outrage.' Spitz then announced that he had swum competitively for the last time.

Shane Gould
At the age of 15, Australian swimmer Shane Gould won five Olympic medals: three gold, one silver and a bronze.

Olga Korbut
Seventeen-year-old USSR gymnast Olga Korbut became an overnight sensation at the Games and was a major contributor to the popularity of gymnastics today. Winning three gold medals and one silver, she was a hit the world over as people followed the emotional highs and lows of her Olympic performance.

Moshe purposely led them past Apartment 2, which housed the fencers and athletes, and instead directed them towards Apartment 3 where the wresters and weightlifters resided. There they met weightlifter Yossef Romano who, along with Weinberg, tried to put up a fight. Six athletes managed to escape but Romano and Weinberg were both killed, and another four were taken hostage. The terrorists took up residence with their hostages in Building 31.

Word was spreading around the village that something was wrong. Three hundred armed police sealed off the area, and hundreds of foreign journalists and photographers gathered on the balconies of the buildings looking down on the Israeli headquarters. The one live (US) ABC-TV camera, which had been filming events in the stadium, was now focused on one window of Building 31, where it would remain for almost 24 hours. The terrorists had nine hostages and were ready to make their demands known to the world.

They asked for the release of 200 Arab political prisoners who were being held in Israeli jails, and they wanted them released by 9 am, after which, if their demands weren't met, they would start shooting the hostages. They also demanded safe passage out of the country. The terrorists were told that the German government was ready to pay any price, to which their leader replied, 'Money means nothing to us, our lives mean nothing to us.'

No Surrender

The president of the International Olympic Committee, Avery Brundage, immediately went into consultation with Munich police chief Manfred Schreiber. Brundage made it clear that he would not entertain the idea of the athletes leaving the village and he maintained that there should be no surrender to political blackmail. As time passed, the deadline shifted from 9 am to 11 am, to midday and then 2 pm. The Israeli Cabinet, led by Prime Minister Golda Meir, decided that they would not give in to the blackmail and also agreed with the German decision that the hostages would not be allowed to leave the country. Marksmen were told by the German Interior Minister, Hans-Dieter Genscher, to 'shoot if you get a chance'.

Despite the hostage situation, and knowing that two athletes were dead, Brundage announced that the Games must go on. At 9.39 am they resumed with the canoe–kayak heats.

Schreiber and Genscher continued negotiating with the terrorists and as the deadlines passed there were no more shootings. They were trying to persuade the terrorists that there was a way of leaving the country safely and the West German Chancellor Willy Brandt flew in to assist negotiations. On his arrival he announced to journalists that 'the happy games are over'. Word was spreading that the police sharpshooters were in position and ready to move if no solution had been reached by 5 pm.

FOR THE RECORD

Athletes killed:

Moshe Weinberg (33) – wrestling coach	Yacov Springer (51) – weightlifting judge
Yossef Romano (31) – weightlifter	Yossef Gutfreund (40) – wrestling referee
Mark Slavin (18) – wrestler	Kehat Shorr (53) – shooting coach
Eliezer Halfin (24) – wrestler	Andre Spitzer (27) – fencing coach
David Berger (28) – weightlifter	Amitzur Shapira (40) – track coach
Ze'ev Friedman (28) – weightlifter	

Meanwhile, many athletes were still unsure of what was happening. At 3.45 pm, Brundage, at the request of Israeli Prime Minister Golda Meir, issued a statement.

The Olympic peace has been broken by an act of assassination by criminal terrorists. The whole civilized world condemns this barbaric crime, this horror. With deep respect for the victims and as a sign of sympathy with the hostages not yet released this afternoon's sporting events have been cancelled.

This was an unprecedented move in Olympic history and one which had huge implications for athletes who had spent their lives training for the events.

Situation Under Control

The terrorists finally agreed to leave the country, but insisted that they take the hostages with them. A helicopter pad was built nearby and at 10.05 pm three helicopters arrived at the village. The German police were hoping to pick off the terrorists as they left Building 31 to make their way to the bus, but the terrorists stayed close to the hostages, ensuring that no sniper could find his mark. Munich police chief Schreiber got into one helicopter, along with the Bavarian Minister of the Interior, Bruno Merk. The terrorists and hostages were in the other two helicopters, and they headed towards Fürstenfeldbruck military airbase on the outskirts of Munich, where a Lufthansa Boeing 727 was waiting to take the terrorists to Cairo.

Thirty-seven minutes later, gunfire was heard coming from the airport. Back at the Olympic Village the journalists were told by Conrad Ahlers, a West German government spokesman, that three of the terrorists had been killed, as well as one German policeman, but that all the hostages had been rescued. The good news was spread around the world and Avery Brundage retired for the night, saying what a tremendous achievement it had been that all the Israeli athletes taken hostage were saved.

ABOVE: A helicopter gutted by a terrorist grenade. In the background, the plane carrying murdered weightlifter David Berger's body prepares to depart.

Bungled Operation

However, four hours later, at 3.22 am, a press conference was called where a very different truth emerged. Things at the airport had not gone according to plan. When the helicopters landed, the pilots were told to stand in front of their aircraft as the terrorists did a reconnaissance of the Lufthansa plane. As the terrorists returned to the helicopters, German sharpshooters opened fire. Bullets flew everywhere, as both sides engaged in a frenzied shoot-out. Three terrorists were gunned down and another rolled back into the shadows under the helicopter. There was an hour of silence before the police implemented the second stage of their attack by bringing in armoured cars. Thinking they were about to be machine gunned, one of the terrorists threw a grenade into one of the helicopters and ran down the tarmac with the helicopter blazing behind him. Four Israeli hostages were in the destroyed helicopter and the remaining five were found still bound together in the other, riddled with bullets. Three of the terrorists were taken into custody.

ABC news reporter Jim McKay, who had been following the story all day, went on air with an unforgettable statement.

When I was a kid my father used to say our greatest hopes and our worst fears are seldom realized. Our worst fears have been realized tonight. They have now said there were eleven hostages; two were killed in their rooms yesterday morning, nine were killed at the airport tonight. They're all gone.

Eleven hostages, five terrorists and one German policeman were dead. As the Olympic Village woke to hear the news, the spirit of the Games was broken. Israel and countries across the world blamed the Germans for what was seen as a botched response to the kidnappings. However, German police saw it differently. They blamed the bungled rescue attempt on an unfortunate combination of political factors: the refusal of the Israeli government to negotiate with the terrorists, the unwillingness of Egypt to assist and the fanaticism of the terrorists, who refused to back down. 'The hostages were as good as dead from the minute the Israeli government refused to hand over the prisoners,' said Schreiber.

However, there was no escaping the fact that the German police had made some startling errors that highlighted their inexperience in an operation of this scale. Communication among the force was poor, and the unit at the airport was never told that there were eight terrorists instead of five, as they'd originally been informed. Consequently, the five marksmen they had in position were at a distinct disadvantage. They also had no radio contact or even night vision for their guns. Another unit of 17 armed police officers waited aboard the plane posing as flight crew. The plan was to ambush the terrorists as they carried out an inspection of the plane. However, this particular group also had no radio contact with the command unit and at the last minute made the fateful decision to abandon their posts rather than put their own lives at risk. Realising that a grenade thrown into the plane would be an immediate death sentence, they chose to ignore their orders. The police had also erected three mobile lighting towers that exacerbated the shadows thrown off the helicopters. Unable to see clearly, they had no idea that some of the terrorists, armed with grenades, were still inside the helicopters with the hostages.

World condemnation resulted. The Philippine and Algerian teams immediately pulled out of the Games as a sign of respect for the dead athletes. Some competitors from Norway and the Netherlands also left, with Dutch runner Jos Hermens quoted as saying, 'You give a party, and someone is killed at the party, you don't continue the party, you go home. That's what I'm doing.' US President Richard Nixon expressed his regret and made it clear that the US would introduce sanctions on any country seen to support the terrorists. An Egyptian spokesman, Mr Youssef, told Australian reporters that there were two sides to every story.

For twenty-five years they have been hoping something will be done for them. They have lost their homes, their rights—and this forced on them by the Israelis has made them desperate. You cannot put all the blame on them. Of course we do not condone such actions—civilians are involved.

I experienced level after level of grief; for my own event, the marathon, those years of preparation now useless; for the dead and doomed Israelis; and for the violated sanctuary of the Games.

– KENNY MOORE, US MARATHON RUNNER, WRITING FOR *SPORTS ILLUSTRATED*

Business as Usual

On 6 September all the athletes gathered in the stadium for a remembrance service. In the centre, 11 chairs sat empty in memory of the Israelis killed. Flags flew at half-mast as the Olympic flame still burnt brightly, flickering to the tune of Beethoven's 'Funeral March'. The speech by German President Gustav Heinemann resonated with everyone.

> *The Olympic ideal has not been destroyed. We owe it more now than ever before. In the incident we have just experienced, no line divides North and South, East and West. Here the division is between the brotherhood of all men who desire peace and those who place in jeopardy the things which make life worth living.*

The names of the hostages were read out by the head of the Israeli delegation and 80,000 spectators stood as a mark of respect.

Avery Brundage's speech unfortunately hit a raw nerve.

> *Sadly in this imperfect world, the greater and the more important the Olympic Games become, the more they are open to commercial, political and now criminal pressure. The games of the XXth Olympiad have been subjected to two savage attacks. We lost the Rhodesian battle against naked political blackmail. We have only the strength of a great ideal ... The Games must go on and we must continue our efforts to keep them clean, pure and honest, and try to extend the sportsmanship of the athletic field into other areas.*

RIGHT: When Abu Daoud, leader of the Black September group, was captured in France in 1977 but quickly released, Israelis demonstrated outside the French Embassy in Jerusalem.

Brundage never once referred to the individual athletes and instead was seen to use the opportunity to praise the Olympic movement, in which he had played a large part. His speech appeared to put the massacre of the hostages on the same footing as the recent Rhodesian controversy, in which he had unsuccessfully opposed the exclusion of Rhodesia from the Games in the face of a threatened boycott by the other African nations. He also announced that the Games would go ahead, just one day behind schedule, and later that afternoon the Games resumed. The Munich Olympics were the 84-year-old Brundage's last.

The *New York Times* said, 'Walled off in their dream world, appallingly unaware of the realities of life and death, the aging playground directors who conduct this quadrennial muscle dance ruled that a little blood must not be permitted to interrupt play.'

'The Olympic idea was murdered in Munich,' said Esther Shachamorov Roth, one of Israel's top runners at the 1972 Games. 'There was a one-day memorial, and then it was business as usual, back to the routine. I was amazed that people were murdered and the Games went on. I was naive, but that experience changed my outlook on life.'

'Incredibly, they're going on with it,' said Jim Murray of the *LA Times*. 'It's almost like having a dance at Dachau.'

However, many thought that Brundage was right and that an institution such as the Olympics should be above political demands. The end of the Games couldn't come soon enough for many of the athletes. The carnival atmosphere of the first week had given way to a grim village surrounded by troop carriers and soldiers armed with submachine guns. Flowers covered the village sidewalks. Five days later the closing ceremony was held, but it had none of the celebratory nature of those of Games gone by.

Just over a month later, on 29 October, a German Lufthansa jet was hijacked and demands were made for the release of the three terrorists awaiting trial. Keen to be rid of the situation, Germany released them all and flew them to Libya. Golda Meir and her Defence Committee retaliated, secretly authorising the Israeli secret service agency Mossad to assassinate all those responsible for the massacre, in a counter-terrorism campaign called 'Wrath of God'.

Twenty-four hours of terror had threatened the very existence of the Olympic Games, left 17 people dead and threatened the future of peace in the Middle East. It showed once and for all that the Olympics and politics are impossible to separate.

OFF THE RECORD

▶ In 2005 Steven Spielberg's film *Munich* was released to high acclaim and six Oscar nominations.

▶ Kevin Macdonald's documentary about the Munich massacre, *One Day in September*, won the Oscar for best documentary in 2000.

BACKGROUND:	Black emancipation in America
EVENT:	World heavyweight boxing championship
OPPONENTS:	Muhammad Ali v George Foreman
ARENA:	Kinshasa Stadium, Zaire (now Democratic Republic of Congo)

Rumble in the Jungle

ZAIRE, 1974

I wanted to establish a relationship between American blacks and Africans. All the time I was there, I'd travel to the jungles, places where there was no radio or television, and people would come up to me, and I could touch them. The fight was about racial problems, Vietnam. All of that. — **MUHAMMAD ALI IN NEWSWEEK**

OPPOSITE: Muhammad Ali (right) in action against George Foreman during the world heavyweight fight at Kinshasa Stadium in Zaire in 1974.

THE YEAR WAS 1974

▶ Richard Nixon became the first US president to resign from office following the Watergate scandal.

▶ Stevie Wonder claimed the Grammy for best album for *Innervisions*.

▶ Francis Ford Coppola's *The Godfather, Part II* won the Oscar for best picture.

▶ It was an American double at Wimbledon, with Jimmy Connors taking out the men's title and Chris Evert winning the women's tournament.

▶ In the United States, Frank Robinson became the first African-American manager in major league baseball.

▶ The British Lions Rugby Union team's tour of South Africa was marred by on-pitch violence as both teams took advantage of the lack of television cameras to settle their grudges physically.

▶ Australia reclaimed cricket's Ashes in the 1974-75 season by defeating England 4-1.

The 'Rumble in the Jungle' is thought of by many as the greatest comeback story of all time. Having won the world heavyweight championship, Cassius Clay converted to Islam and changed his name to Muhammad Ali. When the American military called on him to use his fighting prowess in Vietnam, Muhammad Ali refused to sign up and was consequently stripped of his title by the US government and temporarily banned from the ring. When the ban was lifted, Ali was determined to regain the title. One man stood in his way: the colossus, George Foreman, a man Ali referred to as the 'meanest, baddest boxer on the planet'.

When promoter Don King arranged for the eagerly anticipated fight to take place in Zaire, Muhammad Ali saw it as an opportunity to turn the spotlight on race relations in the United States. Upon his arrival in Africa he quickly started to whip up local support by celebrating the connection between African and American blacks. He spoke of how he and his fellow African Americans had been taken from Africa in shackles but were returning as victors. By the time George Foreman arrived in Zaire, Ali had drummed up overwhelming support and had, incredibly, managed to make many people believe that Foreman was white. Viewed as the underdog and judged even by his own camp as having little chance of victory, Muhammad Ali pulled off one of the most extraordinary wins in history and emerged as a champion for people, black and white, throughout the world.

State of the Nation

The early sixties had seen the first US combat troops arrive in Vietnam. As a growing number of young Americans returned in body bags, many people were asking why they were risking their lives fighting on the other side of the world in a country they knew little about. The intense anti-war feeling was creating divisions in American society, and the war became about race, class, religion and politics. The black civil rights movement, which had made such progress in the fifties, was reeling from the assassinations of the civil rights leaders Martin Luther King, Jr and Malcolm X. The Jim Crow laws which segregated whites and blacks were still in place, and the African-American experience was that of a country divided. The violent backlash against the civil rights movement led to a number of militant separatist black organisations demanding a political voice in a country where the power appeared to be concentrated in the hands of the white man.

King of the World

At the 1960 Rome Olympics, Cassius Clay won the gold medal for boxing and patriotic fellow Americans embraced him as one of their own. He went on to beat the world heavyweight titleholder Sonny Liston in February 1964, and was enthusiastically hailed as the new champion of the world. Clay's speed and mobility in the ring were those of a middleweight, and his outspoken antics out of the ring set him apart from other boxers in the public arena. After winning the world title, Clay announced that he had abandoned Christianity to join the Nation of Islam, becoming a Black Muslim and adopting the name Muhammad Ali. Immediately he became a target for the conservative establishment, who viewed him as a subversive influence capable of inciting race wars. Ali himself proudly and confidently announced that he was 'king of the world'.

In early 1966, while he was in Miami and surrounded by reporters, Ali received the news that he was to be drafted to fight in Vietnam. His spontaneous response instantly became one of the most famous anti-war declarations of the time: 'Man, I ain't got no quarrel with them Viet Cong.' Ali chose to be a conscientious objector to war service, on religious grounds. Already perceived as a contentious figure, Muhammad Ali now found himself accused of being 'un-American'. On 28 April 1967 he was stripped of his heavyweight title, his passport was revoked and he was banned from the ring. For a man at the height of his career the financial losses were huge.

The Olympic hero of the early sixties suffered an immediate loss of public approval, and many now looked on him as nothing more than a coward and a draft dodger. However, he also had many supporters in the United States and across the world who admired his stand against the US government. When a heavyweight champion of the world refuses to fight, he can hardly be accused of cowardice. It seemed impossible to silence the brash, outspoken 'Louisville Lip'. He was charismatic, loud and, best of all, unpredictable. Three years later, the New York Supreme Court ruled that his boxing licence had been unjustly revoked and he was permitted to fight again. Still maintaining his opposition to the war in Vietnam, a much slower and heavier Ali returned to the ring for a series of bouts preparing him for another attempt at the title that he saw as rightfully belonging to him.

The Biggest Prize Purse Ever

In January 1973, the world heavyweight champion Joe Frazier lost his title to George Foreman by a second round knockout, and before Foreman had even left the ring Ali was beside him laying down his challenge. A new promoter, Don King, came on to the scene and Ali and Foreman signed a deal to fight each other for US$5 million apiece, the biggest prize purse to date. The only factors that needed to be decided were where the title bout would be held and who would come up with the money. This was a fight that deserved a dramatic backdrop.

On the other side of the world, in the Republic of Zaire—formerly the Belgian Congo, and nowadays known as the People's Republic of Congo—dictator Mobutu Sese Seko offered to host the fight. As the seventh-richest man in the

---

WHEN WE WERE KING

Due to legal entanglements with the film's financers, it took 22 years for Leon Gast to release the documentary he had shot in Zaire in 1974. *When We Were Kings* won the Oscar for best documentary feature at the 1996 Academy Awards. George Foreman and Muhammad Ali went on stage together to collect the award, with Foreman assisting Ali, who had Parkinson's disease, up the steps.

world, Mobutu was well placed to put up the prize money, especially since he would be dipping into the national coffers. As the leader of an emerging African nation, Mobutu wanted to showcase Zaire as a civilised country ready to compete on the international scene. In fact, Mobutu was a dictator who was anything but civilised. Keen to present his country in the best possible light, he had criminals rounded up and shot before the foreign press arrived, and rumours circulated that hundreds of people were detained in special cells underneath the stadium in the capital, Kinshasa. However, such political and social concerns did not derail the preparations, and the fight was scheduled for 25 September 1974.

King worked with the documentary movie producer Leon Gast and the music festival producer Lloyd Price to turn the event into a celebration of black culture. Conceived of as a 'black Woodstock,' the Zaire '74 Music Festival was staged over the two weeks preceding the fight. A dazzling array of performers including James Brown, the Fanya All-Stars, B.B. King, the Pointer Sisters, Bill Withers and Sister Sledge flew into the country, ready to provide the soundtrack for the drama that was about to unfold.

Foreman's Fists

The fight meant everything to Ali. It was his chance of redemption after having been stripped of the title seven years earlier. He knew that if he could beat Foreman, his claim to be the greatest heavyweight champion of all time would be taken seriously. But at 32, Ali was considered to be past his prime. Foreman, on the other hand, was only 26, and had knocked out both Ken Norton and Joe Frazier in a mere two rounds. Many boxing pundits considered him invincible, and to this day he is often named as the single greatest puncher in heavyweight history. Not only had he never lost, but he had knocked out 37 of his 40 opponents, with his last eight fights finishing inside six minutes. He was a giant of a man whose punching bag had become legendary because of the huge dents he'd left in it with his rock-like fists. 'I've moulded a monster,' said Dick Sadler, his trainer. 'I've taken the best of Joe Louis, Jack Johnson and Rocky Marciano and rolled it all into one.'

The odds were stacked so high against Muhammad Ali that even his trainer was praying that he wouldn't be killed. Many in the boxing world made bets on how long Ali would last before going down for the count.

'Ali, Bomaye!'

When Ali arrived in Kinshasa three weeks before the fight, the documentary team caught it on film. Leon Gast couldn't believe the reaction Ali was receiving. 'They were coming across the roof of the terminal. Ali did this little press conference and then came out and there were people yelling, "Ali, bomaye! Ali, bomaye!"' ('Ali, kill him!') Ali immediately adopted this as his catchphrase for the pre-fight

Mr President, I've been a citizen of the United States of America for 33 years and was never invited to the White House. It sure gives me pleasure to be invited to the Black House.

– MUHAMMAD ALI ON MEETING PRESIDENT MOBUTU

OPPOSITE: Ali shows what he intends to do to George Foreman in the upcoming 'rumble in the jungle'.

> **Some people thought I was a hero. Some people said that what I did was wrong. But everything I did was according to my conscience. I made a stand all people, not just black people, should have thought about making, because it wasn't just black people being drafted. The government had a system where the rich man's son went to college, and the poor man's son went to war.**
>
> – MUHAMMAD ALI

campaign. Foreman hadn't even arrived in the country and Ali's quick talking and amusing antics had already persuaded an entire nation that he was king. Foreman also did himself no favours when he stepped off his plane accompanied by a German Shepherd dog, the breed notorious for its use by Zaire's former colonial oppressors, the Belgians.

Foreman had never excelled at promoting himself. He first caught the world's attention when he won the gold medal at the heavyweight championship at the 1968 Summer Olympics. While athletes Tommie Smith and John Carlos were giving the famous black power salute on the victory dais to protest against the state of human rights in America, Foreman showed his pro-establishment politics by waving two tiny American flags as he strode victoriously around the ring. Many people hated him for it, but Foreman defended his position, saying that he was a living example of the American dream. Being a man of few words, he did little to engage public support while in Zaire and chose to leave the verbal gymnastics to his opponent.

In contrast, Ali spent these weeks concentrating on his PR campaign. At every opportunity he would demean Foreman, calling him 'nothing but a slow-moving mummy'. He maintained that Foreman moved so slowly there was little likelihood of him ever landing a punch on the swift-footed Ali. Foreman had his own comeback, telling the press that he'd developed an 'anywhere punch' that would hurt no matter where it landed.

The fight was going to be broadcast across the world and was getting huge media attention. However, eight days before it was due to happen, Foreman suffered a cut to his eye during a sparring session and the fight was postponed for five weeks, until 30 October.

Watch me dance!

Afraid that he would lose his money, President Mobutu forbade both opponents to leave the country. Although it came out later that Ali wanted to leave just as much as Foreman did, he exploited the delay by mingling with the people, showcasing his extrovert personality, praising black culture and building up a solid fan base. Everywhere he went, he told the people and the worldwide audience the same thing: that he had been taught that blacks were inferior—and yet here he was in Africa where 'they had their own airline, their own post offices, their own supermarkets, and I thought it was just about the best thing I'd ever seen. A country run by blacks!' Meanwhile, Foreman hardly left his hotel room, unaware of the psychological warfare being used against him.

As the musicians and journalists left and the rainy season approached, spirits were dampened. Ali's camp was worried. They knew that the heat would make the ropes stretch and that wet weather would soften the mat and slow down the legendary dance steps which Ali used to outmanoeuvre his opponents. Despite Ali's popularity, Foreman was still the favourite and it was well known that Foreman's camp was predicting a knockout in the third round. Many people assumed this would be Ali's swan song.

The fight was scheduled for four o'clock in the morning so that it could be broadcast on US prime time. Sixty thousand spectators gathered in the open-air stadium. Storm clouds threatened as the monsoon rains approached. As the highly charged atmosphere intensified, Ali's dressing room began to feel like a morgue. His trainers believed Ali would suffer defeat and that the failure would surely break him as a man.

As always, Ali was irrepressible. He made his way to the ring with the chant of 'Ali, Ali, bomaye! Ali, Ali, bomaye!' filling the air. Arriving before Foreman, Ali used the time to dance, shout and whip the crowd into a frenzy of support. As Foreman stepped into the ring, his gigantic frame loomed across the moonlit night and the world's most anticipated fight was set to begin.

Rope-a-dope

As the opening bell sounded, Ali moved quickly. He hit Foreman with a sharp right then peppered his face with jabs. He had the better of Foreman for the first round, but conditions were against him. Ali knew that he had to adjust his tactics. 'The ring was so slow,' he said. 'Dancing all night, my legs would have got tired.' He also realised that Foreman was quicker than he had thought. His entire campaign had revolved around out-manoeuvring Foreman, but the world champion had been listening and had improved his footwork in readiness. Ali chose to ignore the advice coming from his corner, and early in the second round he adopted a tactic which later became known as 'rope-a-dope'. He stopped the footwork and propped himself against the ropes, blocking and covering and leaning as far back as possible. It seemed pitiful to watch him weathering blow after massive blow, but the fact was that Foreman was slowly tiring himself out.

While everyone was screaming for Ali to get off the ropes, Foreman, known for his killer punches, was raining haymakers on his opponent. As he punched, Ali started to goad him: 'You ain't got no punch, you phoney. Show me something, sucker.' At the end of the second round Ali suddenly came back with quick, straight jabs and right crosses straight at Foreman's head. 'Sucker, is that all you got? Is that the hardest you can hit?'

The third round started and again Ali was taking a pounding from the champion. Foreman hit him with an uppercut and for a moment it looked as though Foreman was going to move in and finish off the fight. But suddenly Ali came out from under with straight rights and lefts. Foreman was startled. As he retired to his corner at the end of the round, he knew he was in trouble.

I'm the only black man in the world standin' up for my people.

– MUHAMMAD ALI

RIGHT: Ali let Foreman tire himself out before flattening him with a left-right combo in the eighth round.

FOR THE RECORD

In 1975, Ali met Joe Frazier
and successfully defended his
title in a brutal 15-round battle
called 'The Thrilla in Manila.'
In February 1978, Ali lost his
second championship to a
younger and more powerful
boxer, Leon Spinks, in Las
Vegas, Nevada. However, in
their rematch later that year
Ali regained the title, becoming
the first boxer to be a three-
time world heavyweight
champion. In 1981 he lost his
title to Larry Holmes, and after
one final defeat by Trevor
Berbick in 1981 he retired from
professional boxing.

His boxing record stands
at 108 wins and 8 losses
in his amateur career
(including the Olympic light-
heavyweight gold medal in
Rome in 1960), and 56 wins
(37 by knockout) and 5 losses
as a professional boxer.

In 1996 he carried the Olympic
torch in the last stage of its
journey and lit the cauldron to
announce the commencement
of that year's Games in Atlanta,
Georgia. He was awarded
a replacement gold medal
for the one he had thrown
into the Ohio River in 1960
in protest against racial
discrimination in America.

Ali was refusing to lie down. Foreman's cornermen knew it too. The champion had rarely needed to fight for longer than six minutes and his power punches were only sustainable for a short time.

The next four rounds continued in a similar fashion, with Ali springing to life at the end of each round and inciting the crowd to cry out his name. People around the world could hardly bear to watch as the master of spin took a barbaric beating, rarely moving off the ropes. For seven rounds Ali was a punching bag for one of the heaviest hitters ever to box.

But at the end of the seventh round, there was a shift. It began to look like Foreman was punching himself out. He didn't know what to do: 'I went out and hit Muhammad with the hardest body shot I ever delivered to an opponent. Anyone else in the world would have crumbled.' As Foreman's pace slowed and his punches got weaker, Ali knew that he had to take a chance before the champion had time to get his second wind.

As Foreman lumbered out into the ring for the eighth round, Ali was still taunting him. He stayed on the ropes for most of the round, but with 15 seconds to go he landed a couple of jabs, and then caught Foreman with a sharp right, causing him to stumble backwards. Ali knew that he had him. He charged at Foreman, and landed another right, a concussive left hook and a final right to the jaw that laid the champion flat. Foreman knew that it was all over. 'He threw a left-right combination. It struck ground zero on my chin. I remember thinking, "Boy, I'm going down."'

He was officially counted out with two seconds remaining in the round, still trying to get to his feet. As Muhammad Ali raised his arms in victory, the BBC commentator David Frost announced it to be 'the most joyous scene in the history of boxing'. It had been ten years since Ali had beaten Sonny Liston and seven years since he had been stripped of his title. To the delight of Zaire and the total amazement of the boxing profession, Muhammad Ali was once again the heavyweight champion of the world. He had got what he set out to achieve: validation and redemption. Within hours the rains swept in and the stadium stood in several feet of water.

The Greatest

Foreman came up with excuses for his defeat, claiming among other things that he'd been drugged and that the ropes had been tampered with. But as the years passed he accepted the result with good grace. 'That night, he was just the better man in the ring ... Finally, I realized I'd lost to a great champion—probably the greatest of them all—and now I'm just proud to be part of the Ali legend.'

Fighting in Africa gave Muhammad Ali the opportunity to remind African Americans where they had come from and what they were capable of achieving. By showing the Zaireans running their country efficiently without a white person in sight, he embraced a successful African history and provided a connection between the two nations. His message was clear. As a freedom and justice fighter he told black Americans that they didn't have to be what white America wanted them to be.

> *I was baptised when I was twelve, but I didn't know what I was doing. I'm not a Christian any more. I know where I'm going, and I know the truth, and I don't have to be what you want me to be. I'm free to be what I want.*

2

Waving The Flag

BACKGROUND:	Irish War of Independence
EVENT:	English Crown forces v The IRA
OPPONENTS:	Dublin v Tipperary
ARENA:	Croke Park, Dublin, Ireland

Bloody Sunday: The Croke Park Massacre

DUBLIN, 1920

We understand that Tipperary's superiority over Dublin in football, despite two decisive victories by Tipperary, is being questioned by Dublin. We therefore challenge Dublin to a match on the first available date, on any venue and for any object.

— SIGNED ON BEHALF OF THE TIPPERARY FOOTBALL TEAM, T. RYAN, SEC.

PREVIOUS PAGE: The Argentine team celebrate their 3-2 victory over Germany in the 1986 World Cup.
OPPOSITE: People view some of the damage caused by the 1920 riots in Dublin.

THE YEAR WAS 1920

▶ Martial law was declared in Ireland by the British Government.

▶ Prohibition began in the US as the Eighteenth Amendment made the sale, manufacture and transportation of alcohol illegal.

▶ The first successful transatlantic radio broadcast took place.

▶ The 'unknown soldier' was buried in Westminster Abbey, London.

▶ The Queensland and Northern Territory Aerial Services, later known as Qantas, was founded.

▶ The London Metropolitan Police began introducing cars as an alternative method of transport to horses.

▶ In cricket, Australia defeated England by five Test matches to nil.

▶ The first Olympic Games since 1912 were held in Antwerp, Belgium (the 1916 Games were cancelled due to World War I), with America winning the most medals.

▶ Rugby Union made one of its few appearances at the Olympic Games, with the US team winning gold.

On 24 February 2007 the crowds gathered for a historic rugby union match between England and Ireland at Croke Park, Dublin. It was the 2007 Six Nations Championships and, for the very first time, the Gaelic Athletic Association (GAA) had agreed to host the rugby internationals at Croke Park, while the national stadium at Lansdowne Road was closed for redevelopment. A stadium that came into being solely for the purpose of promoting Gaelic sport, Croke Park was a symbol of Irish independence and allowing the game to take place there signified a new era in Anglo-Irish relations. The Irish Republic, less than a century old, was welcoming the English and proudly taking its rightful place on the international playing field.

However, this match held a special poignancy, being the first time the stadium had hosted an English–Irish confrontation since Irish blood had been spilled in the Croke Park Massacre of 1920. Eighty-seven years prior, on a cold winter's afternoon, English troops had stormed into Croke Park, killing 14 people and injuring up to 100 spectators on the day that became known as Bloody Sunday (a second Bloody Sunday followed 52 years later in Derry). The decision by the GAA to allow the English to play at Croke Park was not without controversy. After the massacre it had been deemed that the Union Jack, a symbol of imperial oppression, would never again fly over the grounds. Consequently, the English agreed to fly their secondary flag, the St George's Cross. But there was another issue: extreme Irish Republicans couldn't countenance the idea of the English national anthem being sung on what was considered to be hallowed ground. There were threats of disruption and police braced for potential violence.

Although for most the animosity was long gone, the significance of the game, both culturally and socially, was lost on no-one. Ireland was again facing the English and everyone present knew that it was a time to honour those lost on the very same turf.

State of the Nation

Twelve months after the official end of World War I, Britain was suffering from a weak economy, with inflation on the rise. The miners and railway workers were on strike and unemployment was high as large numbers of soldiers returned from war.

From January 1919 Ireland was involved in a civil war known as the War of Independence. Tensions between Ireland and England were building and by the early twentieth century the push for Irish independence had become militant. The Irish Bill for Home Rule aimed to grant self-government and national autonomy to Ireland within the United Kingdom of Great Britain and Ireland was set to go before the House of Lords on Tuesday, 23 November 1920. At this time Lord Mayor MacSweeney of Cork was imprisoned by the Crown and died on a hunger strike, sparking a wave of violence in Ireland which lasted for months.

With violence and killings on the increase, the Royal Irish Constabulary (RIC) came under criticism for failing to curb the unrest. Consequently, the government held a recruiting drive in England, offering policing jobs in Ireland to the soldiers returning from World War I. With unemployment rising, it was an opportunity not to be missed.

ABOVE: On the day of the Six Nations rugby match, the Republican organisation Sinn Fein held a protest near Croke Park.

The Black and Tans

In March 1920, despite having little or no training in policing, the soldiers were sent to Ireland to contain the unrest. But many of them were men who had just come off the battlefield, on edge, violent and knowing nothing but hard discipline. They became known as the Black and Tans: the RIC had run out of uniforms and initially clothed them in a combination of the Irish Police and the British Army uniform, and the name stuck. Their rough tactics soon put the Irish population offside as they started to terrorise innocent citizens.

Realising that the Black and Tans were becoming difficult to control, the government introduced ex-officers into the mix, known as the Auxiliaries. The Irish War of Independence had commenced and the behaviour of what were seen as 'Crown forces' did nothing to help stem the tide of hatred building.

The Cairo Gang

On 20 November 1920, the captains of Dublin and Tipperary were preparing for the afternoon match that would take place at Croke Park the following day. It was a match destined for the history books, for all the wrong reasons. That same night Michael Collins, leader of the IRA, was giving instructions for the assassination of the Cairo Gang, a network of British spies posing as travelling businessmen and living in Dublin.

The next morning the IRA rampaged through the streets and, in front of families and neighbours, 14 British agents were gunned down. Michael Collins was unrepentant.

By their destruction the very air is made sweeter. That should be the future's judgement on this event. For myself, my conscience is clear. There is no crime in detecting and destroying, in wartime, the spy and the informer.

Dubliners knew that the British Auxiliaries would be quick to take action, as they were known to be hot-headed and swift to retaliate. But no-one knew exactly when this would happen, and the threat didn't stop 10,000 spectators making their way to Croke Park for the Dublin v Tipperary Gaelic football match.

Troops Mobilise

Gaelic football was incredibly popular and as the War for Independence raged, people clung to anything that represented their grassroots. Families stood together to shout for their team and outside the stadium boys were perched up in the trees, delighted that they were watching the match without having paid.

For Dublin, it was a home game and the support was huge. However, as Michael Hogan led the Tipperary side on to the field he knew that his team stood a good chance, having beaten Dublin in two of their previous games. By all accounts the air was charged and there were high expectations of a good match unfolding. At 3.15 pm the referee blew his whistle and for a time the people of Dublin enjoyed a reprieve from the morning's violence.

However, the spectators were unaware that outside the stadium British security forces were mobilising. As the Auxiliaries were approaching from the north-west, a convoy of troops was coming in from the south. The plan was to raid the grounds, block off the exits and search every man in the crowd. The British forces believed that the men responsible for the morning's bloodshed were hiding within the stadium, supported by the GAA, which they suspected was a front for the IRA.

The crowd tensed as a volley of shots filled the air. They came from outside the stadium. William Robinson, 11, fell mortally wounded from the tree that had given him a much-prized view. Next to go was Jerome O'Leary, 10, who was shot in the head as he sat like a sentry on the wall at the south-west end of the field.

OPPOSITE: Soldiers hold back civilians at a riot in Dublin on 22 November 1920.

As the spectators ran, the British stormed the grounds, firing indiscriminately into the crowd. Many shots were fired over the heads of the fleeing fans, but some bullets found their mark. Caught at the centre of the field and unsure of which way to turn, Tipperary captain Michael Hogan fell to the ground as he took a bullet in the back. As he lay on the ground dying, a spectator, Thomas Ryan, knelt beside him to administer the last rites. He too was shot dead.

Jeannie Boyle, who was at the match with her fiancé—they were to be married the following week—also took a fatal shot. It was 90 seconds of mayhem and carnage. The Auxiliary officers had lost control of the troops and 114 rounds of ammunition had been fired, as well as 50 rounds of machine gun fire from the armoured car stationed outside the gates. When commanding officer Major Mills finally pulled his troops back into line, 14 people were dead and the injured were strewn across the pitch. The pointless mission continued, and men within the crowd were stripped and left shivering on the field. At the end of an extensive search, only one revolver was found and there was no evidence that the men responsible for the morning's killings were present.

When the people who died were examined later, most were found to have been shot in the back as they tried to retreat. It was a total disaster for English–Irish relations and the moment became a tipping point as hatred towards the English increased and support for a republican government spread. Trying to save face, the English tried to push the blame on the IRA and issued a press release explaining the events.

> *A number of men came to Dublin on Saturday under the guise of asking to attend a football match between Tipperary and Dublin. But their real intention was to take part in the series of murderous outrages which took place in Dublin that morning. Learning on Saturday that a number of these gunmen were present in Croke Park, the crown forces went to raid the field. It was the original intention that an officer would go to the centre of the field and speaking from a megaphone, invite the assassins to come forward. But on their approach, armed pickets gave warning. Shots were fired to warn the wanted men, who caused a stampede and escaped in the confusion.*

The world's press devoted its main coverage to the deaths of the British agents, whose bodies were taken back to London, where they received a state funeral at Westminster Abbey. When an Irish politician attempted to bring up the subject of Croke Park in the British Parliament, a fight broke out and his protests fell on deaf ears. For a long time the true story of Croke Park was covered up. The result of a military inquiry was released in later years, which found the actions of the British forces 'indiscriminate, and unjustifiable'.

Lest We Forget

The Six Nations game in 2007 ensured that the story of Croke Park would never again be forgotten. So important was the event that on the day before the match Brian Ashton, a former Irish captain, flew to Ireland to talk with the English team and explain the significance of what was about to take place. Silence fell throughout the ground as a drum roll signified the start of 'God Save the Queen'. The Hogan stand—named for the murdered Tipperary captain—braced itself as the English fans it housed proudly sang their anthem. Irish fans listened respectfully. Then the Irish crowd started up a rousing rendition of 'Amhrán na bhFiann'. Players and fans alike sang their hearts out, with tears streaming down their cheeks. As the singing came to an end, the entire stadium broke into applause that signified mutual appreciation. The riot police surrounding the ground relaxed visibly. Jerome Reilly from the *Irish Independent* echoed the relief felt by many who had predicted violence: 'They played "God Save The Queen" at Croke Park yesterday. And the world did not stop turning.'

The referee's whistle blew and the Irish came out in full force. They had what was possibly the best first half ever seen in Irish rugby history, and as rugby fans the world over watched, it became obvious that an unforgettable match was materialising. Ninety minutes later the game ended with a score of 43–13. It was the biggest win Ireland had ever achieved over their English competitors and for the heroes in green, victory was sweet. The whole stadium, English and Irish alike, acknowledged the moment as one for the history books.

BACKGROUND:	Against fascism
EVENT:	Water polo semi-final
OPPONENTS:	Hungary v USSR
ARENA:	1956 Summer Olympics, Melbourne

Blood in the Water

MELBOURNE, AUSTRALIA, 1956

We felt we were playing not just for ourselves but for every Hungarian. This game was the only way we could fight back. — **ERVIN ZADOR**

OPPOSITE: Hungarian player Ervin Zador bleeds profusely after having been hit in the right eye by the Soviet captain in the Melbourne Olympics water polo semi-final.

The most violent game of water polo in Olympic history took place on 6 December 1956. When Hungary met the Soviet Union in the final round of the Melbourne Olympic water polo competition, the two countries were embroiled in bitter conflict as the Hungarian people rebelled against the harsh Soviet regime and the Soviets dealt with the rebellion by killing thousands of Hungarians. Skirmishes in the water led to Hungarian player Ervin Zador getting hit in the right eye by the Soviet captain. As blood dripped from his eye into the water and a camera clicked, the moment became iconic of the greater struggle of the Cold War.

State of the Nation

The year 1956 was one of intense international crisis, leading to the very first boycotting of an Olympic games. Egypt, Lebanon and Iraq had all withdrawn from the Games over British and French involvement in the Suez Canal crisis. Meanwhile Spain, Switzerland and the Netherlands withdrew to demonstrate their solidarity with Hungary. The President of the Dutch National Olympic Committee voiced his concerns over the IOC's decision to go ahead with the Games: 'How would we like it if our people had been atrociously murdered, and someone said that sports should prevail?'

Since 1948 Hungary had been a People's Democracy under Soviet rule. Free speech was denied and the secret police employed brutal tactics to make sure the Hungarians fell into line. The people of Eastern Europe were ruled by the Communist Soviet Union, but when Stalin died in 1953, the Hungarians hoped for change. When their northern neighbour Poland stood up to the Soviets and successfully installed a change of government with no bloodshed, Hungary felt optimistic and looked to the new Soviet leader, Nikita Khrushchev.

The Hungarian Communist Party wanted a more liberal state of affairs and in July 1956, with Khrushchev's support, the Hungarian party leader Matyas Rakosi was dismissed. By October 1956, there was a move to ban the teaching of Russian in schools, and this led to a students' manifesto. The students put forward 16 demands, including a request for the withdrawal of all Soviet troops.

From late October to early November, all eyes were on Hungary. What started as a student demonstration had quickly evolved into a full-scale rebellion, led by cries of 'Ruszkik haza!'—'Russians, go home!' US President Eisenhower said, 'I feel with the Hungarian people.' John Foster Dulles, American Secretary of State, said, 'To all those suffering under communist slavery, let us say you can count on us.' The Hungarians strove for independence believing that they had the support of the West.

A mass demonstration took place on 23 October in Budapest. Students, factory workers and soldiers gathered outside the Parliament building. The crowd of between two and three hundred thousand was briefly addressed by the man everyone saw as the next leader, the more liberal-minded communist Imre Nagy. Demonstrators turned over a statue of Stalin and tried to have their demands broadcast on national radio. The state police moved in with tear gas and guns. The initially peaceful demonstration spiralled out of control as the Hungarian soldiers sent to aid the police now sided with the crowd.

The next five days saw bitter conflict between the local people and the Soviet troops. Nagy agreed to be the appointed leader of the new movement and, keen to stop the violence, he ordered an immediate ceasefire on 30 October.

After negotiating with the Soviet Union, it seemed that Hungary might be as successful as Poland in their quest for independence. The withdrawal of Soviet troops commenced and the Soviets issued a statement saying they deeply regretted the violence that had occurred and that rather than aggravating the situation with their military presence they would pull out.

Red Army Invasion

When the violence first erupted, the Hungarian water polo team was training high in the hills above Budapest. As they heard volleys of shots and saw the fires burning in the city below, they had no way of knowing what was going on. Their Soviet trainers withheld information, and in the time leading up to the Olympics they were moved to a training facility across the border in Czechoslovakia—which had no pool.

When they flew out of Prague for Australia, limited news had filtered through and many held high hopes that Soviet tyranny was at an end. However, by the time they reached Australia the news was dire. Rather than pulling out, the Soviets had amassed their troops and marched on Hungary. Communist jet fighters, tanks and machine gunners moved in on the protestors. Nagy's fledgling government was overthrown and the Soviet Military Command was now in charge. Thousands of Hungarian citizens were being transported by train to the USSR, never to be seen again, and hundreds were mowed down on the streets. Over the months to come, more than 200,000 Hungarians would flee the country. Citizens left behind would be tried and executed, including Prime Minister Imre Nagy.

Meanwhile, help from the West was nowhere to be seen. As the Soviet Union and America were the world's foremost nuclear powers, America saw the situation as too volatile for it to become involved. In addition, war had broken out in the Middle East after Egypt nationalised the Suez Canal. The British, French and Israelis were determined to maintain control over the only route by which they transported oil from the East. The Suez Crisis commenced with the Israeli invasion of Egypt's Sinai Peninsula—and the Hungarians were left to fend for themselves.

In a 2006 interview with the *Independent* newspaper, Ervin Zador recalled the moment when the Hungarian delegation, then in Darwin, learnt that the Red Army was murdering Hungarian citizens in the streets of Budapest.

THE GREATEST WATER POLO PLAYER OF ALL TIME

Dezsö Gyarmati is the only player to have won medals at five successive Olympic Games. He was also one of the fastest in the world at the time, with a swim time of 58.5 seconds for 100 metres. He went on to coach the 1976 Hungarian Olympic team and later became a Member of Parliament for Hungary.

We were in the restaurant, waiting to change planes, when we heard that the Russians had taken care of the Revolution. I stood up with a glass of whatever I was drinking and announced I was not going home. It had been bad before. Now I felt it was going to be much worse, and that the Russians would never leave. Normally such a statement would have meant no Olympics for a player. But the team officials were still unsure of how things would turn out back home and so I got away with it. Even today I am shivering thinking about the risk I took. Other players felt the same way, but didn't say out loud.

War on Water

As the Hungarians worked their way through the first three group matches, sympathy ran high for the team. The world press was keenly following the conflict and there were many expatriate Hungarians in the audience who identified with their plight. With the crowd on side, the Hungarians put on some dazzling play. Hungary was one of the best teams in the world and, captained by three-time Olympic gold medallist Dezsö Gyarmati, the defending champions were a successful mix of seasoned veterans and brilliant young talent such as Ervin Zador. However, they had strong competition in the Soviet team and when both teams advanced to the semi-final, it was to be a clash of two of the world's best teams. While their Hungarian comrades were embroiled in a landlocked battle in Budapest, Gyarmati and his team were about to fight it out on the water.

What transpired was one of the most violent matches ever witnessed. On 6 December at 3.25 pm the pool arena was packed, with over 5000 fans roaring and waving nationalist flags in support of Hungarian sovereignty. As the game started, so too did the gouging, punching and shoving, both above and below the water.

Dezsö Gyarmati scored the first goal, hitting the Soviet defender in the process. The tone was set, and minutes later the USSR's Vyacheslav Kurennoi was sent to the exclusion box for throwing a punch. The players were swinging at each other whenever they thought they could get away with it. By half time the Hungarians were ahead 2–0. However, the extent of the violence meant that four players—three Soviets and one Hungarian—had spent time excluded from the game, and the police presence was starting to build as the crowd became as stirred up as the players.

When Hungarian player Antal Bolvari was hit by Valentin Prokopov, he suspected that his eardrum had been perforated. Finding it too difficult to mark Prokopov when injured, he asked team mate Zador to take his place. Zador had no problem with the change, as by this time the match was going Hungary's way and victory was only a hair's-breadth away. Zador took up his new position and started to rile his opponent.

So I looked after Prokopov for the last few minutes, and I told him that he was a loser, and that his family were losers and so on ... there was no problem until I made a huge error. I looked up to question why the referee had blown his whistle. I shouldn't have taken my eye off Prokopov. The next thing I saw, he had his full upper body out of the water and he was swinging at my head with an open arm.

Zador, who had scored two of the team's goals, had been sucker-punched. His right eye haemorrhaged and blood flowed into the water. As the referee helped him out of the pool, photographers captured the moment in an

It was not water polo out there, it was pure boxing in the water.

– ERVIN ZADOR

OPPOSITE: Horrified spectators look on as Zador (far right) is led from the Olympic pool after being injured. It was the first incident in what turned out to be one of the most violent matches ever witnessed.

image that reflected the intensity of a much greater struggle. A brawl commenced in the water and angry spectators jumped over the barriers, keen to vent their fury. As the situation deteriorated, the Soviets retreated to the far end of the pool. Police stepped in and attempted to calm the crowd, but the game was out of control. The game came to a halt as the crowd cursed and hissed at the Soviets who nervously trod water at the far end of the pool.

With a minute left on the clock, the referee decided to end the game early and announce Hungary the winners. The noise was such that it was impossible to hear his whistle. Fearful of the crowd's response, the Soviets stayed at one end of the pool until things had calmed down and police protection could be guaranteed. Eventually they were marched single file to the dressing rooms, having lost their dream of Olympic gold. Later, the Soviet team apologised to the Hungarians, saying that the violence was only prompted by one or two team members and wasn't representative of the entire team.

It was a great victory for the Hungarians. As Ervin Zador said later, 'We felt we were playing not just for ourselves but for every Hungarian. This game was the only way we could fight back.' Hungary went on to beat Yugoslavia 2–1 in the final to achieve their fourth gold medal for water polo. The Soviet Union made do with the bronze.

Tears for Hungary

However, the victory was bittersweet and as the Olympics drew to a close, the fate of the Hungarian athletes remained uncertain. Zador shed tears as he accepted his medal. 'I was crying for Hungary,' he said, 'because I knew I wouldn't be returning home.' The Hungarian delegation was divided. When the planes took off for their homeland, they were only half full. Some players decided to head home to their families, but others went to America or stayed in Australia. Emotional scenes occurred at Melbourne Airport as those who felt they had no choice but to go home were farewelled by huge crowds of Hungarian migrants singing the Hungarian national anthem.

The Hungarian section of the Olympic village was in mourning, with many wearing black ribbons across their tracksuits. Avery Brundage, the President of the International Olympic Committee, reminded the world of the purpose behind the Games.

Every civilized person recoils in horror at the savage slaughter in Hungary, but that is no reason for destroying the nucleus of international co-operation and good will we have in the Olympic movement. The Olympic games are contests between individuals and not between nations.

During the closing ceremony the athletes broke from the ranks designated for each specific country and marched together, embracing and holding hands as a symbol of global unity. This became the signature of all Olympic closing ceremonies to follow.

Eight of the 11 members of the victorious water-polo team defected to Australia. They hoped to raise money for Hungary by playing matches in Australian cities. Many of the athletes who returned to Hungary saw the defection as deserting the country when it needed them most, but some athletes were simply too afraid to return. Hungary remained under Communist rule until 1989.

ABOVE: The Hungarian water polo team pose with their gold medals after defeating Yugoslavia 2-1 in the final.

BACKGROUND:	Against colonial oppression
EVENT:	Ethiopia v Mussolini's Italy
OPPONENTS:	Abebe Bikila v The world's best marathon runners
ARENA:	1960 Summer Olympics, Rome

The Barefoot Idealist

ROME, ITALY, 1960

I wanted the world to know that my country, Ethiopia,
has always won with determination and heroism.

— **ABEBE BIKILA**

OPPOSITE: Abebe Bikila runs barefoot through the streets of Rome in the 1960 Olympic marathon. He not only won, but set a new world record in the process.

THE YEAR WAS 1960

▶ France tested its first nuclear bomb in the Sahara.

▶ Three thousand five hundred US troops were sent to Vietnam.

▶ Colonel Joseph Mobutu staged a successful military coup in the Congo.

▶ White South Africans voted that the country should be made a republic.

▶ The US FDA announced it would support the first oral contraceptive pill.

▶ New Zealand's television transmission commenced.

▶ Francis Chichester made a record solo Atlantic crossing in 40 days.

▶ The Oscar for best picture went to *Ben Hur*.

▶ The first episode of the British soap *Coronation Street* aired.

▶ The first Paralympic Games were held in Rome, Italy.

▶ Cassius Clay won his first professional fight in Louisville, Kentucky.

▶ The Soviet Union beat Yugoslavia 2–1 in the first European Football Championships.

When Abebe Bikila ran barefoot through the streets of Rome during the 1960 Olympic Marathon, he became the first black African ever to win a gold medal. Ethiopia was a country suffering from both natural disasters and political instability—it had been rent by wars since Mussolini's attempts to colonise the region in the mid-1930. Against this backdrop, Bikila became an inspiration to his fellow Ethiopians and to black athletes across the world. When he again won gold at the 1964 Olympics, he became the first man to win two consecutive gold medals for the Olympic marathon. Abebe Bikila is considered to be the greatest marathon runner in history, and he paved the way for generations of African long-distance runners.

The State of the Nation

In 1936, Italy invaded Ethiopia and forced the Emperor, Haile Selassie, to seek refuge in England. Despite condemnation from the West, no action was taken and Mussolini's troops remained in Ethiopia until 1941. Finally, British forces, combined with the Ethiopian patriotic resistance forces, were able to defeat Mussolini and reinstate Selassie as Emperor. By the 1960s, Ethiopia was attempting to forge its way as an independent nation.

Realising Ambition

In 1952, aged 16, having spent most of his childhood as a shepherd, Abebe Bikila joined the Ethiopian Imperial Army. Four years later as he watched a parade of athletes returning from the Melbourne Olympics, Bikila asked what they had done and why they were wearing tracksuits emblazoned with 'Ethiopia'. When he learnt that these athletes had represented their country, Bikila immediately set his sights on doing the same.

He was a good athlete and had already been spotted by a Swedish trainer, Major Onni Niskanen, who was employed by the army to develop young talent. For nine years while Bikila served as a member of Selassie's imperial bodyguard in Addis Ababa, he trained at high altitude in preparation for the ultimate test.

In 1960 Bikila competed in the national armed forces championships, at which the favourite was top Ethiopian athlete Wami Biratu. Bikila's performance in the marathon proved to be the upset of the day. As the spectators waited for the competitors to enter the stadium, reports filtered through that an unknown runner had taken the lead. In a shock upset, Bikila entered the stadium well ahead of the pack, with a time that qualified him for the 1960 Olympics in Rome. However, as the top Ethiopian runner was Wami Biratu, Bikila was not part of the Olympic squad until, at the very last minute, Biratu broke his ankle playing soccer and Bikila stepped up as a replacement.

Shoeless Runner

When Bikila arrived in Rome one of the first things he needed to do was meet with the Olympic shoe sponsor, Adidas. With only a few pairs of running shoes left to choose from, Bikila had problems finding a pair that fitted properly. Two hours before the marathon, he decided that he would run barefoot, just as he had when training.

Had Bikila not gone shoeless it is doubtful that he would have received as much media attention as he did, but the idea of this barefooted Ethiopian running 42 kilometres (26 miles) though the cobbled streets of Rome seemed ludicrous to the Western press, who quickly sniffed out a story. No black athlete had ever won an Olympic gold medal, and the barefoot angle was too good to resist. It wasn't only the world press that was sceptical: other competitors also looked down on the shoeless Ethiopian runner, never thinking for a second that he could pose a real threat. However, Bikila and his coach knew that a month prior, in only his second marathon ever, Bikila had recorded a time of 2:21:23 in the high altitude of Addis Ababa. Tough training exercises such as 30-kilometre (18½-mile) runs and 15,000-metre (9½-mile) sprints had paid off.

Echoes of Mussolini

The start and finish line of the marathon stood at the Arch of Constantine. As Bikila waited for the race to commence, he was aware that this was the place at which Mussolini had very publicly paraded his troops as he broadcast to the world his intention to colonise Ethiopia. With echoes of Mussolini resonating in his mind, Bikila was aware that he carried the hopes and dreams of his home country.

Niskanen had told Bikila to look out for three numbers and had made him write them on his hand so as not to forget them: 26, 13 and 69. Number 26 was supposed to identify the race favourite, Moroccan runner Rhadi Ben Abdesellem. Bikila soon broke away from the pack, all the time looking ahead for number 26. At 20 kilometres (12½ miles) he was joined by another runner, wearing number 185. The two men broke further away from the rest of the field and set a convincing lead. Still Bikila kept running with the assumption that number 26 must be somewhere up ahead. He didn't realise that Rhadi was wearing number 185 and had been running alongside him most of the way.

As Bikila passed the Obelisk of Axum, a kilometre from the finish line, he was again reminded of his country's bitter history. The monument had been stolen from Ethiopia by the Italians in 1935 and a burst of nationalistic adrenalin was all Bikila needed for the home straight. Soldiers holding flaming torches lit the route as the lone runner pounded along the ancient Appian Way. Thinking of the honour of an Ethiopian winning on Italian soil, Bikila picked up speed and sprinted to the finish line. He set a new world record of 2:15:16.2, 26 seconds ahead of Rhadi and eight minutes faster than the last Olympic record set by Emile Zatopek.

OBELISK OF AXUM

The Obelisk of Axum is an example of architecture from the ancient city of Axum, and is regarded as one of Ethiopia's national religious treasures. Seventy years after it was removed from Ethiopia, Italy agreed to return it.

After Bikila won the Olympic marathon in Rome in 1960, we Africans all started thinking: 'Look — he is one of us. If he can do it, we can do the same.'

– HAILE GEBRSELASSIE

RIGHT: Bikila approaches the finish line at the Arch of Constantine, Rome.

After the race, reporters questioned him as to why he ran without shoes. He replied, 'I wanted the world to know that my country, Ethiopia, has always won with determination and heroism.' Asked how he felt, he said, 'I ran at my own pace. Towards the end, I put on a spurt, and I still had reserves. I am happy for my country, for my Emperor and for my wife who is waiting for me in Addis Ababa.'

For the first time in history the Ethiopian national anthem resounded through the Olympic stadium and a black African athlete was awarded an Olympic gold medal. Newspapers reported that it had taken an entire Italian army to conquer Ethiopia, but only one Ethiopian to conquer Rome.

A Different Coup

On Bikila's return to Ethiopia, Emperor Haile Selassie promoted him to corporal and awarded him the Star of Ethiopia. Realising the power of sport, Selassie tried to use it to raise his country's profile. Bikila found himself dragged into the politics of his country, being heralded as a figurehead of black African nationalism.

Following the 1960 Olympics, the political scene in Ethiopia quickly deteriorated and a military coup was led by Brigadier-General Mengistu Neway, in which Bikila was forced to take part. When the coup failed, everyone involved was sentenced to death, including Bikila, who had steadfastly refused to kill any dignitaries. Niskanen, his ever-loyal coach, lobbied successfully on Bikila's behalf and Bikila received a pardon from the Emperor.

Bikila felt indebted to the Emperor for saving his life and four years later he set his sights on the Tokyo Olympics, from which he hoped to bring home another medal. However, adversity struck when one month before the race Bikila collapsed with acute appendicitis. Doctors advised him to give up on his Olympic dream and told him that if he attended the Games it would have to be as a spectator. he went to Tokyo regardless, and as Bikila limped off the plane, it was assumed by most that all hopes of a repeat of Rome were left at Japanese customs. However, Bikila had been training at night in the hospital courtyard and when he arrived in Tokyo he continued his training, buoyed by the warm support of the host nation. Barely six weeks after his surgery, Bikila had miraculously recovered in time for the event.

No longer barefoot, but still running against the odds, Bikila pitted his skills against 68 other competitors from all around the globe. Using the same tactics as in Rome, Bikila stayed with the leaders until the 20 kilometre (12½ mile) point. At 15 kilometres (9½ miles) he had broken away from the pack and was running with Ron Clarke of Australia and Jim Hogan of Ireland. By 30 kilometres (18½ miles) he was 40 seconds in front of Hogan and increasing the gap. Basil Heatley of the United Kingdom and Kokichi Tsuburaya of Japan had also made their move and were hot on his heels, but the race belonged to Bikila. He entered the stadium 4 kilometres (2½ miles) ahead of the nearest competitor and 70,000 spectators roared their approval.

Bikila won gold for Ethiopia, and set a new world record of 2:12:11.2. It was the first time that an athlete had ever won two consecutive Olympic marathons. As he finished, Bikila delighted the crowds by doing a callisthenics routine to warm down, and in a post-race interview he claimed that he could have run another 10 kilometres (6 miles).

A National Hero

In 1968, Bikila tried once more to win an Olympic marathon and probably could have done it had he not had to pull out at the 17-kilometre (10½-mile) mark due to a fractured tibia. Instead, he warmly cheered his team mate, Mamo Wolde, on to victory.

Sadly, in 1969 during a period of civil unrest in Ethiopia, Bikila crashed his car, having swerved to avoid a group of protesting students. He was left a paraplegic, but went on to compete in paraplegic archery competitions and often joked that archery would be his next Olympic event.

'Men of success meet with tragedy,' Bikila said. 'I was overjoyed when I won the marathon twice. But I accepted those victories as I accept this tragedy. I have no choice.'

When Abebe Bikila died in 1973, a day of national mourning was announced in Ethiopia. As well as his two Olympic gold medals, he had competed in 26 major marathons. His achievements were extraordinary and to the people of Ethiopia who still remembered the tyranny of their Italian oppressors, the day he ran the marathon through Rome was unforgettable. He was an inspiration to his people, and the reason Ethiopian runners have since dominated long-distance events.

BACKGROUND:	Capitalism v Communism
EVENT:	To re-establish direct communication between the US and China
OPPONENTS:	America v China
ARENA:	The Friendship Matches, China

Ping Pong Diplomacy

CHINA, 1971

A ball bounced over the net and the whole world was shocked. The big globe was set in motion by a tiny globe —something inexplicable in physical but not impossible in politics. — **CHINESE PREMIER ZHOU ENLAI**

OPPOSITE: When the Chinese ping-pong team played in the 1971 World Championships, it was the first time in six years China had taken part in international competition.

When international table tennis players Glen Cowan of the United States and Zhuang Zedong of China exchanged gifts at the World Table Tennis Championships in Japan in April 1971, what followed was to significantly change the course of international politics. For after almost 25 years of self-imposed isolation, the People's Republic of China tentatively extended the hand of friendship to one of its oldest foes, the United States. Publicly, treaties, conferences and negotiations appeared to play little part in proceedings. Instead, Mao Zedong amazed the world by inviting the US table tennis team to Beijing for a series of exhibition matches.

The somewhat unlikely group of diplomats left for China accompanied by a group of excited journalists, including a TV crew. The world held its breath as the country that had remained closed for a quarter of a century once again opened its doors for business. Pictures of China were now beamed around the world as the US team played a series of matches, good-humouredly suffering a series of defeats at the hands of their more skilled opponents.

It was later revealed that, behind the scenes, US President Richard Nixon had been playing a brilliant game of his own, one which was to become known as 'ping pong diplomacy'. By the end of 1971, Nixon became the first US president to visit China. Nobody could have anticipated that a game of table tennis would prove to be a major turning point in world history, one that would result in a sharp U-turn in US foreign policy and the re-opening of Sino–US relations.

State of the Nation

In October 1949, when Mao Zedong and his new communist regime succeeded in overthrowing the Nationalist Government of General Chiang Kai-shek, links between China and the rest of the world were instantly severed. Twenty years later, in March 1969, tension between China and the Soviet Union increased dramatically following a confrontation between troops on the 4,380-kilometre- (2721-mile-) long Sino–Soviet border. Each side blamed the other, and for a while the world seemed to be teetering dangerously on the edge of nuclear war.

US President Richard Nixon viewed this split as the most serious development of the Cold War. Using 'triangular diplomacy' he tried to balance the interests of the three powers who were caught up in this dangerous stand-off. the Soviet Union had one million Soviet troops placed on the Chinese border and missiles were aimed at its cities, poised for the command to launch them. Meanwhile the Soviet economy was stretched and was likely to deteriorate if the ongoing arms race with the United States continued.

Through offering friendship to China and arms reduction and trade to the Soviets, Nixon hoped to establish peace in the Asia–Pacific region by persuading both countries to stop supplying arms to the North Vietnamese. He also envisaged a favourable shift in power to the West.

The Game Begins

When Nixon first came to office, he surprised everyone by making the rebuilding of relations with China a top priority. 'We must not forget China,' he said. 'We must always seek opportunities to talk with her ... If there is anything I want to do before I die, it is to go to China.' Nixon believed that this relationship would bring about a radical change in American diplomacy and that by uniting the world powers, he would ensure that the United States emerged as the new world leader.

On 25 October 1970 President Nixon asked Pakistani President Yahya Khan to pass on a highly confidential proposal to China. Nixon signalled to the Chinese that the US was ready to talk, and promised that if the USSR acted aggressively, America would side with China. The Chinese Premier, Zhou Enlai, discussed the proposal with Chairman Mao and covertly replied that 'We welcome the proposal from Washington for face-to-face discussions'.

Behind the scenes, both countries had now unofficially let it be known that they were open to resuming contact, but neither party knew how to make the first move without losing face. China was quick to spot the opportunity that presented itself through a chance meeting at the World Table Tennis Championships.

A Surprise Invitation

In April 1971, in Nagoya, Japan, the US table tennis team was taking part in the 31st World Table Tennis Championships. As the men's final began, a major upset seemed inevitable as Swedish player Stellan Bengtsson was well on his way to becoming the first non-Asian to win the tournament in 20 years.

However, something even more surprising was happening in the room next door, where members of the US table tennis team had received a staggering invitation: to play some exhibition matches on an all-expenses-paid tour of Beijing. The team sat in stunned silence, many wondering how it was that the game of ping pong had become part of the reconciliation process between two of the world's most powerful nations. As *Time* magazine reported, 'a ping could be heard around the world.'

Players Unite

The Chinese table tennis team was playing in the 1971 world championships—the first time in six years that Chinese athletes had represented their country in international competition. They were undisputedly the best players in the world, and it was felt by many that the championships had been sadly lacking in competitive edge without them. As China began to realise the importance of resuming diplomatic relations with the rest of the world, the team was sent to Japan with strict instructions from Zhou Enlai: 'Friendship first, competition second.' The captain of the Chinese team had interpreted these instructions to

Your handshake came over the vastest ocean in the world — 25 years of no communication.

– PREMIER ZHOU ENLAI
TO PRESIDENT RICHARD
NIXON

ABOVE: The US team pictured with their guides outside the Summer Palace near Beijing

mean extending the olive branch to everyone except their oldest foe, America, and warned the players not to fraternise with the US team.

Nineteen-year-old US team member Glen Cowan was playing a few sets in the joint practice room with English player Trevor Taylor when he suddenly realised that he'd missed his team bus back to the hotel. When Cowan spotted the Chinese team bus going to the same place, he jumped aboard without giving it a second thought. At first no one would speak to him, but as they neared their destination the Chinese world champion, Zhuang Zedong, decided to ignore his team leader's instructions.

The trip on the bus took 15 minutes, and I hesitated for 10 minutes. I grew up with the slogan 'Down with the American imperialism!' And during the Cultural Revolution, the string of class struggle was tightened unprecedentedly, and I was asking myself, 'Is it okay to have anything to do with your No. 1 enemy?'

Zhuang remembered a recent speech in which Chairman Mao had publicly expressed his opinion that China's future lay with the United States. To the amazement of his fellow team members, he walked down the bus and presented the young Californian with a silkscreen print of the Hanchow Mountains. This might have been the end of it, but when the team got off the bus they were met by a horde of journalists and photographers who snapped away as Cowan and Zhuang Zedong exchanged pleasantries. In the interviews which followed, Cowan was asked by journalists if he would one day like to visit China. When he replied that he would, the world press reported that the Americans had expressed a keen desire to visit the People's Republic of China—a place that had been out of bounds to them for 22 long years.

The Perfect Solution

Suddenly the meeting of the two athletes had given their respective governments an opportunity to act without being seen as initiators. It was said that as the ageing Mao took his sleeping pills that night, he came up with the idea of sending out an invitation. He later remarked on Zhuang's diplomacy: 'This Zhuang Zedong not only plays table tennis well, but is good at foreign affairs, and he has a mind for politics.'

On 7 April the Chinese delegation received a message from Beijing. 'Considering that the American team has made the request many times with friendly enthusiasm, it has been approved to invite it, including its leaders, to visit our country.'

Caught in the middle of this political whirlwind, the US team anxiously awaited advice from Washington. It came within hours, when Tim Boggan, Vice-President of the US Table Tennis Association and editor of its monthly magazine, received a phone call, with the message that 'The Department of State views favorably the US table tennis team's trip to the People's Republic of China. This trip is consistent with President Nixon's expressed desire for greater contact between the American and the Chinese people.'

Four days later, on 10 April, the US contingent of nine players, two spouses and four officials left for China. The youngest member of the team, Judy Hoarfrost, 15, later recalled the moment: 'We walked across the Luo Hu Border Bridge to China, accompanied by blaring music, "The East Is Red"—a hymn

OFF THE RECORD

When President Nixon left for China in 1972 he still had no guarantee of an appointment with Chairman Mao.

In 1971 China is stirring, and for the moment it is a friendly giant.

– JOHN RODERICK,
WASHINGTON POST

FOR THE RECORD

In China, much credit was given to top player Zhuang Zedong, who initially broke the icy silence that descended on the team bus when Glen Cowan leapt aboard. Seen as a national hero, he was initially exiled from Beijing after the end of Mao's regime, but after a time was reinstated.

to Chairman Mao. A large red sign proclaimed, "Long Live the Great Unity of the People of the World".' To her, and the rest of the incongruous group of diplomats, it was a bizarre turn of events. 'I felt like we were in a movie,' she said, 'it was all so surreal.' Ten journalists, including five Americans, were also invited to supply coverage to the rest of the world. A mesmerised American public watched as over the next eight days the delegation played table tennis, toured the Great Wall and Summer Palace, chatted with Chinese citizens and attended social events. The information blockade of the Cultural Revolution had reached an end, and it became clear that China was once again ready to take its place on the world stage.

LEFT: Members of the US ping pong team watch a teammate play a Chinese opponent. Out of politeness, the Chinese made sure they never beat the US players by too great a margin.

The Friendship Matches

The Chinese were recognised as the best players in the world, whereas the US men's team ranked twenty-eighth and the women's team twenty-first. But once the games started it immediately became apparent that China, in the interests of diplomacy, had tactfully kept its best players out of the competition. Those who did take part worked hard to ensure that the winning margins were never too wide. The friendship games in Beijing were broadcast throughout the country, and Glen Cowan, the blond Californian who had been instrumental in the diplomatic breakthrough, was particularly popular with the Chinese crowd. At the end of the evening, China had won the men's final (5–3) and the women's

(5–4). The game caller, John Roderick, referred to it as 'an exquisite display of Chinese tact and politeness to guests'.

On 14 April the team members were invited to the Great Hall of the People in Beijing where they were to be received by the Chinese Premier. They waited as Zhou Enlai graciously chatted to the visiting teams from Canada, Colombia and Nigeria before making his way over to the US contingent. The 73-year-old Premier was well versed in the art of diplomacy and sent a clear message to the world. 'The Chinese and American people used to have frequent exchanges,' he said. 'Then came a long period of severance. Your visit has opened the door to friendship between the peoples of the two countries.'

A few hours after the reception, President Nixon announced a relaxation of the trade embargo against China.

The Aftermath of Ping Pong

That same year National Security Advisor Henry Kissinger made two secret visits to China. Up till then, all messages had been passed back and forth through Pakistan, and Richard Nixon had been operating without the knowledge of his ministers. When China sent an official letter saying that it would welcome a special envoy, or the President himself, Nixon made it official. He informed the world that high-level discussions had begun and that he would be visiting China

CONTRIBUTING DIPLOMATS

There are thought to be two other possible reasons for the re-establishment of Sino-US relations.

Welshman Roy Evans, President of the International Table Tennis Federation, was asked to visit China on his way to the World Championships in Japan, at which the Chinese team was playing for the first time since 1965. However, the Chinese were concerned about the participation of South Vietnam. Evans met with Premier Zhou Enlai, who requested that the South Vietnamese be banned from the competition. When Evans refused, the Premier went on to express concern that China had been out of international competition for so long, saying they felt a need to rehabilitate themselves with other countries. Evans suggested that they invite some Western teams to China following the Japan championships. He believed this would help alleviate their isolation, and prepare the Chinese team for further international competition. It was only days later that the Chinese issued the invitation to the US team.

Another possible reason for the thaw in relations involved Leah 'Miss Ping' Neuberger. Neuberger, who was the 1956 World Mixed Doubles Champion and nine times US Open Women's Singles Champion, was travelling with the Canadian team. When the Canadian team was invited to play in China, Neuberger applied for a Chinese visa and it was reported that China issued visas for the entire US team at the same time.

the following spring. At this point, Chairman Mao Zedong was seriously ill and it was said that only the prospect of the meeting with China's 'most respected enemy' was keeping him alive.

In February 1972, as Nixon stepped off the plane in Beijing, the Red Army played 'The Star Spangled Banner' while 350 soldiers gave a guard of honour salute. To the audiences watching throughout China, America and the Soviet Union, the visit represented a shift in world power toward the West. The new relationship between the two powers meant that the threat of Soviet aggression had momentarily abated and that Nixon was one step closer to establishing his dream of peace in Asia.

When Nixon met Mao, the two world leaders shook hands for almost a minute. Kissinger, who was also there, described the meeting as 'our encounter with history'. On the final night of the visit, the US president raised his glass, saying, 'This was the week that changed the world.' Following the event, China resumed diplomatic relations with a further 18 countries. The game of ping-pong had surprisingly played a decisive part in the end of the Cold War between East and West and brought about the restoration of Sino–US relations.

FOR THE RECORD

Table tennis also helped to bring about reconciliation between North and South Korea. A united team played at the 41st World Table Tennis Championships in Japan in 1991. When the women's team won the Corbillon Cup, citizens from both sides of the thirty-eighth parallel celebrated as one, heralding a hopeful shift in relations.

BACKGROUND:	Communism v Capitalism
EVENT:	US v USSR
OPPONENTS:	Bobby Fischer v Boris Spassky
ARENA:	1972 World Chess Championship, Reykjavik, Iceland

The Poisoned Pawn

REYKJAVIK, ICELAND, 1972

My whole career has been building up to this one point. This is really the big match. Even this little thing with me and Spassky is sort of a microcosm of the whole world political situation. They always suggest that the world leaders should fight it out hand to hand. And this is the kind of thing that we are doing—not with bombs, but battling it out over the board.

— BOBBY FISCHER

At the final of the 1972 World Chess Championship in Reykjavik, Iceland, US champion Bobby Fischer was set to meet with the Soviet titleholder, Boris Spassky. The Russians had held the title for 37 years and prided themselves on their success in a game that they used to represent their superior intelligence in the same way that they used their athletic prowess to signify their military strength. As the two major Cold War powers went head to head, the game of chess was catapulted into mainstream sport. Terms such as 'poisoned pawn' suddenly had the power to send ripples of excitement through a hitherto uninterested public. The eccentric personality of Bobby Fischer added to the Cold War drama when he refused to attend the event until an ever-expanding list of last-minute demands had been met. For more than a week Spassky and the Soviet contingent sat in the Icelandic capital waiting for the unpredictable American to make a decision. When United States National Security Advisor Henry Kissinger phoned Fischer and told him that the US needed his services to beat the Russians, Fischer finally relented and agreed to play. Over the next two months the world watched as the tensions of the Cold War were played out in 24 chess games between the two champions.

State of the Nation

A new Cold War era had emerged, one of diplomacy, discussion and alliances. US President Richard Nixon had just made a historic visit to China, and he was courting the communist country in the hope of shifting the power balance against the Soviet Union. The US and the Soviet Union were entering talks to negotiate a strategic arms limitation treaty (SALT), but mistrust was deep-rooted. The US was experiencing civil unrest, US troops were dying in Vietnam and the Watergate scandal—in which Nixon would be forced to resign—was about to hit. Meanwhile, looking for inspiration, US citizens had felt buoyed by unconventional heroes like Muhammad Ali, and were keen for more of the same.

'The Abominable Snowman'

Bobby Fischer was a chess prodigy. At 13, he became the youngest player to win the junior US Open. A year later he was the senior US champion, which qualified him for the Interzonals, the first step in challenging the world champion. To everyone's surprise, Fischer finished fifth and was awarded the title of Grandmaster, another first for one so young. This meant that he was now one of the world's top six players who qualified for the Candidates Tournament. However, for several years Fischer boycotted these qualifying rounds because he felt they were too short and didn't allow for any temporary loss of form. He was also convinced that many of the Soviet players had an agreement to throw games to each other when it suited them. He was already a virulent anti-communist and remained adamant in his beliefs that 'The Russians have fixed world class chess'.

As far as world championship events are concerned, Fischer is in some danger of becoming the Yeti of the chess world. Indeed, to organizers of such events, he must be seen as elusive and as fearsome as the abominable snowman. – Harry Golombek, the Times, *October 1970*

However, by 1972 Fischer was back on the world stage. He was the eight-time winner of the US Championships and was setting his sights on the World Championships. He entertained American audiences by claiming that he was the greatest and would soon win the title, which he boasted was rightfully his. In the run-up to the finals, Fischer wiped out his opponents one by one in spectacular fashion, losing only one game in three matches and experiencing one of the greatest chess runs in history. For the first time in 25 years, the world of chess had a non-Soviet challenger for the title. The chess correspondent for the *Times*, Raymond Keene, described Fischer as 'a kind of angry chess god incarnate ... waging total warfare on the chess board'. Americans began to think that this outspoken, slightly delusional man from Brooklyn could be in with a chance of beating the man who had come to represent the powerhouse of Soviet intellect.

Since the mid-1920s the Soviet Union had set out to dominated world chess, launching a nation-wide program that resulted in an infrastructure of approximately 5 million players. Nikolai Krylenko, founder of the Soviet Red Army, developed the chess system, recognising the game's power as a 'political weapon in the proletarian revolution'. By the 1970s, the Soviets was using their success as a propaganda tool. They promoted the belief that they were masters at the game due to the superior ideology that the players had absorbed, their powerful intellect and nerves of steel, all of which gave them an edge over other countries. The game of chess—involving bluff, intrigue, strategy and entrapment—was the perfect sporting accompaniment to the Cold War.

Soviet Boris Spassky was the current world champion, having beaten Tigran Petrosian in 1969. Fischer and Spassky had met before at the 1970 Chess Olympics, at which both players executed brilliant games before Spassky emerged victorious. In fact, Spassky had beaten Fischer in their last three games. However, when Fischer defeated Petrosian in the 1972 semi-finals in a 6.5–2.5 win it suddenly seemed possible that America could retrieve a title it had not held since 1907.

Political Pawns

Foreign media and press flocked to the Icelandic capital of Reykjavik, which had won the bid to host the match. The event had captured the imaginations of people everywhere. Fischer's face was plastered all over publications such as *Life* magazine, *Newsweek* and *Time*. Chessboards sold out, songs were written and the popularity of the game skyrocketed.

Getting President Nixon and Mr Brezhnev together was child's play compared with the Fischer-Spassky chess summit.

– THE *OBSERVER*, MAY 1972

Despite its being an era of diplomacy, the press and the American public saw the match as full-on war, with two commanding officers standing by for battle. A *New York Times* editorial mused on the implications of Fischer winning: 'Unquestionably, Spassky's loss of the title would be regarded as a major national setback; a sputnik in reverse.'

For Fischer the game eventually represented 'the free world against the lying, cheating, hypocritical Russians'. Richard Nixon showed his support, sending Fisher a congratulatory telegram and assuring him that 'I will be rooting for you'. Meanwhile, Spassky was carrying his own political pressure from the Soviet government—yet he harboured none of Fischer's personal vitriol. Instead, he saw it as a great game between two of the best players in the world.

As time would reveal, this match might have presented the veneer of Cold War drama, but neither player was a true representative of his country's politics. Fischer was a great player, but he was hardly a useful instrument for American propaganda, and Spassky was a Russian patriot who hated the Bolsheviks and never joined the Communist Party.

Mind Games

On 21 June 1972, Spassky and his team arrived in Iceland to acclimatise for the first game, planned for 1 July. However, as Spassky waited in Reykjavik, Fischer failed to show. Instead he missed his flight and hid out at a friend's house in Queens, New York, while the rest of the world awaited his arrival.

Fischer was known to be difficult, his antics often resembling those of a 1970s rock star. His behaviour was totally unpredictable and he would often succumb to depression, disillusionment and paranoia.

As Fischer descended into self-doubt, his list of conditions increased. He wanted to know where the cameras would be, and questioned the light, the shade and the surface of the table. He was also worried about flying, convinced that the Soviets would attempt to blow up his plane. He wanted fresh oranges supplied on the plane, which would then be squeezed in front of him to ensure his juice wasn't deliberately contaminated.

As time went on, the Russians became convinced that the American was playing mind games with Spassky. But the title meant everything to Fischer, and the mind games were not of his own making. Instead, he was a victim of an uncontrollably obsessive personality, and tried to micromanage every tiny detail in the quest for perfection.

As Fischer continued to list his demands from New York, Icelandic officials started to worry that he might not turn up and postponed the opening of the championship to midday on 4 July. The Soviets were furious, and there were mutterings that Fischer should be disqualified for his absence. However, Spassky was adamant that the match should be played and agreed to the delay.

Still Fischer wasn't satisfied, and as the new date drew closer and press attention increased, he demanded an increase in prize money from his Icelandic hosts. He wanted restrictions on TV coverage and 30 per cent of the spectator revenue for himself and Spassky. Icelandic officials began to wish the championships were being held elsewhere.

A Call to Arms

As the media reported the latest twist in the chess saga, British business tycoon Jim Slater heard the development on the radio and stepped in to double the prize money. Slater was an avid follower of chess and was later responsible for the development of the game in the United Kingdom. 'Fischer is known to be graceless, rude, possibly insane,' he said. 'I really don't worry about that, because I didn't do it for that reason. I didn't do it because he was polite; I didn't do it because he was graceful. I did it because he was going to challenge the Russian supremacy, and it was good for chess.'

The champions would now be competing for an unprecedented amount of prize money, but there was still no assurance that Fischer would come. Iceland decided to put in a last-minute call to the White House in the hope that they would give Fischer the push he needed. A phone call from Henry Kissinger restarted the proceedings with opening lines that have since become legendary: 'This is the worst player in the world calling the best player in the world. America wants you to go over there to beat the Russians.' Fischer reacted like a soldier being called for battle and later explained to his camp that 'I have decided that the interests of the nation are greater than my own.'

'The Match of the Century'

A collective sigh of relief was heard from the Icelandic organisers as Fischer finally arrived. Chess etiquette states that opponents should personally attend the draw at which it is decided who plays White in the first game. However, Fischer chose to sleep in his hotel room, sending Grandmaster William Lombardy in his place instead. The Russians were so furious that again it looked as if the match would be cancelled. Only when Fischer wrote a letter of apology to Spassky did things get back on track. By now, few people were unaware of the Cold War soap opera of Spassky v Fischer, with its twists and turns and daily cliff-hangers.

At 5 pm on 11 July the match finally commenced as Fischer took the stage, having kept Spassky waiting for ten days. It was to be the first of 24 games stretching from July through to September. To everyone's shock, Fischer lost the first game in the twenty-ninth move by making the elementary mistake of taking a poisoned pawn with his bishop.

OFF THE RECORD

On 20 July somebody leaked Fischer's list of demands. They included a private swimming pool, a wider range of restaurants, pocket money to be paid up-front and a new car.

Fischer blamed the defeat on the distracting sound and presence of the TV cameras and demanded that the cameras be removed. There was a certain irony in this, considering that Fischer had done some hard negotiating to ensure that the players would benefit financially from the TV rights. On day 2 he boycotted the game and stayed in his hotel room. Spassky turned up to play, and because Fischer was due to make the first move, the referee, Lothar Schmid, started Fischer's clock. Spassky sat on the stage, alone and uncomfortable as the audience watched the seconds pass. Five minutes later, when Fischer had failed to appear, Spassky left the auditorium.

As an hour passed, Schmid announced that Spassky was the winner of the second game. The crowd gave the referee a standing ovation, disgusted by Fischer's behaviour. Schmid later spoke of how he had agonised over that moment. 'I remember, that night, when I had woken up, I had tears in my eyes— my face was full of tears—because I had the feeling that perhaps I could have destroyed a genius.'

Following the forfeit, Fischer was ready to head to the airport but without his knowledge, Bill Lombardy removed the distributor from Fischer's car and spent the evening persuading him to stay. Fischer's aides kept him up all night, virtually brainwashing him into completing the tournament.

Diva Antics

With Spassky ahead 2–0, Fischer was now in trouble. But Spassky was also struggling; he had felt the pressure mounting as the tournament approached. The long, uncertain wait had shot the champion's nerves to pieces and he was struggling to keep it together.

When Fischer returned for the third game Spassky was feeling vulnerable. Fischer again complained about the conditions in the exhibition hall and demanded that the game should take place in a small back room. The Icelandic Chess Federation had no choice, as there was no guarantee that Fischer would turn up if they refused. Keen to complete the match, Spassky complied with Fischer's request. The two players retired to a small room from which the only pictures broadcast were from a single closed-circuit security camera. Still, Fischer felt obliged to thoroughly check the room. As Lombardy later said:

When Bobby arrived, Boris was, as usual, seated at the table. Bobby did not sit down but went around inspecting the television equipment, and at this point Boris betrayed indignant agitation. Bobby tested the remote-control camera for possible sources of noise. Schmid watched the proceedings and became anxious. He felt the match once more was in jeopardy. Schmid took Bobby by the arm in an effort to get him to the playing table.

OPPOSITE: Boris Spassky in the week before he arrived in Iceland to play against Bobby Fischer. Fischer's grandstanding during the event played havoc with Spassky's nerves.

All this nonsense ... all this delay ... all this haggling ... I think had an adverse effect on Boris Spassky, who was a very straightforward, decent, certainly a brilliant chessman and very nice man ... I think this was against his character.

– PAUL MARSHALL, FISCHER'S ATTORNEY

Bobby objected to the referee's interference, telling him to 'shut up'. Spassky later recognised this moment as the major turning point for him in this psychological marathon. He didn't like the way Fischer was talking to Schmid and he didn't like the conditions. From then on he played, he said, 'like a rabbit caught in the gaze of a boa constrictor'. The Russian press attacked Spassky's play, giving an early indication of the treatment he could expect if he lost.

Mozart Symphony

From game 4 onwards, the match returned to the main hall, where Fischer's game went from strength to strength. All cameras were removed except for the single closed-circuit TV camera. Game 6 was thought to be one of the most beautiful games ever played when Fischer for the first time ever played the Queen's Gambit Declined as White. The *Times* referred to the game as 'a Mozart Symphony', and after the final move Spassky stood up and applauded Fischer along with the audience, something no one had seen happening at any previous championship. Fischer liked Spassky and later commented on his reaction: 'Did you see that? That was class.'

By the end of July, Spassky was looking exhausted and asked for a postponement of the ninth game on medical grounds. Rather than see their player lose, Moscow tried to encourage Spassky to return to the Soviet Union, but he refused, determined to do the right thing and complete the match. He resumed the match, but looked troubled. By the tenth game Fischer had come back from 0–2 to take a 6.5–3.5 lead. During game 11 Spassky surprised everyone by playing and winning a game that was described as 'deep and profound'.

In game 14 Fischer made a mistake on his nineteenth move and people assumed he would resign the game. However, Spassky then made a mistake with his twenty-seventh move. Realising that victory could have been Spassky's, the Russian team saw their player was in trouble and decided to drastically switch tactics.

Transmitting Brainwaves

As the seventeenth game progressed, the Soviets accused the Americans of using 'electronic devices and a chemical substance' which were affecting Spassky's performance. They demanded that experts strip the room.

Spassky's assistant, Efim Geller, commented: 'Having known [Spassky] for so many years, it is the first time that I observe such unusual slackening of concentration and display of impulsiveness in his playing which I cannot account for by [Fischer's] exclusively impressive playing.'

On 24 August, light fittings were taken apart and the men's chairs were X-rayed. Fischer's was a special chair, which had been flown in from New York and was a duplicate of the one he used in the match against Petrosian. A bag of air from the stage was taken for analysis. After close examination, nothing was found and play recommenced.

A New Champion

Game 20 saw another draw, the seventh in a row, and Fischer only needed one point from the remaining four matches to claim victory. The twenty-first game commenced and Spassky initially played absorbing chess. However, another draw looked imminent as Spassky started to underplay, giving Fischer the edge. At the adjournment, the champion assessed the game and realised there was no point in continuing. Spassky phoned in his resignation and a new world champion was announced.

Fischer had taken the title held by Russia for the last 35 years. He had combined seven victories with eleven draws to gain the 12.5 points he needed. The final score was 12.5 for Fischer and 8.5 for Spassky, with Fischer winning seven games, Spassky winning three, and eleven draws.

At the banquet following the tournament, Fischer moved to sit beside Spassky and got out his pocket chess set. Twenty-one games weren't enough— Fischer wanted to go over some of the earlier moves. As the Icelandic Chess Federation gave their speeches, Fischer merely tore open the envelope containing the cheque and scrutinised the figure.

After the match Fischer boasted that 'The Russians are wiped out' and 'They probably now feel sorry they ever started chess.' Had Fischer viewed the game more as Spassky did, it could have been seen as a rare moment of cordial diplomatic relations between the two countries. Instead the *Washington Post* speculated that Fischer's behaviour had been responsible for the game escalating 'from a sport into a revival of the Cold War'.

Behaviour aside, Bobby Fischer was single-handedly responsible for the transformation of the future of chess. He showed that it could be among the most nail-biting of sports; that it contained skill, strategy, drama and tension.

Playing 'to the Kings'

Spassky later left the Soviet Union and moved to Paris with his third wife. He was allowed to keep his Soviet passport and even carried on playing competitive chess, occasionally acting as an honorary representative for his country. He considered himself in self-exile, never comfortable with the Communist regime. He had nothing but admiration for Fischer and his fellow chess masters.

In a long match a player goes very deep into himself, like a diver. Then he comes up very fast. Every time, whether I win or if I lose, I am so depressed I want to die. I cannot get back in touch with other people. I want the other chess player. I miss him. Only after a year will the pain go away. A year.

> **MORE MOVES TO COME**
>
> The 1972 Fischer–Spassky match inspired the West End musical *Chess*, by Tim Rice and Andrew Lloyd Webber. 'The good guy was the Russian, who was meant to be the bad guy, and the bad guy was the American, who was meant to be the good guy,' said Rice. 'It was all very confusing and a perfect illustration of how politics creeps into everything.'

ABOVE: Spassky (left) shakes hands with Bobby Fischer at the beginning of their famous rematch in 1992. Fisher won, but experts who watched the game said he was past his prime.

In the years that followed, Fischer refused to play a game or even to be seen in the public arena. In 1975 Anatoly Karpov challenged him for the title and, as expected, Fischer started on his list of extravagant demands. When some of these demands couldn't be met, Fischer refused to play and was consequently forced to relinquish his crown to Karpov, having not played a single game. Fischer disappeared from public life for about 20 years until he returned briefly in 1992 for a rematch with Spassky, which he again won. Twenty years later, world champion Garry Kasparov summed up what had happened when he wrote in the *New York Journal*, 'Fischer demolished the Soviet chess machine but could build nothing in its place. He was an ideal challenger—but a disastrous champion.'

Grandmaster Larry Evans had once said that what made Fischer different to all other players was that 'he has been willing to give up his personal life' for chess. Now, having reached the pinnacle of his chess aspirations, there was nothing left to do and no life to fall back on. As Fischer himself admitted, 'The only thing I can do is play chess … but I do that rather well.' Ironically, it was Fischer's opponent Spassky who seemed to understand Fischer better than most, having studied him from across the board for months at a time. While the Russian camp analysed Fischer's chess moves, Spassky remarked that Fischer was 'very lonely. That is one of his tragedies.'

In 2005 Iceland offered Fischer instant citizenship as he sat in a Japanese jail awaiting extradition to the US for tax evasion. He had become a recluse and increasingly deranged in his outspoken anti-Semitism. Former chess champion Bill Hartson seemed on the mark when he said, 'Chess doesn't drive people mad. It keeps mad people sane.' Bobby Fischer died in 2008 at the age of 64—incidentally, the number of squares on a chessboard.

Chess is war over the board. The object is to crush the opponent's mind.

– BOBBY FISCHER

BACKGROUND:	Cold War
EVENT:	Olympic basketball final
OPPONENTS:	US v USSR
ARENA:	1972 Summer Olympics, Munich

The Great Gold Robbery

MUNICH, GERMANY, 1972

The American team was offended, and it wasn't right.
It was the Cold War. Americans, out of their own natural
pride and love of country, didn't want to lose and admit loss.
They didn't want to lose in anything, especially basketball.

— IVAN EDESHKO, USSR OLYMPIC BASKETBALL TEAM, 1972

OPPOSITE: The US basketball delegation celebrate, believing they had won the Olympic basketball final. But the last seconds of the match were replayed and Russia took the gold.

The US men's basketball team arrived at the 1972 Olympics with a perfect track record and the unabashed confidence of an adoring American public. They were the best in the world, with a 63–0 Olympic record and seven consecutive gold medals. However, when they met the Soviet Union in the finals, events took a shocking turn. With the Americans leading 50–49 and only three seconds to go on the clock, a drama unfolded which resulted in the most controversial basketball game in the history of the sport. As the final seconds passed, play was stopped twice. Each time the US team celebrated victory, only to be told that the game was not yet over. A confused dismayed US team went back on court and resumed play each time. To their disbelief, as the final horn sounded the Soviets won the game and claimed the gold medal. Outraged, the US team boycotted the medal ceremony, saying that it was gold or nothing! To this day their medals have never been collected.

State of the Nation

When the USSR entered the Olympic Games in 1956 at the height of the Cold War, inevitably politics and sport became intertwined. Over the next three Olympics, tension rose as leaders from the East and West put increasing stress on the role sport had to play in demonstrating their superiority and dominance. When it was announced that the 1972 Olympics would be held in West Germany, the US entered the games expecting political grandstanding and judging bias from East Germany.

All American Game

Having introduced basketball to the Olympics in 1936, the United States had never lost a game and had won a gold medal in the sport at every Olympics since. The press and the American public were confident that this winning streak would continue. However, many experts in the basketball world were aware that the Soviets were beginning to build an increasingly formidable side, which had practised together for over a year and won eight out of their nine games in a US tour. The US team was made up of collegiate players, the youngest athletes ever sent, who had only played together for 12 exhibition matches and the Olympic trials. There was speculation later that the US had been lax in their selection criteria.

As competition got underway, both the United States and the USSR stormed towards the finals. The US won their first seven games, after which the competition was halted for two days, due to the massacre of Israeli athletes by the terrorist group Black September. When the Games recommenced, the US beat Italy and took its place in the final against the Soviet Union. Both teams entered the finals with eight wins and no losses.

Stop the Clock

On Saturday 10 September the crowd gathered for the much-anticipated final. From the start of the game the Soviets surprised the Americans by using an effective pattern offence and a strong defence, which resulted in them gaining a ten point lead twice in the game. Tension was high and play was aggressive. Both teams had a player ejected due to fighting on the court and one US player, Jim Brewer, was knocked unconscious, rendering him unable to return to the match.

With ten minutes to go, the Soviets were ten points ahead. In the last four minutes of the game the US, led by Kevin Joyce, decided to change defensive tactics, and this had immediate results. Joyce hit a pair of baskets, bringing the US closer to the Russians at 44–36. With 55 seconds on the clock, the US narrowed it to 49–46. When Forbes hit a jumper from the top of the key to make it 49–48 with only 38 seconds left, it was turning into an extraordinary final. Knowing that it was essential to keep possession away from the Americans, the Soviets attempted to freeze the ball for as long as possible.

Then, with only ten seconds of the game to go, Doug Collins of the US got the ball after a mid-air collision and raced down the left-hand side of the court. As he tried to make the lay-in, he was slammed headfirst into the basket supports by Soviet player Zurab Sakandelidze, and was awarded two penalty throws.

Still feeling dazed, Collins managed to sink the first of two free throws, and brought the score to 49 all. Despite the horn going off mid-shot, he sank the second and put the US in the lead for the first time in the game. It was 50–49 and the US had every chance of winning gold.

With only three seconds on the clock, the Soviets took possession and played the ball from under their basket, managing to get it as far as mid-court. However, as they passed inbounds, play was suddenly stopped with one second remaining, due to the Soviet coach signalling from the bench for time out. Thinking they had won, the entire US delegation ran on court in jubilation. However, confusion reigned when the secretary general of the International Federation of Amateur Basketball (FIBA), Robert Jones, ordered the play to restart and informed the officials and coaches that the clock should be set back three seconds to when the Soviet coach said he had been trying to get the referees' attention, which was just before Collins had made his free throws. Jones had no legal authority to decide the matter, but the timers followed his orders.

The US coach, Hank Iba, who had coached the winning 1964 and 1968 teams, protested, but the protest was overruled and the clock was reset so that the final three seconds of the game could be replayed. Play commenced with the Soviets throwing a desperate long ball to the other end of the court. When the ball went wildly astray, the Americans again assumed victory.

> It was sort of like being on top of the Sears tower in Chicago celebrating and then being thrown off and falling 100 floors to the ground. That's the kind of emptiness and sick feeling I felt.
>
> – DOUG COLLINS, US TEAM MEMBER

However, Jones stunned the Americans when he decided that the Soviets hadn't been given a fair go and blamed an error with the clock. Apparently it had still been in the process of being reset when the referees put the ball back in play. He informed the officials that there would be another three seconds of play.

Exhausted and confused, the two teams once again took up their positions. Play commenced as Sakandelidze quickly fired a long pass to Alexander Belov, who was standing under the US basket. He neatly popped in the short lay-up, winning the game for the Soviet Union 51–50.

This time it was the Soviets who were embracing each other as the US team stood in disbelief, many reduced to tears. After 63 games in eight Olympics, the Americans had lost for the first time and couldn't believe how the final seconds had played out. Furious at the debacle, Hank Iba stormed up to the officials. 'Certainly, we're protesting,' he said. 'I've never seen anything like it in my entire life. There is no possible way this ball game could have been won by those people.'

It wasn't just the players and coaches who were confused at the result. For the first time in Olympic history one of the two officials, Renato Righetto, refused to sign the scorecard. 'I'm not signing this paper,' he said. 'I'm protesting.'

Gold or Nothing!

The US put in an official protest, and announced that it would be a 'gold medal or nothing'. The US agreed that the game should have continued after the court

THE US PROTEST

'The US is protesting the extra three seconds granted because the game, according to FIBA rules, was over.

The US was shooting the second of a two-shot foul. This free throw was made. At the point the free throw was made, there were three seconds remaining.

At this point, according to FIBA rules, neither team can call a timeout. The official score sheet does not show a timeout in the last three seconds.

The opponents played the ball and ran off two seconds. According to FIBA rules, this was the only official way to continue the game.

With one second remaining, spectators ran onto the playing court and referees stopped the game at this time. At this point, with one second remaining, according to FIBA rules, they acted correctly.

When the spectators were removed, the game was started with only one second to go.

The one-second was played and the horn sounded, officially ending the game. The official score was US 50, Russia 49.

According to FIBA rules the game is officially over.'

invasion and that play should have carried on for one second. However, they protested that Jones had then put the clock back three seconds. Iba later said, 'We should have just walked off the court. The game was over and we had won it. I don't know why we ever went back on the court again.'

The five-member FIBA jury of appeals consisted of representatives from Poland, Hungary, Cuba, Italy and Puerto Rico and it took 14 hours for them to reach a decision. It was believed that the secret ballot was a 3–2 result, with a Communist bloc vote swaying the outcome. At the press conference later that day, Ferenc Hepp from the Board of Appeals broke the news that the Soviet Union would be awarded the gold medal and that the US would get the silver.

A heated debate broke out between journalists, the coaches and the Olympic officials. Hepp claimed that the decision to turn the clock back three seconds had come from referee Renato Righetto, but the German scorekeeper then spoke

ABOVE: Russian players celebrate having won gold, while stunned US players look on.

up, saying, 'No-one at the table ordered three seconds. There was a signal made for three seconds, but it did not come from the table.' He blamed Jones for the signal, which had left the referee with no choice but to continue.

US team manager Herb Mols also blamed Jones. 'Jones is the dictator of FIBA,' he said, 'and he rules it with an iron hand. He made a mistake in calling for three more seconds and he did not want to back down.'

Everyone was blaming Jones for the initial mistake, but there was also a lot of debate regarding a possible bias from the FIBA jury. 'Everything progressed according to strictly Cold War politics,' said *Sports Illustrated* writer Gary Smith. 'There were three Communist Bloc judges. It's a three to two vote. America loses. The Soviet Union wins the gold medal, and at that point the American players are facing a stark reality. Do they accept the silver medal?'

No Show

Rumours of a US boycott of the medal ceremony quickly spread. Kevin Joyce expressed the sentiments of the whole US team:

> *Everyone in the world except for those poor deprived people in Russia knows that we are still Olympic champions ... We voted quickly and unanimously not to take the silver medal since we legally and morally won the gold.*

> **If we had gotten beat, I would be proud to display my silver medal today. But we didn't get beat, we got cheated.**
>
> – MIKE BANTOM,
> US TEAM MEMBER

RIGHT: The US team refused to accept their silver medals and were absent from the presentation ceremony.

Although a few of the US Olympic officials tried to rally support for the medal ceremony, all the players felt the same way. Team captain Kenny Davis said, 'We felt like they just did something to us that was illegal and we didn't know any other way to protest than to say that you're not about to get us to show up to take that silver medal.'

When it was announced that the medal ceremony would be moved to the Olympic Stadium, basketball chairman Bill Summers made the announcement everyone knew was coming. 'The United States team, I regret to say, cannot accept the silver medals.' He went on to say, 'We feel we are entitled to the gold. We will protest, if only silently, by our absence from the ceremony.'

In the Vault

Over 30 years later, the silver medals still sit unclaimed in a vault in Lausanne, Switzerland. On the thirtieth anniversary of the 1972 Olympics, the IOC again offered to present the US team with their silver medals, but although two team members said they'd vote for accepting the medals, the team always said it would have to be a majority vote. Some players, such as Kenny Davis, remain insistent that the medals will never arrive on American shores: 'I have placed it in my will that my wife and my children can never, ever receive that medal from the '72 Olympic Games.'

The Russians felt they had won fair and square. Despite press speculation, there was never any evidence of definite fixing or bias, but the result remained a bitter pill for the US and the players of the time.

FOR THE RECORD

US basketball results, 1972 Olympics:

USA 66	Czechoslovakia 35
USA 81	Australia 55
USA 67	Cuba 48
USA 61	Brazil 54
USA 96	Egypt 31
USA 72	Spain 56
USA 99	Japan 33
USA 68	Italy 38
USA 50	USSR 51

BACKGROUND:	Cold War
EVENT:	Olympic ice hockey medal round
OPPONENTS:	US v USSR
ARENA:	1980 Winter Olympics, Lake Placid

Miracle on Ice

LAKE PLACID, NEW YORK, USA, 1980

It's the most transcending moment in the history of our sport in this country ... For people who were born between 1945 and 1955, they know where they were when John Kennedy was shot, when man walked on the moon, and when the USA beat the Soviet Union in Lake Placid. — **DAVE OGREAN, EXECUTIVE DIRECTOR OF USA HOCKEY**

OPPOSITE: The US ice hockey team, jubilant after their 'miracle' victory against the USSR in the 1980 Winter Olympics.

Having dominated ice hockey since 1964, the USSR was everybody's tip to win a fifth successive gold medal at the 1980 Winter Olympics at Lake Placid in upstate New York. Although they were officially amateurs, the Soviet team consisted of legendary veterans and giants of the game who were respected throughout the world. As the relatively inexperienced US collegiate team started to carve its way through the competition, the American public sensed a potential upset at hand. When the two teams were scheduled to meet in the medal round, the impending clash attracted unprecedented interest in the game of ice hockey.

With political relations between the two countries strained and the arms race exacerbating tensions between them, the game took on a new meaning for the American public, who saw the game as representing good versus evil, capitalism versus communism and East versus West. The idea of beating the mighty USSR had seemed an impossibility, yet the US public held its breath hoping that the time for a miracle had arrived. When 'Team USA' beat the Soviet juggernaut 4–3, Americans felt as if a war had been fought and won.

State of the Nation

The American public was disillusioned. In November 1979, Islamic revolutionaries in Iran had stormed the American Embassy in Tehran and taken more than 60 people hostage. By the start of the Winter Olympics in February 1980, the hostages had been held captive for more than 100 days and there was no end in sight for the crisis. The Soviets had invaded Afghanistan in 1979, a move that President Carter referred to as a 'grave threat to peace'. Subsequently, Carter would announce a trade embargo and a US boycott of the Moscow Summer Olympics, which were due to take place in July 1980. Relations between the two countries had not been so tense since the Cuban missile crisis of 1962. At home, Americans were struggling with domestic inflation, the rising price of petrol, and economic uncertainty. For a country that was usually so deeply patriotic, America had little to celebrate.

Team USA!

As journalists and spectators turned up for the Winter Olympics in Lake Placid, deep in the Adirondack Mountains, the talk was about how badly the event had been organised. Apart from unstoppable US speed skater Eric Heiden, who ended up winning five gold medals, the US public had few sporting achievements to cheer at the Games. However, this started to change as the young, inexperienced US ice hockey team began to climb its way through the competition.

The 12 teams of the tournament were divided into two divisions, with the US in the Blue division and the USSR in the Red. Almost unnoticed by the general public, the US team drew their first match against Sweden in spectacular fashion when defenceman Bill Baker equalised with only 27 seconds remaining, tying the game 2–2. This draw was to prove crucial to the US chances in the later medal round of the competition. Their next game was against Czechoslovakia, which was considered the odds-on favourite to top the Blue division. The Czechs had already thrashed Norway 11–0 and they looked set to continue winning. However, the US team was gathering momentum and they created a buzz across the nation by beating Czechoslovakia 7–3. Next to fall to the Americans were Norway, followed by Romania.

With one more game to go in their division, against the struggling West Germans, the US started to get a sense that maybe they could be in with a chance of a medal. However, after the first period the Germans were leading 2–0, having scored with two stunning 20-metre shots from beyond the blue line. In the second period US player Rob McClanahan got one back, and Neal Broten equalised with 1 minute 29 seconds remaining. In the third period, to the home crowd's relief, McClanahan and Phil Verchota both scored, and the US won by 4–2. It was the ninth day of competition and the win saw the team finish in second place in Blue division.

'Team USA', as they were now known, had won 4, lost 0 and drawn 1 to finish on 9 points, the same as the Swedes. However, the Swedes took first place in the division due to a better goal difference. Suddenly all eyes in the country were on the US team, and on the top two sides from the Red division who would now play against the US and Sweden in the round robin medal round.

Meanwhile, with seven players from the 1976 Olympics and one veteran who had played in the last three Olympiads, the Soviets had been storming through the Red division. Japan fell to them 16–0, the Netherlands 17–4 and Poland 8–1. By the end of the divisional round the USSR had won every game and finished top of their division, with Finland holding onto second place by goal difference over Canada.

The top two teams from each division progressed to the medal round. The leaders of each division would now play the runners-up from the other division, and then the final games of the tournament would see the division winners face off against each other in one game while the runners-up contested the other match. The team with the most points after these games would win the gold medal.

Team USA had hoped to top the Blue division to give themselves an easier first-up game against the Red division runners-up. In that way, they would hold off on meeting the Soviets until the final game, when they might both be fighting for gold. But the competition structure meant that an early clash with the USSR was inevitable. And so the medal round got under way, with Sweden facing Finland and the US up against the mighty Soviets, knowing they had to avoid defeat at all costs if they were to retain any hope of winning a gold medal.

RIGHT: Goalkeeper Vladimir Myshkin was brought on to replace Vladislav Tretiak in the second period. Here he defends against a US attempt to score.

Machiavellian Tactics

Coach Herb Brooks from the University of Minnesota was familiar with Olympic competition, having played for his country in 1964 and 1968, but this time he had been faced with a different type of challenge: he had to build the US national team. Six months prior to the competition, Brooks assembled a team of college graduates from the surrounding universities of Minnesota, Wisconsin and Boston. He had spent 18 months hand-picking the athletes through a series of tryout camps and psychological tests. He then took them across Europe and North America to bring them up to speed through playing exhibition games.

With the players coming from competing universities, Brooks figured that the only way to unite the team was to give them a common enemy. Consequently, he made himself as unpopular as possible. Military in his coaching style, he played the part of a boot camp sergeant, putting the players down whenever possible on the assumption that their anger would turn into the determination necessary to see them through the competition. 'He messed with our minds at every opportunity,' said starting defender Mike Ramsey. 'If Herb came into my house today, it would still be uncomfortable,' explained captain Mike Eruzione, years after the event. The team kept a record of 'Brooksisms', full of legendary putdowns such as, 'You're playing worse and worse every day and right now you're playing like it's next month.'

His psychological games also focused on the Soviet team. They were the strongest team in the world, with players such as Boris Mikhailov, goalkeeper Vladislav Tretiak, Aleksandr Maltsev, Vladimir Petrov, Valery Vasilyev and Valeri Kharlamov. These were men who had become legends in the game and were highly respected by the American students. Brooks knew that he had to 'break down the Soviets to mortals' if the US was to have any chance of beating them.

A week before the start of the Olympics his team played the Soviets in an exhibition game at Madison Square Garden. The game ended in an embarrassing defeat, with the USSR winning 10–3. When the US team applauded their opponents off the ice, it appeared that the young players still had stars in their eyes. The Soviets were in peak form. As well as their established veterans, they also had some brilliant young players coming through, and most importantly they had the greatest goalkeeper in the history of the game, Tretiak, as their last line of defence.

Perhaps the US had already made it as far as they were going to go. The day before the match Dave Anderson wrote in the *New York Times*, 'Unless the ice melts, or unless the United States team performs a miracle ... the Russians are expected to win the Olympics gold medal for the sixth time in the last seven tournaments.'

STORY OF THE CENTURY

In 2008, the International Ice Hockey Federation voted the event as the century's top international hockey story.

'The Moment Is Yours'

On Friday 22 February at 4 pm the game commenced, with standing room only in the Olympic field house at Lake Placid and TV cameras at the ready to beam it across America, albeit at a slightly later time. Moments before the match, Brooks inspired the team by giving what has been called 'the speech of a lifetime'. The players listened as he told them, 'You were born to be a player. You were meant to be here … The moment is yours.' The speech had the desired effect. As goalkeeper Jim Craig remembered, 'You didn't just want to check a guy into the boards, you wanted to check him through the boards.'

The game started and both teams flew out across the ice. Nine minutes into the first period Vladimir Krutov deflected a slap shot by Aleksei Kasatonov into the goal, giving the Soviets a 1–0 lead. Their confidence was sky-high after the exhibition game at Madison Square Garden, and perhaps it made them a little too complacent, because the US replied five minutes later with a goal from Buzz Schneider. The Soviets realised that something had shifted, and stepped up a gear. Sergei Makarov restored the Soviet lead four minutes before the end of the first period. It appeared that they would go into the break with a vital one-goal advantage.

However, as the clock was winding down, Dave Christian took a massive shot from the blue line, which Tretiak kicked out with his pad. Mark Johnson saw the puck coming his way and he collected it, glided straight through the USSR defence and slammed it into the goal with just one second left in the period. The Soviets put in a protest that the goal was late, but officials gave it the thumbs up and the score was level again at 2–all.

The USSR appeared to go into shock. Half the team headed for their dressing room while the rest remained on the ice to face off for the final second of the first period. When the teams returned after the intermission, everyone present was astounded to see that the Soviet coach Viktor Tikhonov had put Tretiak on the bench. 'He [Tretiak] was not playing well in previous games,' Tikhonov later explained, 'and my feeling is he was probably too nervous at this tournament.' This rocked the confidence of the Soviet team and boosted the spirits of the Americans, who couldn't believe their luck.

The second period started with Vladimir Myshkin in goal. 'I don't think I should have been replaced in that game,' Tretiak wrote in his autobiography. 'I had made so many mistakes already, I was confident my play would only improve. [Myshkin] is an excellent goalie, but he wasn't prepared for the struggle, he wasn't "tuned in" to the Americans.'

Despite the apparent upheaval in the team, the USSR scored a third goal two minutes after the restart and went on to dominate play for the entire second period. However, they found US goalie Jim Craig in outstanding form, saving shot after shot. It was to Brooks's credit that he had spotted and maximised

Craig's potential. He knew how to manipulate Craig, having told him prior to the Games, 'You are playing tired, and your curveball is hanging'—a baseball slight, meaning that he was leaving himself open to the opposition. Craig reacted with angry bursts of energy, making sure he never looked tired, and his defence had never been tighter than it was against the Soviet onslaught in this game.

Seven minutes into the third and final period, Dave Silk hit the puck towards the goal and it ricocheted off the skate of a Soviet defenceman into Johnson's path. Johnson became the top US scorer in the tournament by blasting it past Myshkin, and the Americans had brought the scores level yet again at 3–3. While the Soviet coach was keeping his players out on the ice all the time, Brooks was short-shifting his team, which meant that he had fresh, energetic players to bring on at the end of the game.

Two minutes after Johnson's goal, Eruzione came back on after a spell on the bench. Eighty-one seconds later, the 25-year-old Eruzione, the oldest man on the team, scored his third goal of the Olympic tournament, putting his team ahead with ten minutes left on the clock. The 6-metre slapshot hurtled past Soviet defenceman Vasili Pervukhin and goalkeeper Myshkin. In an interview later with Leonard Shapiro, Eruzione explained what happened: 'Pavelich [at the side boards] just tipped it into the middle. I got it at the blue line and I think their defenseman was screening the goalie. I don't think he [Myshkin] saw it.'

With ten minutes to go in the game, everyone in the stadium was sensing an American victory and the US team were desperate to hold off the Soviets, who were hell-bent on scoring. Two minutes after the US goal, Aleksandr Golikov tested Craig with a backhander, which the US goalkeeper saved spectacularly. With 57 seconds to go he was again tested by a backhand from Petrov and again he pulled off an incredible save. As the final seconds approached, the crowd started to join in the countdown and ABC commentator Al Michaels embarked on what has become one of the most famous sporting commentaries of all time.

> ... *dumping it in to the American end again. Morrow is back there, now Johnson. 19 seconds. Johnson over to Ramsey. Letinov gets checked by Ramsey. McClanahan is there, the puck is still loose, 11 seconds! You got ten seconds! The countdown going on right now! Morrow up to Silk, 5 seconds left in the game! Do you believe in miracles? Yes!*

When the final horn sounded, Craig and the team were mobbed as coaches and team officials rushed onto the ice. The whole team was caught up in a moment of pure jubilation. People took to the streets waving massive American flags and hugging each other. Unbelievably Craig had saved 36 of the Soviets' 39 shots. 'He was a tower of strength for us, no question,' said US coach

Right after we won I got bags of mail. It was like in the movie *Miracle on 34th Street* when they bring in all that mail to Santa. That's what I used to get.

– MIKE ERUZIONE

Herb Brooks. 'For an American team to be successful, the catalyst has to be the goalkeeper ... Craig told me yesterday, "You wait, wait till tomorrow, Coach. You haven't seen it."'

Pressure Mounts

To America it felt as if they had already won the gold that night, but the team still had to face Finland in the final game of the medal round. The Finns had drawn with Sweden and were at the foot of the medal table on 1 point. The USSR and Sweden were on 2 points, with the US now on top of the table with 3 points. With 2 points up for grabs, a win would secure the gold medal for America, no matter what happened in the other match between the USSR and Sweden. Eruzione and Brooks knew that it was essential to keep the team focused. After the win over the Soviets, US captain Eruzione told an interviewer:

> *Right now I'm a little confused, everything happened so fast. I don't think you can put into words what this means. But I know this, we can't forget we've got one game left. I'll be damned if I'll let them get lazy now. We're one more day away from a dream.*

'There was incredible apprehension before this game,' said backup goalie Steve Janaszak. 'We were horrified by the thought that we'd be sitting around 10 years later and wondering how we could lose the gold medal after coming so close.' Brooks pushed his players through a tough practice routine, needling them by saying 'You're too young. You can't win this.'

When the game started, Finland came out with every intention of winning and keeping their medal hopes alive. After two periods they had built a 2–1 lead. In the interval before the final period, Brooks motivated his players by warning them of the consequences of losing. They skated out to play the last 20 minutes of their tournament with his words ringing in their ears: 'This will haunt you the rest of your lives.' Brooks got the result he wanted, and the team lifted to completely outplay the Finns. Verchota, McClanahan and Johnson each scored a goal, bringing the final score to 4–2 to the US.

The victory sealed the gold medal for the US. In the other match, the USSR thrashed Sweden 9–2 to give them the silver, while the Swedes took the bronze. Eruzione took to the winner's podium for the medal ceremony. As the American anthem came to a close, he beckoned for the rest of his team mates to join him. It was almost impossible to believe that a bunch of college students had not only beaten the mighty Soviets, but had also won gold for America. As commentator Al Michaels said, 'No scriptwriter would ever dare.'

OPPOSITE: Team USA celebrates their 4-3 victory over the Russian team in the Olympic semi-final. The US went on to beat Finland in the final and take the gold.

Post Miracle

The Soviet players reacted to their failure with good humour, but they had been surprised by the ability and determination shown by Team USA. Russian player Valery Vasilyev later asked US team doctor V. George Nagobads, 'What did you give your players to eat or drink so in the third period they can skate like that? Last period is always ours. In second period, when we were ahead 3–2, we celebrate.' Nagobads replied, 'It's called the fountain of youth.' Despite the Soviet players' outward display of sportsmanship, there had been a lot of pressure on them to win. Their position on the national team saved them and their families from poverty, and in losing they knew they would have to face the wrath of Tikhonov, who ran his team like a dictatorship.

The US win seemed to raise the morale of the entire country, making up for America's absence in the upcoming Moscow Olympics. The *LA Times* ran a cartoon depicted the US team as the soldiers at Iwo Jima, raising the American flag with a hockey stick. Seen to represent victory during the Cold War, the spirit of the win was not really in keeping with the IOC's ethos that sports and politics shouldn't mix in the Olympic arena. As journalist Thomas Boswell said, 'The US versus USSR game duplicated, in miniature, many of the emotions and motivations that have fed the fires of every war in history.'

Thirteen of the US players went on to play professionally in the NHL. Eruzione, however, retired from the sport one week after the Olympics, wanting to go out on top and enjoying the press coverage. E. M. Swift wrote in *Sports Illustrated*: 'With one seemingly harmless shot, Mike Eruzione staked the US to a lead and a Miracle on Ice.' Little did Eruzione realise that the shot would still be talked about 30 years later.

'MAGIC' JOHNSON

US forward Mark Johnson feared that he would never make the Olympic team. His father was legendary American coach Bob Johnson. Despite Mark being the best of the college hockey players, his dad had kept him off the 1976 team because he feared people would accuse him of nepotism. Bob Johnson and Herb Brooks were arch rivals and when the 1980 Olympics neared, Mark Johnson feared that this time it would be this rivalry that would prevent him from being chosen. However, Brooks was more concerned with winning and Johnson was the perfect player in many ways. For example, he wasn't intimidated by the Soviets. Every Sunday he had played 'the Russian game', in which his dad had made his players wear the names and numbers of the USSR squad members. It was good preparation for the famous battle. Johnson turned out to be the Americans' top scorer in the tournament, with team mates calling him 'Magic' Johnson after the champion NBA basketballer. Years later Johnson played in the NHL for the New Jersey Devils. Two of the Soviet players who had lined up against him in the 1980 game were now his team mates: Slava Fetisov and Alexei Kasatonov. He asked them why the goalie had been pulled in 1980. They replied, 'Coach crazy.'

Months after the win, Herb Brooks wrote each player a letter, in which he said:

This year was a challenge for all of us. A challenge to: Live and work as a unit. Play a positive game—a creative way. Make the most out of our dreams. You met those challenges and conquered them. If there was a team I ever wanted to identify with on a personal basis, this was the team.

Brooks had done everything in his power get the best out of his team. His psychological approach combined with his tactical expertise resulted in one of the most famous wins of all time. In later years Brooks was interviewed by the *Minneapolis Star Tribune* at his home where he had just watched *Willie Wonka and the Chocolate Factory*. 'You know, Willie Wonka said it best: We are the makers of dreams, the dreamers of dreams ...' Brooks said. 'We grew up as kids having dreams, but now we're too sophisticated as adults, as a nation. We stopped dreaming. We should always have dreams. I'm a dreamer.'

BACKGROUND:	The world against South African apartheid
EVENT:	New Zealand pro-tour v anti-tour protestors
OPPONENTS:	The All Blacks v The Springboks
ARENA:	Eden Park, Auckland, New Zealand

'The Tour': 1981 Springboks v All Blacks

AUCKLAND, NEW ZEALAND, 1981

When we came out of the game, the fighting was all over. We had no idea how bad it had been. But as we walked down Onslow Road, we realised we were walking over broken glass. We saw cars over-turned, fence-posts smashed, the street was littered with helmets and broken shields. It looked more like Soweto than New Zealand.

— SPECTATOR AFTER THE EDEN PARK FINAL TEST

OPPOSITE: Flour bombs were dropped onto the playing field during the third test between the All Blacks and the Springboks in 1981. All Black Andy Dalton tries to keep his focus on the game.

When South African rugby team the Springboks toured New Zealand in 1981, their visit resulted in an unprecedented period of civil unrest and division throughout the country. Prime Minister Robert Muldoon believed that politics should stay out of sport, but by the end of what became known as 'the Tour', 54 per cent of the population had started to think otherwise. By hosting the Springboks, many New Zealanders believed they were not only seen to be supporters of the South African apartheid system but that they were also supporting racial prejudice and discriminatory practices going on in their own country. Over a period of 56 days, more than 150,000 people took part in over 200 demonstrations as sport and politics became inextricably linked and the hitherto peaceful country of New Zealand descended into near civil war.

State of the Nation

Since the 1960 All Blacks tour of South Africa, tension had been mounting over the sporting rivalry between the two countries. In what was seen as a nod of approval towards apartheid, New Zealand rugby selectors had sent an 'all white' team to compete in South Africa and had continually overlooked Maori players in order to compete with their most worthy opponents. Despite a petition called 'No Maoris, No Tour' signed by 150,000 people, the selectors carried on their relationship with the Springboks, touring with no Maori players until 1970. Throughout the controversy the selectors maintained they were trying to protect the Maori players and save them from embarrassment.

The South African racial prejudice regarding Maoris was evident as far back as 1921. After the Springboks defeated a New Zealand Maori eleven, a South African reporter sent a telegram home complaining about the support from white New Zealanders:

BAD ENOUGH HAVING TO PLAY OFFICIALLY DESIGNATED NEW ZEALAND NATIVES, BUT SPECTACLE THOUSANDS EUROPEANS FRANTICALLY CHEERING ON BAND OF COLOURED MEN TO DEFEAT MEMBERS OF OWN RACE WAS TOO MUCH FOR SPRINGBOKS WHO FRANKLY DISGUSTED.

By the 1970s, South Africa found itself increasingly isolated from world sport as the rest of the world started to voice opposition to the apartheid system by banning the country from sporting competitions.

The legally sanctioned system of racial segregation had existed in South Africa since 1948, when townships had been set up in which almost three million people had been forced to live. Not allowed to vote, black people were dominated by the white upper classes. Anti-apartheid activist Nelson Mandela had been imprisoned since 1964 and came to symbolise the plight of black people. In 1976, the country descended into violence as the Soweto riots broke out and hundreds of black protesters were killed, many under the age of 18.

Despite often espousing the theory that sport and politics should not be mixed, the International Olympic Committee controversially decided to ban South Africa from the upcoming 1976 Summer Olympics in Montreal. Meanwhile, New Zealand naively extended its support to another All Blacks tour of South Africa. International condemnation was immediate when more than 20 African nations boycotted the Olympics due to New Zealand's participation. They firmly believed that New Zealanders were staunch advocates of apartheid and considered them to be 'the worst racists in the world'. Prime Minister Robert Muldoon had seriously underestimated the amount of feeling regarding the oppression of black people in South Africa and unless he acted quickly, his country would be politically isolated.

The Gleneagles Agreement

In 1977, pressured by the Olympic controversy, Muldoon joined other Commonwealth world leaders to produce the Gleneagles Agreement (or Gleneagles Accord) by which Commonwealth Prime Ministers agreed to join together in an international anti-apartheid campaign. While it stated that each government could interpret the agreement to suit their own needs, it also said that 'there were unlikely to be future sporting contacts of any significance between Commonwealth countries or their nationals and South Africa while that country continues to pursue the detestable policy of apartheid.'

The agreement was applauded and most New Zealanders thought it marked the end of Springboks tours. However, when the New Zealand Rugby Football Union (NZRFU) invited a 'merit-selected' Springboks side to tour in 1981, the issue once more divided the country. People looked to the government to intervene, but Muldoon refused, saying that it wasn't his place to 'interfere with the freedom of our sportsmen'. He told the NZRFU that he was clearly opposed to the tour, but on the other hand he wasn't going to stop them. It was no coincidence that Muldoon and his Nationalist party were campaigning for re-election that very same year and knew that if they went with the majority opinion over the tour, they stood to win.

Dissension broke out as New Zealanders started to see the tour as being representative of far more than apartheid. Despite being a national sport, New Zealand rugby was seen as a bastion of conservative and traditional values. The whole protest became part of something bigger as traditional attitudes were pitted against liberal, post-colonialist ideals. Many women, Maoris and New Zealand youth identified with the oppression felt by the black South Africans and joined the swelling anti-tour movement.

SPORTING BOYCOTTS

The pressure from sporting bodies on the apartheid movement started in 1964, when South Africa was banned from the Olympics. The frequency of disruptions to sporting events increased throughout the 1960s. In 1969 the Springboks' tour of the UK was continually impeded by pitch invasions by anti-apartheid campaigners. In 1970, the MCC withdrew its invitation for the South African cricket team to tour England. Sporting boycotts had a considerable impact on the final abolition of apartheid in 1994.

'Be strong, be patient, be steadfast'

Until now, the players themselves had tried to stay out of the politics, but emotion was further ignited by the announcement from All Blacks captain Graham Mourie that he would not play against the Springboks: 'I believe the tour is wrong—for morality, for rugby ... the controversy and the effects of the tour will be bad for the game.' Mourie felt supported by a letter he received from New Zealand's High Commissioner in London, who condoned Mourie's decision, believing that it could define a turning point in New Zealand's international relations. He said, 'Kia kaha, kia manawanui, kia u ... Be strong, be patient, be steadfast.'

This heartfelt decision on the part of the New Zealand captain divided his friends, family and supporters. Following his lead, two more All Blacks, Bruce Robertson and Gary Seear, also announced that they wouldn't be available to play.

With the heat rising, the police warned the NZRFU that they would have to introduce costly preventative measures to ensure safe and peaceful demonstrations. Police numbers would need to be increased and specially trained riot squads would be introduced. The NZRFU proceeded with their plans, and in July 1981 the Springboks arrived in New Zealand, having been forced to fly via the United States due to Australia's boycott of transport facilities for the team.

Battle Lines Drawn

As the Springboks prepared for a series of matches leading up to the first Test, New Zealanders realised the time for debate was over. A groundswell protest movement began as clashes broke out between fans, police and protesters.

On 22 July at the first game at Gisborne against Poverty Bay, the Springboks gave their full attention to the game at hand, winning 24–6. However, tension was mounting outside the field when pro-tour and anti-tour protesters came face to face. At this stage the group of anti-tour protestors was relatively small, but numbers were rapidly increasing across the country.

On 25 July, the Springboks faced Waikato at Hamilton, but this time the protest was much larger. The pitch was invaded by hundreds of protesters who stormed the ground, having used boltcutters to get through the surrounding fence. Rumours that a low-flying aircraft was approaching proved too much for the police and to the shock of players and fans, the game was cancelled. There were angry confrontations as avid rugby supporters attacked the arrested protesters on their release from the police station.

On 29 July New Zealanders were so angry over the tour that a large crowd had started to gather outside the New Zealand Parliament in Wellington. As the anti-tour protesters edged their way closer to Parliament on what was meant to be a peaceful march, police had been ordered to stand their ground and to use their batons if necessary.

The demonstration descended into chaos as police lashed out at the crowd. Schoolchildren and the elderly were among the victims as batons rained down. The crowd retaliated with shouts of 'Shame! Shame! Shame!' What was intended to be a 'freedom and democracy' march now highlighted aggressive policing tactics and the loss of a basic right to protest. Meanwhile, Muldoon was in London attending the royal wedding of Prince Charles to Lady Diana Spencer, and was reportedly furious that the Hamilton match had been called off. Security was increased as New Zealand prepared for the first of three Test matches.

Setting the Stage

The first Test took place in Christchurch at Lancaster Park on 15 August 1981. Prior to the start of the game, thousands of protesters broke through the surrounding barbed wire and scattered fragments of glass around the field. Many normally law-abiding citizens were now prepared to risk arrest for the principle they were defending. The police moved in, cleared the area of demonstrators and deemed the area safe. The All Blacks defeated the Springboks 14–9.

When the two sides met again for the second Test in Wellington on 29 August 1981 at Athletic Park, the Springboks hit back at the host nation, winning 24–12. The stage was now set for one of the most dramatic and controversial series deciders ever to be held in the game's history.

FOR THE RECORD

Date	Game	Score
22 July	v Poverty Bay at Gisborne	24-6
25 July	v Waikato at Hamilton	Cancelled
29 July	v Taranaki at New Plymouth	34-9
1 August	v Manawatu at Palmerston North	31-19
5 August	v Wanganui at Wanganui	45-9
8 August	v Southland at Invercargill	22-6
11 August	v Otago at Dunedin	17-13
15 August	v All Blacks at Christchurch	9-14
19 August	v South Canterbury at Timaru	Cancelled
22 August	v Nelson Bays at Nelson	83-0
25 August	v New Zealand Maoris at Napier	12-12
29 August	v All Blacks at Wellington	24-12
2 September	v Bay of Plenty at Rotorua	29-24
5 September	v Auckland at Auckland	39-12
8 September	v North Auckland at Whangarei	19-10
12 September	v All Blacks at Auckland	22-25

A BITTER AFTERTASTE

At the closing banquet of the 1995 World Cup, Louis Luyt, the South African rugby president, arrogantly asserted that 'There were no true world champions in the 1987 and 1991 World Cups because South Africa were not there. We have proved our point.' The All Blacks captain responded by leading his team out of the room. The French and English followed. To make matters worse, Luyt then singled out Welsh referee Derek Bevan for being the 'best referee in the World Cup'. Bevan had disallowed a last-minute French try against South Africa in the semi-finals. Rather than accept the gold watch, Bevan also left the room. 'It was something I could have done without,' he said. 'It came out of the blue: I have no idea why he singled me out. It could be misconstrued, and if that is the case, it leaves a bitter taste.'

Stopping a Nation

On 12 September 1981, police presence at Eden Park, Auckland, was the highest it had ever been. It was the fourth anniversary of the murder of black activist Steve Biko and now that the tour had come down to this final deciding game, the stadium and city were on high alert. For safety reasons the Springboks had been taken to the stadium the night before, where they had slept on concrete floors, waking throughout the night to the chants of the anti-tour protesters outside the grounds.

Welsh referee Clive Norling signalled that South Africa had won the toss, and a titanic struggle commenced. Outside the stadium, protesters threw rocks and overturned cars. Inside, balloons inscribed with 'Biko' hovered around the ground. As the players demonstrated some of the best rugby ever seen, a low-flying Cessna 192 swooped in over the stadium and dropped flour bombs and flares onto the pitch. At the half-time whistle the Springboks were down 3–16, and the atmosphere was electric.

When play resumed, the pitch resembled a war zone. Acrid pink smoke poured from the flares scattered across the pitch and white lines of flour were streaked across the turf. Despite the chaos, play continued. Rather than being put off, the Springboks rallied and came from behind by scoring three tries and levelling the score at 22–all with only moments to go. If the Springboks could convert the try, the game was theirs. However, Naas Botha's shot misfired and the ball drifted outside of the right upright.

The crowd watched in suspense, afraid that the action-packed game might end in a disappointing draw. To the relief of the spectators, Norling called for extra time, later saying that the Cessna had lost the game valuable minutes. With seconds to go the All Blacks were awarded a penalty and chose to take a quick tap. Caught off guard, the Springboks were then penalised for not having retreated the full 10 metres (33 feet).

All Black player Allan Hewson took the kick from 45 metres (148 feet) out. The ball soared effortlessly through the posts, putting the All Blacks ahead at 25–22. One minute later the final whistle blew and the Tour was finally at an end. The rugby that was played that day is often forgotten, but it was thought to have been the best ever played in the history of the All Blacks–Springboks rivalry.

As the crowd left the ground they were shocked at the scenes of devastation outside the stadium. 'The Tour' had gone ahead, but it had torn apart the fabric of New Zealand society and the wounds would take many years to heal. In 1996, New Zealand Prime Minister Jim Bolger said that the tour had 'reached into—and often divided—families, friends and communities throughout New Zealand, perhaps more than anything else in our recent history'. But it wasn't just New Zealanders who felt the effect of the tour. The advent of television in South Africa in 1976 meant that by 1981, South Africans who had become isolated in

TOP: Protesters pull down a fence around a football park during the Springboks' first game, against Poverty Bay.

BOTTOM: Police wearing riot helmets, and with batons drawn, confront anti-apartheid protesters during the Springboks' third match, against Manawatu.

their political views now witnessed first-hand how passionately opposed many countries were to their polices.

Had New Zealand boycotted the Springboks earlier, it would no doubt have had a huge impact. But what they did in 1981 had great significance in speeding up the closing years of apartheid. As South African captain Wynand Claasen later reflected: 'I think what happened on the tour and the anti-South Africa feeling, that was the start of the final change. After that we were basically totally isolated from all sport.'

February 1990 saw the beginning of the dismantling of the apartheid system in South Africa and the release of Nelson Mandela after 27 years in prison. He later recalled receiving the news in his prison cell that the Hamilton game had been cancelled. He said it was 'as if the sun had come out'.

One Team, One Country

Only a month after Nelson Mandela became the South African President in 1994, he invited the Springboks captain Francois Pienaar to his office and charmed the young blond Afrikaner into joining him in an ambitious plan to use the game of rugby to unite the nation.

When Mandela spoke to the black South Africans and claimed that the 'Boks' belonged to them as much as the whites, his own people booed him. The game of rugby was seen as a symbol of the abolished apartheid system, and it seemed extremely unlikely that black South Africans would ever embrace the Springboks team, which they had despised for so many years. To make the possibility even more remote, Mandela was asking them to support a team that was all white, apart from winger Chester Williams.

But Mandela was determined, and when South Africa hosted the 1995 World Cup, the elder statesman pulled out an amazing bag of tricks. The CEO of the South African Rugby Union came up with the inspired slogan, 'One Team, One Country' and, having established the support of the team, Mandela gradually got the entire country behind his vision.

The Springboks reached the finals on 24 June at Ellis Park, Johannesburg, and for the first time South Africans, black and white, stood united to cheer on the 'national side'. Moments before the match the team had impressed spectators by singing the new national anthem, which was a song of black resistance—'Nkosi Sikelel' iAfrika' ('God Bless Africa').

After the anthem, Nelson Mandela stunned everyone by walking onto the ground to greet the players, wearing the hated Springboks jersey. The entire stadium, made up of 95 per cent whites, fell into an uneasy silence. Seconds later, a cry went out: 'Nel-son! Nel-son! Nel-son!' Mandela had achieved his dream: having already established black support for his politics, this now signalled that he also had the white vote.

Tokyo Sexwale—who was imprisoned with Mandela and was later to become the first black premier of the Johannesburg region—described the match in an interview with the *Guardian*.

Only Mandela could wear an enemy jersey. Only Mandela would go down there and be associated with the Springboks. The liberation struggle of our people was not just about liberating blacks from bondage, but more so it was about liberating white people from fear. And there it was. Fear melting away. People were shouting, 'Nelson! Nelson!' And who were these people, these rugby crowds? They were our jailers, our oppressors; the people guarding the borders, the police stations. But it was, 'Nelson! Nelson!' We stood there and we didn't know what to say. As President of the country, he could have just ended up in the box and given them the cup. But to stand with them, to move his hands in the air, to wear that jersey, to have that cap, to lift the cap for them and to greet the people ... you sat there and you knew that it was worthwhile. All the years underground, in the trenches, denial, self-denial, away from home, prison: it was worth it. For truly, that day, we supped with the gods.

The final was an epic match between age-old opponents South Africa and New Zealand. By the end of the match, the two teams were level at 9–all. The first half of extra time saw both teams dropping penalty goals, but it was South Africa who finally emerged victorious, with a drop goal from Joel Stransky.

At the end of the match, Nelson Mandela, President of South Africa, still wearing the Springboks shirt, awarded the William Webb Ellis Cup to South African captain Francois Pienaar. As Mandela handed the cup over, he said: 'Francois, thank you for what you have done for our country.' Pienaar quickly replied: 'No, Mr President. Thank you for what you have done.' It is considered one of the most symbolic sporting moments of all time.

BACKGROUND:	The Falklands/Malvinas War
EVENT:	FIFA World Cup
OPPONENTS:	Argentina v England
ARENA:	Mexico City, 1986

The Hand of God

MEXICO CITY, MEXICO, 1986

In the pre-match interview we had all said that football and politics shouldn't be confused, but that was a lie. We did nothing but think about that. Bollocks was it just another match!

— DIEGO MARADONA

OPPOSITE: Diego Maradona, the Argentinian captain, scores his first goal in the 1986 FIFA World Cup match against England with the 'hand of God'.

THE YEAR WAS 1986

▶ A nuclear explosion destroyed the Chernobyl nuclear reactor, exposing thousands to deadly radiation.

▶ The space shuttle *Challenger* broke apart in midair, killing all seven crew members.

▶ *Platoon* won the Academy Award for Best Picture.

▶ The winner of Song of the Year at the Grammy Awards was 'We Are the World'.

▶ *The Oprah Winfrey Show* debuted on US national television.

▶ President Ferdinand Marcos and his wife, Imelda, fled the Philippines after mass demonstrations against his leadership.

▶ Russia launched the *Mir* space station.

The quarterfinals of the FIFA World Cup of soccer, 1986, became the arena for a confrontation between the national teams of Argentina and England. Although the countries had met three times in previous World Cup matches, this was their first encounter since their armies had fought a war for sovereignty over the Falkland Islands four years earlier. It was impossible to downplay the political significance of the game, and it was obvious to all that this game would be an epic contest—particularly for the Argentinians, who saw it as an opportunity to avenge their loss in the war. The English felt quietly confident of their ability to progress to the semifinals, but were also wary of the threat posed by Argentina's talented captain, Diego Maradona. And their concern proved to be well-founded. England not only lost the game and exited the competition, but in the process were forced to stand by and watch in awe as Maradona scored two of the most famous goals in the history of the sport. The first was a blatant case of handball that Maradona notoriously ascribed to 'the hand of God', while the second is still spoken of as the most beautiful goal ever scored at the World Cup. Despite claims from both sides that it was only a game, both players and fans knew that there was far more at stake than a mere soccer contest.

State of the Nation

The Falkland Islands, known in Argentina as the Islas Malvinas, are about 400 kilometres (248½ miles) east of Cape Horn, deep in the south Atlantic Ocean. They were first discovered in 1592 by the English navigator John Davis. In the ensuing centuries, the islands were sporadically colonised by France, Spain, Great Britain and Argentina. This resulted in occasional outbreaks of violence between the rival powers, but there were also periods when settlers from various nations were able to coexist there peacefully. By 1811, all the colonists had withdrawn, with the British and Spanish each leaving behind plaques asserting their respective sovereignty over the islands.

Argentinian sailors arrived on the abandoned islands in 1820 and established a penal colony there over the next ten years. In 1832, the British returned and reasserted their claim to the islands. The Argentinian settlers were permitted to remain and continue their business ventures, while the British established a naval base, which was eventually used to service ships fighting the Germans in both world wars. With the establishment of the United Nations in 1945, Argentina took the opportunity to argue its right to sovereignty over the islands. Negotiations dragged on without any meaningful conclusions, while the 2000 mostly British inhabitants stated their preference to remain under British control.

Then, on 2 April 1982, the Argentinian military dictator General Leopoldo Galtieri shocked the world by ordering his troops to invade the islands. Galtieri underestimated the strength of the British response, and in particular the determination of Prime Minister Margaret Thatcher to hold on to the islands. Highly unpopular at the time due to the raft of free-market reforms that her government had introduced, she spotted an opportunity to restore her approval rating before the 1983 election by leading the country to a military success. On 3 April 1982 she declared war on Argentina. According to her daughter, Carol, Margaret Thatcher had to consult an atlas on the eve of the invasion in order to find out where the islands were located.

After World War II, the British had gradually removed their naval presence in the south Atlantic Ocean region, including the Falklands. To retake the islands from Argentina, it was necessary to assemble a naval task force with sufficient air cover. The task force eventually arrived in the south Atlantic and landed on the island of South Georgia on 19 April. After confrontations with the Argentinean forces at sea and on land, the British took control of the island on 25 April. The conflict escalated into an air war in May, with losses of aircraft and ships on both sides. The major event of the war was the sinking of the Argentinean light cruiser *General Belgrano* on 2 May, with the loss of 323 lives. The decisive land battle was at Goose Green, East Falkland on 28 May, with the British taking over 1000 Argentinean prisoners.

On 14 June 1982, Argentina was forced to surrender, and British forces marched into Port Stanley, the principal town of the islands. All in all, the conflict resulted in 258 British and 649 Argentinian deaths. Many soldiers on both sides returned home suffering terrible injuries and psychological trauma. The war marked an all-time low in British–Argentinian relations, and it ultimately led to the fall of the right-wing military junta that had ruled Argentina since 1976. The return of democracy was some consolation for the Argentinian people, but the popular resentment of Britain remained strong. This spilled over into protests against Chile and the United States—countries that had supported Britain in the war. Meanwhile, in Britain, the war was a massive popular success for Margaret Thatcher. With the jingoistic backing of the tabloid press, she went on to win the 1983 British election, holding power for the Conservative Party until her resignation in 1990.

Mexico City

The 1986 FIFA World Cup finals were originally going to be held in Colombia. However, in 1983 the country announced that it was bankrupt and could not afford to stage the Cup. Mexico, which had hosted the tournament in 1970, stepped into the breach and offered to act as host again. However, there were many in the international soccer community who thought Mexican conditions were unsuitable for the world's most watched international sporting event. The tournament was to be held in June, when competitors would have to contend with searing temperatures. The stadiums in Mexico City, Puebla and Toluca were over 2000 metres above sea level, which presented significant breathing difficulties for athletes unaccustomed to the thinner air. FIFA was also criticised for scheduling games to start in the midday heat so that they could be broadcast at prime time in the soccer-mad countries of Europe. Argentina was one of the many competing nations to air its grievances publicly, particularly through its captain Diego Maradona. However, once the tournament started it became obvious that the great player's skills and conditioning more than equipped him to deal with the harsh conditions.

Whether he could deal with the dubious tactics employed on the pitch by some of Argentina's opponents was another question. Their first match in the opening group stage was against South Korea, relative minnows in the global football pond. Argentina ended up winning the contest 3–1, but as soon as the game had started it became evident that the Koreans were targeting Maradona with constant aggressive fouling. This trend would continue throughout the tournament, as team after team used all their defensive energies to prevent Maradona from displaying his remarkable talents with the ball. In the second game, Argentina met Italy, one of the heavyweights of world soccer and a nation renowned for its miserly defensive strategies. Despite constant attention from the Italian midfield and backline, Maradona managed to get free to score a goal that remains one of his personal favourites, and the game finished 1–1. This was enough for Argentina to make it through to the second-round knockout stage, where in an ill-tempered match they beat their South American neighbours Uruguay by a solitary goal and advanced to the quarterfinals.

Meanwhile, England had made a slow start in their group, losing their first game 0–1 to Portugal and then only managing a scoreless draw with Morocco. It took a hat-trick by their star striker Gary Lineker for them to win their final group match 3–0 against Poland and reach the knockout stage. There they came up against another South American nation, Paraguay, two days after Argentina had beaten Uruguay. A victory for England would set up a quarterfinal showdown between the two combatants in the Falklands War. The English duly dispatched Paraguay with another 3–0 scoreline, and tensions began to bubble over in Mexico, Argentina and England in anticipation of the big game.

Battle Cries

As the two countries moved through the group stage and it became apparent that they could meet in the quarterfinals, the press in Argentina and Britain inflamed the patriotic sensibilities of their respective publics, knowing that memories of the Falklands War were still raw and emotionally charged in both countries. The British press cast their travelling fans as soldiers, with headlines such as 'Mexico alerts 5000 troops!' The Argentinian press came to the party by likening Maradona to their national revolutionary hero, General José de San Martin, who had fought for Argentinian independence against the colonial powers in the nineteenth century.

With the press doing their best to fan the fires of nationalist sentiment, diplomats from the two countries were working behind the scenes to defuse the political significance of the match. Instructions were issued to the coaches of the two teams, Carlos Bilardo and Bobby Robson, to tell their players to keep out of politics and remain focused on the game. However, once Argentina and England had won their respective knockout matches and the predicted encounter became a certainty, it was impossible to escape the broader implications. As Robson recalled, 'No matter how hard I tried to avoid the political undertones, I couldn't hide the fact that four years ago we had fought a war with Argentina.'

As the match drew closer, commentators and fans singled out Maradona and English goalkeeper Peter Shilton as the two players most likely to influence the outcome of the match. While Shilton was one of the best goalkeepers ever to play for England, Maradona was now emerging as one of the greatest attacking midfielders the world had ever seen. Though perhaps not in a class all of his own, he was being named alongside Pelé as the greatest in the history of the game. Robson was confident that England could win, provided the English defence concentrated on keeping Maradona away from their goal. He warned his team that the Argentinian captain had the capacity to turn the result of a game inside 5 minutes, and he opted against the common tactic of man-marking him with a single player. Instead, the whole team was to take responsibility: 'The nearest man goes to Maradona, kills him, and if he doesn't, the next one does, simple as that.' As Maradona remembers, 'The next game was against England, on 22 June 1986, a day I will not forget for as long as I live, ever.'

Divine Retribution

As the unrelenting summer sun beat down on Mexico City's Azteca Stadium on 22 June, everyone was prepared for an epic match. The World Cup was televised live across the globe, so in addition to the 114,580 spectators gathered in the stands, many millions more were watching the action on televisions around the world. The inflammatory press coverage and the politically charged nature of the game had prompted the Mexican authorities to send 15,000 police and soldiers to the stadium to maintain order. However, the drama of the day was not to take place in the stands—it all unfolded in the middle of the pitch.

The match began slowly, with England relying on a long-ball strategy and keeping most of their players in defence whenever Argentina had the ball. When they won possession, they would simply bang the ball up the field in the hope that their solitary striker, Lineker, could hold onto it while his teammates ventured forward to join him. This was less risky than moving forward in formation via dribbling and short passing, but also less likely to produce goals.

SIMPLY THE BEST

Gary Lineker went on to win the 1986 World Cup Golden Boot. He was the tournament's leading scorer, with six goals to his name.

Maradona played in four World Cups. In 2000, FIFA presented him with an award for being the best footballer of the twentieth century.

LEFT: Just a few minutes after the 'hand of God' incident, Maradona easily passes English defender Terry Butcher (far left) and moves towards goalie Peter Shilton (right) on his way to scoring the 'goal of the century'.

The first yellow card of the match was shown to the English defender Terry Fenwick after a mere 9 minutes, and there was some feeling in the English camp that the Tunisian referee was penalising them unfairly and favouring the Argentinians. The first half ended scoreless, but within 5 minutes of the restart the match delivered the first of its two defining moments. Maradona took possession in the England half and moved unerringly through their defence toward the top of the penalty box. Before he reached the wall of defenders in front of the goal, he laid the ball off to the right to his teammate Jorge Valdano, who was just inside the penalty area. England midfielder Steve Hodge managed to get a foot to the ball but only succeeded in hooking it dangerously back over his head towards his keeper.

Shilton came out to punch the ball away, but Maradona had continued his run into the penalty area and he leapt for the ball at the same time. As they met in midair the ball came off Maradona, looped over Shilton's outstretched fist, and bounced into the goal. As it did, Maradona gave a nod of the head as if to make out that he had headed the ball—a well-known yet obvious trick.

Maradona hit the ground with arms raised, claiming the goal, and then shot a quick look towards the referee before racing towards the sideline to celebrate. Shilton and coach Robson also looked towards the referee, fully expecting him to disallow the goal for handball. But the referee gave the signal that the goal had been scored, and turned to run back to the centre circle for the restart. Shilton, usually a very composed player, ran after the referee to protest. He was joined by Fenwick, Glenn Hoddle and Peter Beardsley, who were all convinced that the ball had hit Maradona's outstretched left hand as he leapt up with Shilton. However, the English protests were lost in the thunderous applause of the crowd as the referee and the linesman both confirmed that it was a goal. From their viewpoints, it appeared that Maradona had headed the ball legitimately into the net.

The Argentinian players went to congratulate Maradona on the sideline, although some of them were visibly slow to join him, as if they too had expected the goal to be disallowed. The crowd simply went wild, Mexicans and Argentinians joining in the celebration of Argentina's one-goal lead, while whistles and jeers of protest from the English supporters rang around the ground.

Maradona later said that this most controversial of goals was scored 'partly by the head of Maradona and partly by the hand of God', implying that it wasn't his hand that put the ball in the net but the will of a divine entity. He later described how his teammates were a bit timid in their celebrations of the goal: 'They came over to embrace me but it was as if they were saying: "We've robbed them,"' he said. 'But I said to them: "Whoever robs a thief gets a 100-year pardon,"' Maradona might have stayed out of politics prior to the match, but on the field the war was in full swing.

English commentators at the time expressed their suspicion that Maradona had played the ball with his raised left hand rather than his head, and television replays and still photographs confirmed that was indeed the case. The English players were shell-shocked by the goal, and the English press accused Maradona of cheating, referring to the incident as 'The Hand of the Devil'. No matter how many times the nation reviewed the moment in slow motion, the result always seemed gut-wrenchingly unfair.

However, for all Argentinians, both on and off the pitch, robbing the English in this way was a deeply satisfying experience. That spirit was even manifested in the commentary of the legendary Argentinian broadcaster Victor Hugo Morales. 'I ended up saying something not very professional,' he recalls. 'I was on a high with emotions that the war might have set off and I said, "What can I say?— against the English, we even use the hand."' In Argentina, the goal was seen as a prime example of the concept of *viveza*, meaning something between sharpness and craftiness. According to Jorge Valdano, viveza 'is deeply rooted in the average Argentinian, and when you get away with it, you celebrate: you are "smartest" compared to others.'

'Turns like a little eel ...'

The emotions running around the stadium after Maradona's 'hand of God' escapade were turned on their head just 4 minutes later by a goal of an entirely different nature from the Argentine maestro, one which is generally considered to be the 'Mona Lisa' of the soccer universe, the so-called 'goal of the century'.

It took Maradona 10 seconds to score this goal—a long time to be in possession of the ball at any level of the game, but which in a quarterfinal of the World Cup seems an eternity. Sports journalist Brian Glanville later described the goal as a historically significant moment. It was:

> ... astounding, so unusual, almost romantic, that it might have been scored by some schoolboy hero, or some remote Corinthian, from the days when dribbling was the vogue. It hardly belonged to so apparently rationalised an era such as ours, to a period in football when the dribbler seemed almost as extinct as the pterodactyl.

At the 9-minute mark of the second period, Maradona received the ball 5 metres inside his own half and executed a neat 180-degree spin which took him away from the England midfielders Peter Beardsley and Peter Reid. Reid tried to track back with him, as did the left-back Kenny Sansom, but Maradona left them both in his wake. The ball seemed to be attached to his left foot as he approached Terry Butcher, and four tiny touches saw him cut inside the experienced defender with ease. A little shimmy took him past Fenwick, who flung out his left arm in a futile attempt to impede Maradona's progress into England's penalty area.

By then, English captain and goalkeeper Peter Shilton was the only man standing between Maradona and the goal which would earn him the slack-jawed admiration of everybody who witnessed it. Shilton came quickly off his line, narrowing the angle to goal and spreading himself wide. Maradona shaped to shoot past Shilton's right glove, but then adjusted and tapped the ball to the keeper's left. He ran onto it just before Butcher caught up with him and lunged at him from behind, trying to make contact with ball, legs, feet—anything. But Maradona had judged his final manoeuvre to perfection, and he just had time to get his left boot to the ball and slide it into the net ahead of a despairing Stevens.

The cheering in the stadium had been deafening when Maradona produced that spin back at the halfway line, and from there it had swollen with every touch, every shimmy, every wrong-footed defender. When the ball went into the net, the volume needles on every sound-recording device in the Azteca flew into the red. Everyone watching knew they had just been privy to a rare display of magic. The English and the Argentinian commentaries bear witness to the effect that the goal had on the hearts and minds of their respective compatriots. In England, Bryon Butler's calling of the goal for BBC Radio was recently voted as one of the most memorable pieces of sporting commentary ever:

GOAL OF THE CENTURY, MOVE BY MOVE

1. Maradona (M.) receives 5 metres inside Argentinean half, facing right touchline and facing Beardsley.

2. With left foot, M. taps back towards goal (Argentina). Beardsley goes goal-side (England) of him.

3. Now facing Reid, M. continues clockwise turn. Left tap out toward right touchline, passing Beardsley on right.

4. With left, M. plays into open space on right wing. Reid follows at safe distance.

5. With left, M. continues straight ahead. Two tiny left touches. Lines up Butcher.

6. With two left, M. goes around Butcher easily on left. Butcher turns to pursue.

7. With left, M. shimmies and rounds Fenwick on right, who clutches at him with left hand.

8. Shilton comes out of goals. M. shapes to play/shoot to left. With left, M. rounds Shilton on right. Butcher tackles from behind.

9. With left, M. shoots into goal, ahead of Stevens, who is tracking back too slowly. Burruchaga and Valdano are both available and unmarked in front of goal.

Maradona turns like a little eel, he comes away from trouble, little squab man, comes inside Butcher and leaves him for dead, outside Fenwick and leaves him for dead, and puts the ball away ... and that is why Maradona is the greatest player in the world.

Meanwhile, in the Argentinian television booth, Victor Hugo Morales was again beside himself with emotion as he produced a commentary that has become the defining soundtrack to Maradona's remarkable goal:

Genius! Genius! Genius! Ta-ta-ta-ta-ta-ta ... GOOOOOOOOOAL! I am going to cry! Oh, my God! How beautiful football is! What a goal! Diego! Maradona! I am crying, forgive me please ... Maradona, with a memorable run, with the most beautiful play of all time ... What planet are you from, to carve through so many English, and the whole country is a closed fist, is screaming for Argentina ... Thank God, for football, for Maradona, for these tears, for this Argentina 2, England 0!

The players themselves were stunned at what they had seen. Midfielder Jorge Burruchaga recounts the moment. 'When he finishes the goal and goes to the corner flag I was the first one to reach him. I was happy, shouting, joyous, and then I said to him, "It's impossible what you've just done, you son of a bitch."'

The first goal of the match had been scored with a single touch of Maradona's left hand, but the goal of the century required 10 seconds of magical dribbling and about 11 touches of the ball, all with his left boot, twisting and turning and sending opposition players the wrong way while he sailed past them without missing a stride.

Gary Lineker will never forget it:

The second goal was, and still remains, the best goal ever scored. You have to take into account the significance of the football match and the conditions, as it was unbelievably hot and we were playing on a pitch that moved with you every time you put your foot down to go the other way. It was pretty unplayable. To do what he did was just extraordinary. I have to say I just stood there on the halfway line and thought, 'Wow.' That could have meant we were out of the World Cup, but it was just breathtaking.

The Gambetta

There was nothing anyone could have done to stop the goal. 'There was no lack of discipline on our part, no errors,' said English coach Bobby Robson, 'just the genius of one player who went through half our team to score the best goal of the competition.' However, it was a bitter pill to swallow for Peter Shilton, England's captain on the day and the man who carried the ultimate responsibility for stopping Maradona. The 'hand of God' goal had happened not long before, and Shilton said he was feeling rattled and unprepared. But Shilton (not to mention Beardsley, Reid, Butcher and Fenwick) was really the victim of a technique Maradona had been working on since he was a boy. It was the Argentinian art of dribbling known as the *Gambetta*, or sending one's opponent the wrong way and sidestepping past them—something every young boy practised for hours, and something that was part of the Argentinian way of life.

Defeat of a Country

Lineker clawed back a goal for England in the eighty-first minute, but Argentina held on to win the match 2–1. They overcame Belgium 2–0 in the semifinal, and then went on to beat West Germany in the final to claim the World Cup for the second time. The 'hand of God' goal was the subject of endless discussion, but Maradona stuck to his story that 'it was 100 per cent legitimate because the referee allowed it and I'm not one to question the honesty of the referee'. By the end of the tournament, Maradona was not only one of the greatest players in the world, but in his own country he had become almost a minor deity. He even adopted the habit of referring to himself in the third person, as 'Maradona'.

Treated like a king, seen as a maverick, it was hardly surprising that he escaped direct criticism in FIFA's official report on the controversial quarterfinal. The governing body was too scared to censure either him or the referee, for the age of commercialisation had arrived and Maradona was hot property. No-one could touch him. In Buenos Aires he was given a hero's welcome, standing on the balcony of the presidential palace and raising the treasured World Cup for all to see.

After the game, Maradona admitted his true feelings and those of all of his teammates when he referred to the game against England as 'the final':

I say a final because for us, because of everything it represented, we were playing a final against England. More than defeating a football team it was defeating a country. Of course before the match, we said that football had nothing to do with the Malvinas War, but we knew a lot of Argentinian kids had died there, shot down like little birds. This was revenge. It was like recovering a little bit of the Malvinas.

Twenty years later, on his own talk show, Maradona finally admitted to the handball and the Argentinians just seemed to love him all the more for it. He was a boy from the slums who had led the charge against Argentina's colonial oppressors. He not only spoke to Argentina, but he gave hope to every kid growing up in the developing world aspiring for success. Always a straight talker, Maradona quickly put paid to the most discussed goal of all time:

At the time I called it 'The Hand of God'. Bollocks was it the hand of God, it was the hand of Diego! And it felt a little bit like pickpocketing the English ...

Postscript

In 2008, Maradona was appointed head coach of Argentina's national soccer team. One of his first engagements was a friendly match against Scotland, whose assistant coach was Terry Butcher, one of the English defenders in the 1986 match. Before the Scotland game, Butcher told an interviewer that he still hadn't forgiven Maradona for the handballed goal. Maradona's response, as mischievous as ever, was to point out that England's third goal in their only World Cup final victory in 1966 should have been disallowed as it had not crossed the line. For English football supporters, this is the equivalent of denying the authenticity of the Bible to a devout Christian. Maradona's second jibe, at the post-match press conference (after Argentina had beaten Scotland 1–0), was to ask 'Who is Butcher? Who is Butcher?' His cheek was better received by the Scottish fans and press, whose longstanding enmity with England had led many in 1986 to loudly celebrate the 'hand of God' goal.

Footballs and Bullets

BACKGROUND:	World War I
EVENT:	Britain v Germany
OPPONENTS:	Allied Forces v Germany
ARENA:	The Western Front

Christmas Truce Football Match

BELGIUM, 1914

It is thought possible that the enemy may be contemplating an attack during Xmas or New Year. Special vigilance will be maintained during these periods. — **BRITISH GENERAL HEADQUARTERS, ST OMER, 24 DECEMBER 1914**

PREVIOUS PAGE: Zvonimir Boban kicks a Serbian police officer while defending a Croatian fan when a riot broke out between the fans at a football match between Croation club Dinamo Zagreb and Serbian club Red Star Belgrade.

OPPOSITE: German soldiers decorate a Christmas tree at the front line.

THE YEAR WAS 1914

▶ Britain's House of Commons passed the Irish Home Rule Act.

▶ On 28 July, Austria-Hungary declared war on Serbia, beginning World War I.

▶ The Ford Motor Company introduced measures for a minimum wage of $5 a day and a maximum working day of 8 hours.

▶ J. T. Hearne of England became the first bowler in first-class cricket to take 3000 wickets.

▶ Baseball legend Babe Ruth made his major-league debut with the Red Sox.

▶ The English Rugby Union team achieved their second consecutive Five Nations Grand Slam.

The story of the 'Christmas Truce' of World War I and of a game of football played between the enemy sides seems to many like the stuff of legend, invented by soldiers in desperate need of life-affirming news as they experienced the full horrors of war in the Flanders mud. However, first-hand accounts from troops on both sides of the conflict provide us with startling proof that this miraculous event did indeed occur. On Christmas Day 1914, troops stationed along the 800-kilometre (497-mile) Western Front climbed out of their rat-infested trenches and celebrated Christmas with a temporary ceasefire. As many as 10,000 men, German and Allied Forces alike, swapped photos, rations and cigarettes, sang Christmas carols, and then kicked makeshift soccer balls across the area known as 'no-man's land', from which they had just cleared their dead. The truce spread up and down the front from Belgium to the Swiss border, but many of the most poignant and vivid accounts of that extraordinary Christmas came from soldiers stationed near the Belgian town of Ypres.

The Lead-up

In August 1914, the assassination of Archduke Franz Ferdinand while he was on a state visit to Bosnia was to result in the violent fracturing of the intricate web of treaties and colonial affiliations that had been built up between the Allied Powers, led by Britain, France and Russia, and the Central Powers, led by Germany and Austria–Hungary. Control of the Balkans had seemed vital to both sides and the assassination had effectively put an end to weak attempts at maintaining a peaceful 'balance of power'.

Austria–Hungary now declared war on the prime suspect for the murder, Serbia, drawing the latter's ally, Russia, and subsequently the Allied Powers into one of the bloodiest and most widespread conflicts in history. Trenches were dug in battlefields that stretched from the muddy marshes of France to the deserts of Africa and the Middle East, and the fighting would involve troops from as far afield as Australia, New Zealand, Canada, South Africa and the United States.

As 1914 was drawing to a close, it became apparent that promises that the war would be over by Christmas were cruelly over-optimistic. The 'Great War', as it came to be known, would rage on for four more devastating years, involving 73 million military personnel and 38 countries, before the Central Powers were finally defeated, bringing to an end a conflict that had resulted in the deaths of more than 15 million people and effectively destroyed a whole generation of young men.

The Greatest Gift

As Christmas 1914 approached, the British Army was occupying an area of the Western Front in Belgium that ran south from the Ypres Salient to the La Bassée Canal. Huddled behind earth ramparts and barbed wire, they shot at the enemy troops positioned in trenches some 65 metres (60 yards) away, or were sent over the top to attempt a usually abortive—and in terms of casualties, always costly—attack. It was still early in the conflict and although there had been thousands of deaths, the poison gas and aerial bombardment that would cause young men to 'die as cattle'—as the war poet Wilfred Owen described it in his 'Anthem for Doomed Youth'—were not yet in use. But conditions that December were appalling: the soldiers in the trenches had scant protection against the sub-zero temperatures of that harshest of winters and they watched with sick horror as rats scavenged in the mud beside them. As they huddled together on that Christmas Eve, memories of Christmases past must have haunted both sides, uniting them perhaps with an intense longing for home and for a respite from the living hell in which they found themselves.

While the British troops received gifts in a brass box from King George V, the German troops opened their presents from the Kaiser and discovered plum puddings, cigarettes, cigars, warm blankets and small Christmas trees to symbolise the family festivities of happier years. By the time night fell on Christmas Eve, the rain had stopped and the ground was covered in hoarfrost which glittered in the moonlight. As they kept watch, tired eyes fixed on the enemy trenches, the British were suddenly amazed to see tiny flames begin to flicker in the darkness. The Germans were decorating their trenches by setting up their miniature Christmas trees, lighting the candles attached to the branches and placing them on top of the parapets. There was still some distant gunfire, but in many areas of the front there fell a tense, expectant silence.

And now, in what must have seemed like the greatest Christmas gift of all, the ordinary soldiers of both sides made peace for that night. Against all odds, and to the consternation of both British and German military commanders, an impromptu ceasefire was established along the Western Front. Accounts of these extraordinary truce negotiations pepper the letters and the diaries of soldiers from both sides, the descriptions varying according to where the writer was stationed. One account tells of how a German officer sent some chocolate cake over to the British, inside which was a note suggesting a ceasefire at 7.30 pm to enable everyone to celebrate. The British accepted with alacrity, sending a gift of tobacco in return.

According to Captain Josef Sewald of the 17th Bavarian Regiment:

> I shouted to our enemies that we didn't want to shoot and that we should make a Christmas truce. I said I would come from my side and we could speak with each other. First there was silence, then I shouted once more, inviting them, and the British shouted 'No shooting!' Then a man came out of the trenches and I on my side did the same and so we came together and we shook hands—a bit cautiously!

Play the greater game and join the football battalion.

– RECRUITMENT POSTER FOR WORLD WAR I

RIGHT: During the Christmas truce, German and British troops ventured onto no-man's-land, shaking hands and exchanging gifts before impromptu football matches broke out up and down the lines.

Silent Night

The British troops stationed outside La Chapelle-d'Armentières in northern France listened in astonishment as the Germans began to sing. As Albert Moren of the 2nd Queen's Regiment recalled:

> *It was a beautiful moonlit night, frost on the ground, white almost everywhere; and ... there was a lot of commotion in the German trenches and then there were those lights—I still don't know what they were. And then they sang 'Silent Night'— 'Stille Nacht'. I shall never forget it. It was one of the highlights of my life.*

The British troops shouted over the barbed wire which lined the ramparts of the trenches that they wanted more, firing flares to show their appreciation. Soon there was virtually a concert taking place as songs from both sides ricocheted back and forth across no-man's-land. Officers who were safely ensconced well behind the front line soon heard of the fraternisation between the troops. Some sent orders forbidding the contact, but many officers from both sides, no doubt sickened too by the carnage, turned a blind eye or even joined in. As the troops lay down to

WHEN SPORT STOPS WAR

The Australians reluctantly called it a draw and retired for tea. – Bill Gammage

Gallipoli, December 1915, saw the most unusual game of cricket ever played. Britain's General Kitchener gave orders that the Anzac soldiers should be withdrawn from Gallipoli after the disastrous campaign in the Dardanelles. Over 11 nights, 35,445 Anzac troops were to be evacuated from the area and redeployed to the Western Front in France. However, after the mismanagement that had seen troops paying a terrible price against the Turks, who had now entered the war on the German side, it was vital that casualties be kept to a minimum. Orders went out for the remaining troops to be as active and visible as possible in order to convince the Turks that no withdrawal was in operation. While many took up sentry duty or made sure that they were visible patrolling the trenches, the men from the New South Wales 4th Battalion were more inventive, and decided to engage in a game of cricket.

On 17 December, the men made their way to an area of ground known as Shell Green, set up the stumps and sent the first man in to bat. It was an extraordinary test of nerve, as the Green was well within enemy range and under constant fire. The Turks watched in some confusion as the 4th Battalion stepped out with their makeshift bats and balls and proceeded to play.

For an area usually bombarded, Shell Green was unusually quiet. For two hours the Turks ceased their fire and watched the game unfold. Finally, they seemed to lose interest and started firing, sending shells ricocheting onto the 'pitch'. The Anzacs responded in a daredevil fashion, pretending to field the mortars as they dodged the bullets. At the end of the game, the players retired without a single injury and the Turks were left deeply puzzled. Two days later, all of the Anzacs were successfully evacuated. Today, Shell Green serves as a cemetery for the Anzac troops who lost their lives in World War I.

sleep that night, they took comfort from the knowledge that they would survive another day at least. For many, it reaffirmed their belief in the human spirit and the fact that camaraderie might exist even in such a hellhole. All who witnessed it reported that it was the strangest and most memorable night of their lives.

Christmas Day

As dawn broke on Christmas Day, soldiers who had slept soundly for once peered out of the trenches and stared in disbelief. Bruce Bairnsfather of the Royal Warwickshire Regiment was one of them:

> *I awoke at dawn, and on emerging on all fours from my dugout, became aware that the trench was practically empty. I stood upright in the mud and looked over the parapet. No Man's Land was full of clusters … of khaki and gray … pleasantly chatting together.*

Cautiously at first, a few men had ventured out onto no-man's-land to be met by members of the opposing army. Enemies shook hands, swapped cigarettes, exchanged gifts and told stories of home. And those in desperate need of a haircut or shave found that soldiers who had been barbers in their civilian lives were setting up shop and offering their services. 'Tommy' or 'Fritz', they were warmly welcomed as customers and must have enjoyed the sense of being smartened up for this special day. Many of the Germans had until recently been working in England and been forced to leave on the outbreak of war. As a result, they spoke good English and had much in common with the 'Tommies' they were fighting.

As Bryan Latham of the London Rifles took in what was happening, he remarked that no-man's-land 'had the appearance of a football pitch at half-time'. However, the festive spirit did not reach all parts of the Front. French and Belgian troops, who were fighting along parts of the Western Front with the British, were less willing to join the festivities: they had already lost 400,000 people, and the enemy troops that occupied their homeland were wreaking devastation.

Alfred Anderson of the 5th Battalion of the Black Watch describes the unique stillness of that Christmas morning as seen from his position some distance behind the front line:

> *I remember the silence, the eerie sound of silence. Only the guards were on duty. We all went outside the farm buildings and just stood listening. And, of course, thinking of people back home. All I'd heard for two months in the trenches was the hissing, cracking and whining of bullets in flight, machinegun fire and distant German voices. But there was a dead silence that morning, right across the land as far as you could see. We shouted 'Merry Christmas', even though nobody felt merry.*

'HOW DO YOU SPELL PELÉ? G-O-D!'

Not many people can stop a war, but when the Brazilian soccer legend Pelé was invited in 1967 to accompany his club side, Santos, to an exhibition match in Nigeria, that's exactly what happened. With the Biafran Civil War raging, Pelé was worried and expressed his concern to his agent, who confidently replied, 'Don't worry. They'll stop the war.'

The agent was right: hostilities came to an official standstill for three days. Pelé himself couldn't believe what was happening. 'Apparently there really was a temporary ceasefire, just for us. My team mates remember seeing white flags on the streets and banners pleading for peace, just so people could go and see Pelé.'

Despite playing in a FIFA World Cup final at the age of 17, and being the only three-time winner of the World Cup, Pelé must look back on the ceasefire in the Biafran War as one of his greatest achievements.

RIGHT: German soldiers and British
soldiers from the 11th Brigade,
4th Division, at Ploegsteert in
Belgium on Christmas Day, 1914.

Germany Wins, 3–2

Once presents had been swapped and stories told, impromptu football matches broke out up and down the lines. Many of the players had no ball, so they improvised with tins, jam boxes, their helmets or lumps of straw tied together with string. A German soldier, Johannes Niemann, told of his experience:

> *A Scot dragged out a football ... and soon there was a proper game of football in progress with helmets for goalposts. It was such a sight on the frozen mud. One of us had a camera, and the two teams of footballers quickly assembled themselves into a single group of pretty colorful rows with the football in the middle ... During the game, our lancers soon discovered that the Scots wore no underwear beneath their kilts, so that their rears were clearly visible as soon as their kilts started fluttering. That amused us greatly, though at first we could hardly believe it.*

The men rediscovered a fleeting joy in life as they chased madly after the makeshift soccer balls, skidding over the icy ground. As Kurt Zehmisch of the 134th Saxons recorded in his diary:

> *The English brought a soccer ball from the trenches, and pretty soon a lively game ensued. How marvelously wonderful, yet how strange it was. The English officers felt the same way about it. Thus Christmas, the celebration of Love, managed to bring mortal enemies together as friends for a time ... I told them we didn't want to shoot on the Second Day of Christmas either. They agreed.*

This game lasted for an hour before the soldiers collapsed, exhausted from months of sleep deprivation and weakened by meagre rations. Many football matches took place on the front, but it seems this was the only one to occur between the two opposing sides. The letters from German and English soldiers seem unanimous in recording the score as 3–2 to the Germans. On 1 January 1915, the *London Times* published a letter from a major quoting the same result.

Back to the Fighting

Just as there were varying accounts of how the 1914 Christmas truce began, there were also different versions of how it ended. A popular version is attributed to Captain J. C. Dunn, the medical officer in the Royal Welsh Fusiliers, whose unit had received two barrels of beer from the Saxon troops opposite:

> *At 8.30 I fired three shots in the air and put up a flag with 'Merry Christmas' on it, and I climbed on the parapet. He [the German] put up a sheet with 'Thank you' on it, and the German captain appeared on the parapet. We both bowed and saluted and got down into our respective trenches, and he fired two shots in the air, and the War was on again.*

The Christmas truce has become legendary, mainly because it was a ceasefire called by the troops themselves, not by their commanding officers or government ministers. Some worried that there might be a reprimand, but most knew that the people waiting at home on all sides would be thankful that their loved ones had had a moment of relief. Few spoke out against the truce, but it was said that a young Austrian soldier stationed near Ypres—one Adolf Hitler—complained that such an understanding 'should not be allowed'.

The truce lasted for different lengths of time at various sections along the Front. Many troops did not want the war to begin again, and in some areas the truce extended up to a week before fighting resumed. Even then, it was said that in the days that followed, many of the bullets fired were aimed high into the air. For a short time the fraternising and the football had united the two sides, allowing them a precious opportunity to glimpse the person behind the uniform and share their yearning for all that they had left behind. But it was not long before the soldiers would have to put such feelings aside. As British soldier Alfred Anderson observed, 'The silence ended early in the afternoon and the killing started again. It was a short peace in a terrible war.'

Such a truce did not happen again until the final Armistice on 11 November 1918. That football game in no-man's-land on the first Christmas Eve of the war remains unique in the history of this most terrible of wars. For those hours, ordinary soldiers from both sides defied the orders of generals and governments, reaching out across the frozen, corpse-strewn wasteland that divided them.

BACKGROUND:	World War II
EVENT:	Nazism v Ukrainian communism
OPPONENTS:	FC Start (Kiev) v Flakelf (Germany)
ARENA:	Zenit Stadium, Kiev

Game of Death: Germany v Ukraine

KIEV, UKRAINE, 1942

Red sport will never die! — **THE LAST WORDS OF UKRAINIAN GOALKEEPER NIKOLAI TRUSEVICH BEFORE BEING CLUBBED TO DEATH**

When Nazi Germany invaded the Soviet Union in 1941, the Ukrainian city of Kiev fell under German occupation. Months later, players from the Dynamo soccer team of Kiev, which had previously been one of Europe's best football clubs, reunited to form a team. When they beat the Germans in a 'friendly', they were seen to be undermining the Nazis' claims of representing a 'master race'. The Ukrainians were warned not to win again. The Germans assembled a top team of their best athletes and challenged the impoverished players of Kiev to a rematch. As the crowds cheered, the Dynamo players chose to ignore the warnings from their German oppressors and ran rings around the opposing team. For a moment they experienced the elation of victory, but in the months following, many of the players paid the ultimate price—they were systematically rounded up and killed by the Nazi occupiers.

State of the Nation

By the time World War II erupted in 1939, the Soviet Union was frozen in the iron grip of communist dictator Joseph Stalin, who had particular contempt for the people of the Ukraine. In the early 1930s the region had suffered great famine due to Stalin's agrarian policies, which had resulted in the deaths of an estimated 14 million people. In 1937, Stalin mounted a campaign of political repression, under which anyone seen to be in opposition to the government was liable to be executed. No Ukrainian citizen was exempt.

On 22 June 1941, the Germans caught Stalin unawares and declared war on the Soviet Union, launching an invasion of the vast country. By way of a three-pronged attack named Operation Barbarossa, Hitler's troops drove deep into Soviet territory. The Red Army was defeated, the air force was destroyed, enabling the Germans to establish strongholds in key cities throughout the country.

Hopes Dashed

Soccer was a popular sport throughout the Soviet Union, and the Ukraine was no exception. The city of Kiev boasted a team called Dynamo Kiev which had featured prominently in the first USSR championships of the mid-1930s. Despite experiencing an unsettling run towards the bottom of the league since then, they were hopeful of making a comeback. However, as 1941 approached, all hopes of a revival were blighted by the German invasion of Russia. Kiev became a primary target, and all young men were called to defend their country.

As German troops drew closer, the team was disbanded and some players headed to the front lines, while others stayed behind. Three months later Kiev fell in a bitter battle, and the Ukraine was occupied by the German forces.

Many Ukrainians thought life might be better under Hitler, thinking that no-one could be worse than Stalin. When the Germans ordered all Jews in Kiev to report to an appointed location, many Ukrainian nationalists who harboured

THE YEAR WAS 1942

▶ At the Wannsee Conference, German leaders decided that the 'final solution' to the 'Jewish problem' was to relocate them, then to kill them.

▶ Anne Frank received a diary as a birthday present.

▶ The United Nations was formed, with 26 countries agreeing to join.

▶ The Australian cities of Sydney and Newcastle were damaged when they were shelled by Japanese submarines.

▶ The Oxford Committee for Famine Relief, known as Oxfam, was established.

▶ The Statute of Westminster Adoption Act formalised the independence of Australia's parliaments from Great Britain.

▶ The movie *Casablanca* premiered in New York City.

▶ Orson Welles's *Citizen Kane* won the Academy Award for best writing for an original screenplay.

▶ Joe Louis knocked out Buddy Baer in the first round to win the heavyweight boxing title.

anti-Jewish sentiment saw the Nazis as potential allies. Consequently, many citizens chose to act as informants, despite the hardships imposed by the Germans. By November 1942, an estimated 100,000 Ukrainians had been killed; 75 per cent were Jews. Hopes of kinder dictators appeared to have been in vain.

FC Start

As the Germans secured their grip on Russia, some Soviet prisoners of war were released from the POW camps and sent home. They returned weak, starving and exhausted; as none of them had work permits, most were facing starvation. When ardent Dynamo fan Iosif Kordik spotted one of his favourite players, Nikolai Trusevich, walking the city streets in 1941, he offered him a job sweeping floors in Kiev's huge Bakery Number 3. The Dynamo goalkeeper immediately accepted the offer and the two men became firm friends.

As they discussed the glory days of football, Kordik came up with the idea of getting a team together to represent the bakery. Together he and Trusevich trawled the streets in search of the rest of the Dynamo players, as well as some from the former Locomotiv Kiev team. Slowly the men were found, and offered jobs in the bakery and a place on the team. By June 1942, Trusevich and Kordik had enough players to take part in the local league organised by the occupiers.

Called FC Start, the team may have lacked equipment, but was certainly not short on skill. The first match was against a team called Rukh, who were supported by the organiser of the local league—Georgi Shvetsov, a German informant. When the undernourished and physically exhausted FC Start beat Rukh 7–2, Shvetsov was furious and persuaded the Germans to ban the newly formed team from training at the local stadium.

The ban did nothing but fire the team's determination to succeed, and as the season commenced they went on to beat the Hungarian garrison team 6–2 and a Romanian side 11–0. On 17 July 1942 they took on PGS, a German military team, and shocked the enthusiastic locals by winning 6–0. Now on a roll, they went on to beat a much-favoured Hungarian team, MSG Wal, by 5 goals to 1. FC Start had become the runaway favourites in the league, and they were whipping up nationalistic sentiment at every match.

Knowing that FC Start were beginning to symbolise far more than just football success to the oppressed locals, the Germans introduced a newly formed side called Flakelf. The team was selected from the ranks of the champion players in the German Luftwaffe (air force), and the Germans were confident that they could teach the Start players a lesson.

When the teams met on 6 August, shocked German troops watched as FC Start embarrassed their hand-picked opposition, winning 5–1. With Hitler's claims that Germany was home to a master race now called into question, a date was set for a rematch—and the Germans were determined to win at any cost.

Red Army Battle Cry!

As the Kiev crowds flocked to the Zenit Stadium on 9 August for the rematch, Nazi guards patrolled the area and Ukrainian police monitored the mood. It was tense, with everyone expecting trouble—none more so than the Start players. Before the game, the German referee (who was also an SS officer) marched into the FC Start dressing room and instructed the players that they would be expected to greet their opponents 'in our fashion', alluding to the famous Nazi salute. The request divided the Kiev team. Some refused the idea of the salute and were all for winning on the field. Others thought it wiser to perform the salute and also let the Germans win the game. After a heated discussion, the dissenters relented and abandoned all notion of appeasement. From the beginning of the match, it became apparent that the FC Start players were there to make a statement.

As the Flakelf team acknowledged their leader with a 'Heil Hitler', FC Start answered as one with a Soviet slogan and the battle cry of the Red Army. The players had decided to oppose the Nazi regime and embrace the spirit of the locals, who had gathered in their thousands to watch the game.

Biased refereeing was evident from the start. When a German forward kicked Nikolai Trusevich in the head, the goalkeeper could only watch blearily as the first German goal flashed past him into the net. FC Start quickly retaliated, scoring with a long shot from a free kick by Ivan Kuzmenko. Then Makar Goncharenko, in a moment of inspiration, dribbled the ball through the Flakelf defence and placed it neatly in the German net for a 2–1 lead.

ABOVE: Members of the Dynamo Kyiv squad, one of Europe's best football clubs, in 1929

Forfeit or Else

At half time, with the score 3–1 in their favour, the FC Start players were feeling confident. However, their mood soon changed when they received two ominous visits to the dressing room at half-time. The German informant Shvetsov appeared first and advised them to forfeit the match. The second visitor was an SS officer who warned them that it was impossible for them to win and that they should be wary of the consequences of even trying.

FC Start were being bullied into giving the game away, but they refused to do so lying down. Leading 5–3 deep in the second half, the Start players added insult to injury by showcasing their superior skill. When the Ukrainian defender Aleksei Klimenko dribbled the ball through the entire field and around the German goalkeeper, everyone waited for him to push the ball into the goal. Instead, he stopped it before the line, and booted it back towards the centre circle.

The Germans were furious. This play was more insulting than a win. The referee called time early and the Flakelf players quickly left the pitch, fearful at the increasing hostility from the Ukrainian crowd who had by this time realised that their players must be under threat. As the spectators cheered for FC Start and yelled insults at their German oppressors, the Nazis unleashed their guard dogs and chaos ensued.

The Interrogation

The players nervously awaited the German backlash, but for the next fortnight life went on as normal. However, after the Starts played their final fixture of the season on 16 August, beating Rukh 8–0, the SS proved that it had merely been biding its time. Straight after the game, they raided Bakery Number 3 and arrested the entire team. Each player was interrogated under torture as the SS tried to force confessions that would officially allow them to execute the Ukrainians. Despite the players closing ranks and refusing to cooperate, it was only a matter of time before an excuse would be found to kill them. Nikolai Korotkykh became the first player to die, having been exposed as a former officer of the Soviet secret police organisation NKVD.

Trusevich and his team were taken to a labour camp at nearby Syrets, which was renowned for the cruel and sadistic treatment of its prisoners. Few people ever left; most died from exhaustion and hunger. In February 1943, the camp commandant decided to shoot every third prisoner as a result of a local protest. The first to go was FC Start striker Kuzmenko. The Germans hadn't forgotten the goal he had scored against them in the rematch. The second was Klimenko who, in his moment of brilliance, had broken through the ranks of the entire German team only to decide not to take a shot at goal. Finally, still wearing his goalkeeper's jersey, Nikolai Trusevich turned to his execution squad with the words 'Red sport will never die!' and was clubbed to death.

A few other ex-Dynamo players made it through the Nazi occupation. Goncharenko, Fedir Tyutchev and Mikhail Sviridovsky hadn't been taken to the camp, and instead were in a work squad in the city. They went into hiding until Kiev was freed from German occupation in 1943. Another, Pavel Komarov, was suspected of being a German informant and simply disappeared, as did the former Locomotiv players who were never seen again.

The Aftermath

Stalin came back into power in 1943, and the people of Ukraine continued to live under his oppressive regime. The FC Start team had paid a high price for their win against the Germans, but for a fleeting moment these skilled and determined players had given hope to the people of Kiev—and had themselves experienced the long-suppressed pleasure of exercising their freedom of expression.

COMMUNISM V NAZISM

In 1972 a monument was erected outside the Dynamo Kiev stadium in honour of the FC Start players. It represents the victory of communism over Nazism.

BACKGROUND:	Border dispute between Honduras and El Salvador
EVENT:	The 'Futbol Wars'
OPPONENTS:	Honduras v El Salvador
ARENA:	Stadiums in Tegucigalpa, San Salvador and Mexico City

The Futbol Wars

TEGUCIGALPA, SAN SALVADOR AND MEXICO CITY, MEXICO, 1969

Soccer may be just a game in other parts of the world, but in Central America it's an endemic form of madness ... Locally known as 'futbol', there is nothing else in the form of sports that can begin to approach the levels of passion it evokes in the land. It isn't hard to imagine a soccer game serving to start a war in this region. **— LORENZO DEE BELVEAL, JOURNALIST**

OPPOSITE: Honduran women and children flee towards the Guatemalan border the day after El Salvador's troops invaded Honduras in 1969. Clashes at the recent international soccer match between the countries precipitated the outbreak of war.

In the late 1960s, immigration and border disputes between El Salvador and Honduras were threatening to drive the two neighbouring nations into all-out war. The tipping point came when they went head-to-head in three soccer World Cup qualifiers in June 1969. When the second match ended in the burning of national flags and the victimisation of fans, diplomatic relationships between the countries came to a screeching halt. Known as the 'Futbol Wars', the matches ignited the building hatred between the Hondurans and the Salvadorians, and two weeks later war broke out, resulting in thousands of casualties.

State of the Nation

El Salvador in the 1960s was a small country with an ever-growing population and a burgeoning economy. However, inequities caused by the Central American Common Market, which had also spurred on the country's growth, had left almost half of El Salvador's peasantry without land due to the rapid expansion of the export crop economy. Honduras, to its east, was a much larger country, with a smaller population and an underdeveloped economy. As a result, increasing numbers of Salvadorians were flooding into Honduras. Border disputes had occurred ever since the two countries had become independent nations 130 years before, as both countries had laid claim to border regions and islands along the Pacific coast.

By the late 1960s, an estimated 300,000 Salvadorian immigrants had crossed the border into Honduras. Salvadorians were working on Honduran land and setting up flourishing businesses. The majority of the migrants were seen as squatters with no legal rights and as such were heavily resented. As the numbers of Salvadorian migrants increased, the Hondurans felt they were in danger of being overrun, and they targeted the illegal immigrants as the reason for the economic disparity between the two countries. In fact, the Salvadorians were being used as scapegoats for the inadequacies of the dictatorial governments, led by Oswaldo López Arellano in Honduras and Fidel Sánchez Hernández in El Salvador.

In early 1969, the government of López Arellano reinstated a land reform law in a bid to evict all of the Salvadorian squatters from Honduras. Constituting almost 20 per cent of the Honduran population, the Salvadorians were suddenly given 30 days to leave their homes. The prospect of up to 300,000 peasants returning en masse to El Salvador was a situation the Salvadorian government would find difficult to handle.

Three-Game Elimination

In June 1969, the tension between Honduras and El Salvador increased further when the national soccer teams of the two countries were engaged in a three-game qualifying round for the 1970 World Cup in Mexico. The first match was to take place on 8 June at the Honduran national stadium in the capital, Tegucigalpa.

The Salvadorian team arrived the night before and, as was customary, Honduran fans intent on keeping the opposition awake all night targeted their hotel. The tactic worked, and in the last minute of the game a livelier Honduras team scored the winning goal and won the game 1–0.

The crowd went wild, the stadium was burned and fights broke out. For many Salvadorians, it was a tragic blow, but for 18-year-old Amelia Bolanios it was too much to bear. Taking her father's pistol, she shot herself in the heart. Seen as a martyr for the sacred sport, Bolanios was given a state funeral, attended by El Salvador's president and the Salvadorian soccer team. By the time of the second match, the Salvadorians were not only playing for their country, but defending the loss of innocence and honouring the memory of their young fan.

As the teams prepared for their second encounter, there were reports in El Salvador that paramilitary groups, partly made up of an extreme right-wing group called La Mancha Brava, were evicting Salvadorian farmers from the Honduran land they had been farming for years. Thousands of Salvadorians started a mass exodus over the border from Honduras, and news of violent displacements and terrible atrocities began to filter through. The press responded with a war of words and insults, using every opportunity to inflame Salvadorian nationalism.

Dead Rats and Rotten Eggs

On 14 June 1969, the Honduran soccer team arrived in the Salvadorian capital, San Salvador, for the match the next day. As expected, Salvadorian fans surrounded their hotel throughout the night. However, this time the campaign of terror was carried out with military precision. Led by General José Alberto Medrano, chief of the intelligence services and director of the National Guard, gangs of Salvadorians did their utmost to make sure the Hondurans received no sleep. Dead rats and rotten eggs were thrown through the broken windows of the hotel before it was finally torched and the players forced out into the night. As the disturbance intensified, two people were killed and seven were injured by police.

Game Two

The next day, the Honduran team entered Flor Blanca stadium in front of an overwhelmingly hostile crowd. The Honduran flag had been burned by the Salvadorian crowd, and no-one could hear the Honduran national anthem above the sound of the booing. The Hondurans didn't have a chance and lost to El Salvador 3–0. As Honduras's coach Mario Griffin Cubas observed, it was the best result possible for his team, who may not have survived had they won: 'We're awfully lucky that we lost.'

The Salvadorian fans celebrated the win by destroying the area surrounding the stadium, and singling out the visiting Honduran fans for beatings. Cars were overturned, shops were burned and windows smashed. The Honduran

SOCCER WAR

The Futbol Wars were also known as the Soccer War and the 100-hours War.

SOCCER TROOPS

The warlike rhetoric which
accompanies the world of
soccer is demonstrated all
over the world. For example,
the most prominent fan club
of Team USA is called 'Sam's
Army'. At the 2006 FIFA
World Cup, American striker
Eddie Johnson announced
to the US troops stationed
at Ramstein Air Base in
Germany that his team had
arrived at the World Cup
ready for a 'war'.

'Whenever you put your
jersey on and you look at
your crest and the national
anthem's going on, and
you're playing against a
different country, it's like you
do or die, it's survival of the
[fittest] over 90-minutes-
plus. We're going to go
out there and do whatever
we've got to do.' Johnson
concluded by saying, 'It's do
or die … I don't want to go
home early.'

players escaped over the border in armoured cars, thankful to be alive. When their tales of victimisation reached their fellow Hondurans, the hatred that had built up for years between the two countries started to manifest in violent outbursts throughout the region. In Honduras, Salvadorian residents were reportedly assaulted or killed by La Mancha Brava, which had strong links to the government.

The Salvadorian press reported three days of atrocities akin to genocide, but the Hondurans continually denied the charges. By 17 June, the local press in San Salvador was demanding that the government should 'take drastic measures against Honduras'. Huge numbers of Salvadorian refugees were flooding back to El Salvador. In late June, all diplomatic relations between the two countries were severed.

The Decider

With the deciding match to be played in Mexico City on 27 June, Central America came to a virtual standstill. Anyone who could get to Mexico City did, and 'futbol' fever ruled the region.

The play on the field was as dirty as the rules would allow. When El Salvador won 3–2 in the final seconds of extra time, there was mayhem in the stadium and throughout the surrounding area. Fights, rapes and murders ensued as the city became a battle zone, with no Geneva Convention in sight. The Hondurans accused the Salvadorians of biased refereeing and cheating. The insults from both sides quickly escalated, and were taken up by the Honduran and Salvadorian governments.

Tales of atrocity on both sides were thought to have been heavily exaggerated by the press, and inflammatory broadcasts and news stories weighed heavily in the conflict. Honduran radio even urged listeners to 'pick up a plank and kill a Salvadorian'.

100-hours War

On 14 July, the Salvadorian army invaded Honduras as a Salvadorian plane dropped its first bomb over Tegucigalpa. The city went into blackout, and stood by nervously as a tropical storm lit the city for the enemy pilots.

Quickly asserting its military capability, El Salvador bombed the Honduran air force while the planes were standing by in their hangars. Moving into Honduran territory, the El Salvadorian army cut off the roads from Honduras to Guatemala and Nicaragua. However, five days into the war, Salvadorian troops ran out of ammunition, petrol and resources. They had shown their military strength by occupying the land, but no change of government resulted. Instead, the Organisation of American States (OAS) arranged a ceasefire and the United States put pressure on El Salvador to withdraw. The troops pulled out and the

OPPOSITE: Salvadorean soldiers at a frontier post near El Poy, El Salvador aim their machine guns towards Honduras.

LOSING THE WORLD CUP: THE ULTIMATE PRICE

In Colombia, football can be a matter of life or death—as defender Andrés Escobar Saldarriaga found out in the aftermath of the 1994 FIFA World Cup.

Rife with corruption, Colombian soccer has a history of being linked with money laundering, gambling and drug cartels. When the major Colombian cartels were disbanded in the late 1980s and the 1990s, it was hoped that the level of corruption in Colombian soccer would be reduced. However, disengaging proved difficult and the close ties remained. As the 1994 FIFA World Cup approached, many of the Colombian players were chosen from Atlético Nacional, a team sponsored by drug lord Pablo Escobar. In fact, in 1997 a Colombian government report found that drug traffickers still controlled between 70 and 80 per cent of shares belonging to the five biggest soccer clubs.

When the Colombian team arrived at the 1994 World Cup, they were playing with such brilliance and flair that many tipped them as the tournament favourites. In the qualifying round, they had decisively beaten Argentina 5-0, and pressure was building on their opening game against Romania. However, when the match started, the players seemed different. Gone was the carefree style they had demonstrated in the qualifying matches, and in its place was an apparent nervousness. It transpired that the team coach, Hernán Gómez, had received death threats over his selection of the squad, and betting syndicates and drug cartels were trying to control the game. The pressure proved too much and the team lost 3-1.

The second match was against the United States. With the score sitting at 1-1, Colombian defender Andrés Escobar accidentally deflected the ball into the back of the Colombian net, scoring a disastrous own goal. The number 2 player, nicknamed 'the Gentleman of Football', was devastated. Colombia was out of the World Cup.

Ten days later, on 2 July 1994, Escobar was gunned down outside a club in his hometown. He was shot 12 times. Every time the killer released a bullet, he reportedly shouted 'GOAL!' In June 1995 Humberto Muñoz Castro was sentenced to 43 years for Escobar's murder, but he was released in 2005.

two nations were left to make sense of the short-lived carnage. The Honduran peasants were the worst affected—in five days, 2000 were killed, and at least 100,000 were displaced by the advancing Salvadorian army.

Aftermath

World media coverage of the 'Futbol Wars' of July 1969 was limited due to other significant events: as El Salvador invaded Honduras, other borders were crossed and territories claimed as the Americans successfully completed the first moon landing. El Salvador went on to compete in the 1970 World Cup, their first ever World Cup appearance. They lost to Belgium, Mexico and the USSR and were eliminated after the first round, having scored no goals.

OPPOSITE: Colombian defender Andrés Escobar accidentally scored an own goal in a match against the US in the 1994 World Cup. He paid for it with his life.

BACKGROUND:	The Yugoslav Wars
EVENT:	Croatia v Serbia
OPPONENTS:	Dinamo Zagreb v Red Star Belgrade
ARENA:	Maksimir Stadium, Zagreb, Croatia

The Kick Without a Ball

ZAGREB, CROATIA, 1990

Here I was, a public face prepared to risk his life, career, and everything that fame could have brought, all because of one ideal, one cause, the Croatian cause.

— ZVONIMIR BOBAN

OPPOSITE: The Dinamo Zagreb captain, Zvonimir Boban, clashes with a Serbian police officer during the match against Red Star Belgrade in 1990.

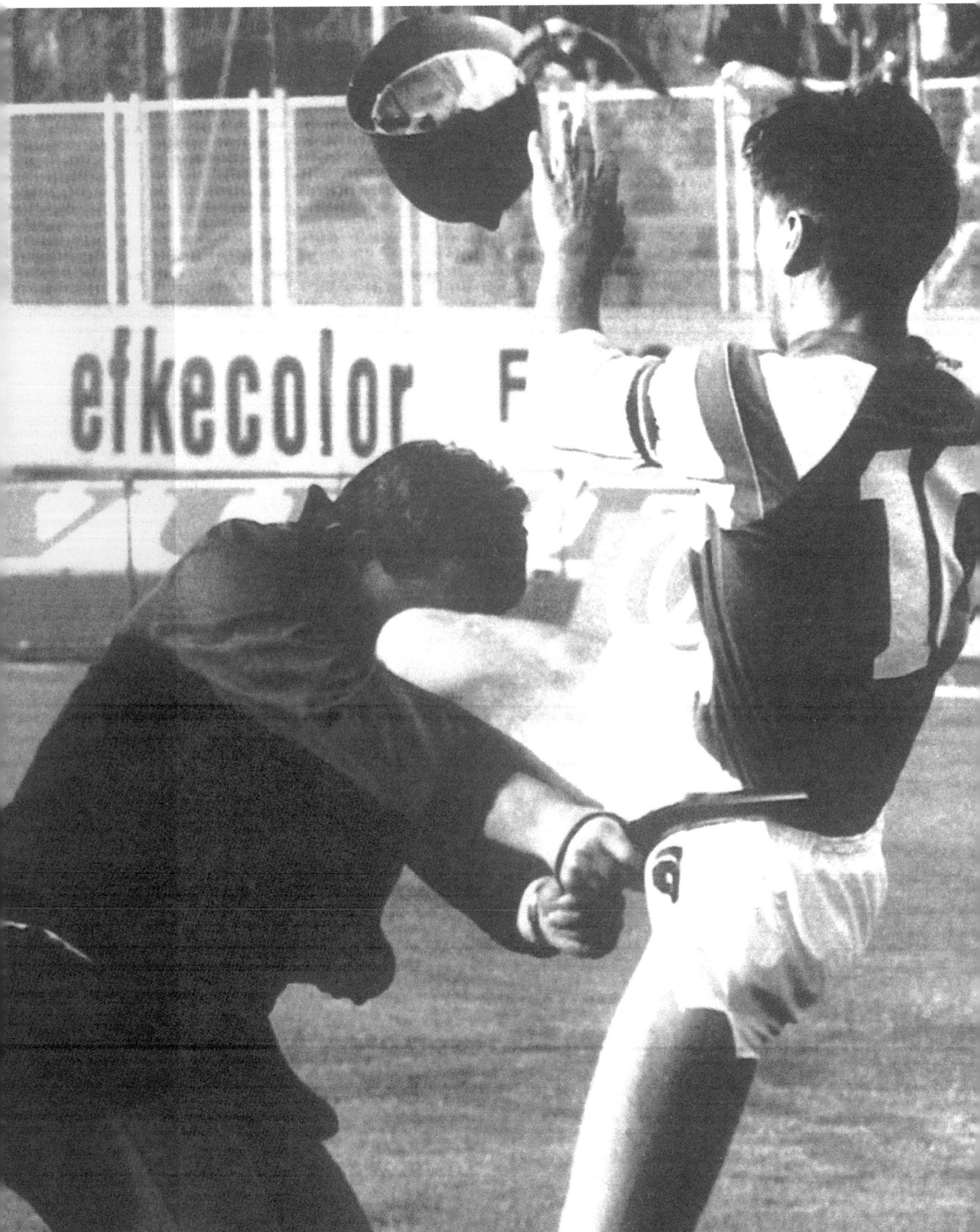
efkecolor F

On 13 May 1990, a skirmish broke out on a Croatian soccer field in Zagreb that many people believe marked the beginning of the Croatian War of Independence against Serbia. It all began when the visiting fans of Serbia's Red Star team, from Belgrade, started to tear up the stadium belonging to the Croatian home side, Dinamo Zagreb. The resulting battle quickly turned into the biggest pitch invasion in history.

As the conflict escalated, the Serb-dominated police force stood by and watched. No goals were scored that day, yet the Dinamo Zagreb captain, Zvonimir Boban, became famous for the most dramatic kick of his career when he defended a Croatian fan by dropping a karate kick on an offending policeman. The kick was caught on camera and broadcast throughout the region, immediately being interpreted by the Croats as a demand for the end to Serbian dominance.

State of the Nation

Since 1943, Yugoslavia had been a socialist republic united under the banner of communism. It was made up of six constituent republics—Bosnia and Herzegovina, Croatia, Montenegro, Macedonia, Slovenia and Serbia—and was led by Josip Broz Tito from 1945 to 1980. After Tito's death, however, the republic's delicate stability broke down. Croatia started to canvass for the independence it had previously experienced under the Nazi regime of World War II, but this affiliation with the Nazis made the Serbs anxious—more than half a million people from the region, both Serbs and Croats, had perished at the hands of the Nazis. In this climate of instability, the tensions of World War II resurfaced.

During the 1980s, nationalist sentiments in the region increased. When the Berlin Wall was torn down in 1989, signalling the end of 'official' communism, Yugoslavia was completely destabilised. Slovenia and Croatia became the leading forces behind a drive to reorganise Yugoslavia into a confederation and to vote against communism. However, they were opposed by Serbian leader Slobodan Milosevic, who identified with the still-powerful residual communist system.

As the break-up of Yugoslavia gained momentum, Croatia held its first elections in 1990. Franjo Tudjman, a Croatian nationalist, became the first president of Croatia by defeating the communist opposition. The red-and-white chequered flag of Croatia was once more displayed proudly, but the Serbian minority living in Croatia began to fear the worst. Conflict in the Balkans seemed inevitable, as the simmering ethnic tensions and antagonisms came ever closer to tearing the region apart.

Militant Fans

On 13 May 1990, the Croatian capital of Zagreb was preparing for a first-division match in the Yugoslav football league between two of the competition's top teams: Red Star Belgrade (Serbia) and Dinamo Zagreb (Croatia). It promised to be a good match; however, violence was common in the Yugoslavian league and police manned the stadium in readiness.

Fans of the Dinamo team, known as the Bad Blue Boys, started to congregate in their allotted area in the Dinamo stadium as 3000 Red Star fans from Serbia, known as Delije, gathered on the other side. Fighting had already broken out in the Zagreb streets, but it wasn't until 25,000 fans had gathered inside the stadium that the tension began to take effect.

The game had barely started when Delije began to shout nationalistic slogans, hoping to get a rise out of the Dinamo fans. They chanted that Zagreb was a Serbian city and demanded the death of the newly elected Croatian president. When the Bad Blue Boys started to throw stones and retaliate with similarly nationalistic slogans, Delije started to tear up the stadium. As advertising billboards were torn down and chairs hurled across the stands, the Serb-controlled Yugoslav police stood in their riot gear and for 30 minutes did nothing to stop the unfolding mayhem.

When Delije broke down the fence that separated them from their rival supporters, then set upon the local fans in the southern stand, the Blue Boys became incensed. They mowed down a huge fence dividing the northern stand from the grounds and, in their thousands, spilled onto the field, streaming over to the southern stand where their fellow fans were being assaulted.

The Only Kick of the Match

When the riot began, the game was immediately halted, and the Red Star players fled to the locker room. Some of the Dinamo players stayed on the pitch, which was now covered with crazed fans and an even greater presence of riot police, who finally called for back-up. Thousands of fans broke into violent scuffles. Armoured vans, water cannons and tear gas were all deployed as the pitch started to resemble a battlefield. In the ensuing chaos, helicopters were brought in to evacuate the Serbian players as the fighting escalated both inside and outside the stadium.

Dinamo captain and midfielder Zvonimir Boban was trying to make sense of the chaos when he saw a Croatian fan being attacked by a Serbian policeman. In front of TV cameras, Boban deftly landed a karate kick on the truncheon-wielding officer. Helping the fan to his feet and surrounded by other Bad Blue Boys acting as his bodyguards, Boban retired to the locker room, unaware that the incident had been captured on film.

Prior to the Croatian election, Franjo Tudjman had promised to limit Serbian presence in Croatian public life. The public saw Boban's kick as signifying an end to Croatian acceptance of Serbian dominance. He was treated as a national hero, but would suffer for his decision—he was suspended from playing for six months, which put him out of the World Cup in Italy. The

A NOTORIOUS WARLORD

The president of the Delije fan club was a Serbian nationalist named Zeljko Raznjatovic, also known as 'Arkan'. Raznjatovic used the fan club to build a base of Serbian paramilitary troops known as Arkan's Tigers, and later became a notorious warlord. In 1999, he was indicted by the International War Crimes Tribunal for his part in the ethnic cleansing of non-Serbs during the war, but his indictment was only made public after his assassination in 2000.

policeman he kicked was not in fact a Serb, but a Bosnian Muslim. Years later the man publicly stated that he forgave Boban and that he understood the captain's actions.

The invasion of the pitch lasted 70 minutes, resulting in hundreds of casualties on both sides. As people watched the events unfold on national television, they feared that the violence would spark a civil war in the Balkans.

Aftermath

In the days that followed, the Serbian and Croatian press expressed vastly different views on the events at Maksimir Stadium. The lack of police intervention led to Croatian political parties calling for all Serbs involved in ministerial or police affairs to resign. Meanwhile, the Serbian press claimed that the riot had been preplanned and financed by Tudjman's followers, who had manipulated the outcome to purge the government of Serbs. There was no doubt that both sides were using the game to further their political objectives.

The US Joins the Game

Soccer and the Balkans conflict were yet again inextricably linked on 16 October 1990, when Tudjman invited the US soccer team to play the Croatian national team at an exhibition match in Zagreb. The match was to be combined with the restoring of a national monument of a nineteenth-century hero, Ban Josip Jelacic, which had been removed by the communists. At a time when Croatia was still officially part of the Yugoslav republic, the US visit to Croatia was seen as unofficial support from the West for the country's independence. Tudjman drummed up such fervent national spirit that over half a million Croats made their way to the capital city.

As the Croatian players came onto the field, they wore the same jerseys previously worn under the Nazi regime during World War II, and the chequered design that once formed the flag of the Nazi-sponsored Independent State of Croatia was once again proudly worn. The Yugoslav Football Committee was heavily criticised for allowing the game to take place, as it was seen as jeopardising the politics of the region which, by this time, were hanging by a thread. When Croatia beat the United States 2–1, it was all Tudjman needed to demonstrate that the country was strong enough for independence.

From Soccer to All-out War

On 25 June 1991, Slovenia, Croatia, Macedonia, and Bosnia and Herzegovina claimed independence from Yugoslavia. In Croatia, many of the Bad Blue Boys joined the Croatian police and army forces; similarly, members of Delije joined with the Serbian equivalents. According to Paul Mojzes, a US academic who has studied ethnoreligious conflict in Yugoslavia, 'some of the nationalistic

OPPOSITE: The pitch invasion during the match was the largest in history, and the riots resulted in hundreds of casualties on both sides.

soccer fans quickly became some of the earliest nationalistic warriors—and war criminals'.

In 1992, the European Community formally recognised Croatia as an independent nation, but the Croatian War of Independence continued for three more years. On 14 December 1995, the leaders of Croatia, Bosnia and Serbia signed the Dayton Peace Accord, which provided a framework for peace in the

ABOVE: Boban kicks a Serbian police officer while defending a Croatian fan.

region. It had taken five years since the riot at Maksimir Stadium for Croatia to gain its independence and to establish an almost Serb-free zone. In the four years of the Croatian war, more than 10,000 people were killed, and thousands more are still missing.

Out of the Ashes

Croatia had gained independence, but was left a shadow of its former self, seen by the rest of the world as a war zone or an insignificant former Yugoslav republic. However, when the Croatian national soccer team, captained by Zvonimir Boban, beat Germany 3–0 in the quarterfinals of the 1998 FIFA World Cup, the team was again linked with the national psyche. The win was considered a major upset, and symbolised the possibility for change. A sense of elation and optimism flooded the country, which intensified a week later when Croatia's win against the Netherlands moved the World Cup debutantes into overall third place.

In 1999, the Serbian-based Yugoslavia national football team and Croatia played against each other in a qualifying match for the Euro 2000 championship. Once more, the battle lines were drawn. The second qualifying match took place in Zagreb, but by this time Yugoslavian fans needed visas to enter the country and the audience was made up mostly of Croatian supporters. President Tudjman used the event as an opportunity to commemorate the Croats lost in the war, knowingly inflaming the political passion surrounding the game. However, his political manipulation backfired when this time it was Yugoslavia who won a place in the championship with a 2–2 draw, eliminating Croatia in the process. Yet again soccer and politics had been intertwined, but this time the goals had gone Serbia's way in what must have felt like a political own goal for Tudjman.

Soccer was never the cause of conflict in the Balkans, but it was certainly used as a vehicle for expressing beliefs on religion, ethnicity and nationalism, and many felt the aftermath of Zvonimir Boban's legendary kick. Fifteen years after the 1990 match, the Zagreb newspaper *Vecernji list* observed:

> *The game that was never played will be remembered, at least by the soccer fans, as the beginning of the Patriotic War, and almost all of the contemporaries will declare it the key in understanding the Croatian cause.*

Gender
and Sport

BACKGROUND:	Votes for women
EVENT:	The first martyring of a member of the suffragette movement
OPPONENTS:	Suffragette movement v The Establishment
ARENA:	Epsom Downs Racecourse, 1913

Deeds Not Words: Emily Davison and Derby Day

EPSOM, UNITED KINGDOM, 1913

There will be a public funeral in honour of this soldier fallen in a war of freedom. — **CHRISTABEL PANKHURST**

PREVIOUS PAGE: Bobby Riggs poses with supporters before the famous 'Battle of the Sexes' tennis match with Billie Jean King.

OPPOSITE: The king's horse, Anmer. The suffragette Emily Davison tried to grab its reins as it passed her during the Epsom Derby in protest against the government's refusal to grant women the vote.

The 4th of June 1913 was the day of the prestigious Epsom Derby in Surrey, England, just south of London. King George V sat in the royal box, keenly anticipating the performance of his own horse, Anmer, in the race. The 16 horses got off to a clean start, but as they hurtled around Tattenham Corner, a woman stepped out from behind the rails and attempted to grab the reins of the king's horse as it galloped past. The crowd watched in horror as Emily Wilding Davison was trampled under the pounding hooves, then rushed to hospital, where she died four days later. Shocking news footage of the day showed a grainy figure jerkily stepping out into the path of the powerful thoroughbreds in one swift and brutal moment. Having given her life in her belief that women should be able to vote, Davison certainly brought attention to the suffragette movement. Whether she intended to die for the movement is still debated to this day.

The State of the Nation

Although women were first given the vote in 1893, in New Zealand, on the other side of the world British women were involved in a bitter battle to secure the same rights as their sisters in the southern hemisphere. By the early twentieth century, women in Britain were allowed to serve on boards and even become mayors, but the vote remained elusive. Clearly, an attention-grabbing strategy was needed to further the cause of the campaigners for women's suffrage, or 'suffragettes' as they came to be known.

In 1903, the leaders of the Women's Social and Political Union (WSPU), led by Emmeline Pankhurst and her daughter, Christabel, held an inaugural meeting at which it was decided that women campaigning for the vote were 'guerillists', and as such could employ all methods of war deemed necessary to achieve their goal—apart from the taking of a human life. They were to act 'through deeds, not words'. This militancy increased when the suffragette headquarters relocated to London in 1906.

Despite the seriousness of this mission, the movement was viewed by conservative Britain as a bunch of old maids with nothing better to do. However, when a deputation of women representing over 100,000 suffragists presented their case to the Prime Minister, Sir Henry Campbell-Bannerman, in 1906, the PM realised that this was a significant campaign, difficult to ignore. Despite being swayed by their arguments, he found himself with a divided cabinet that would never take the idea of women having the vote seriously.

Having failed to achieve their goal through peaceful and diplomatic negotiations, the suffragettes were forced to resort to other means. A desperate series of incidents followed, including hunger strikes, vandalism, women chaining themselves to railings in protest, and even bombings.

Cat and Mouse

Emily Davison joined the WSPU in 1906. Three years later she gave up her teaching profession, deciding instead to work full-time for the suffragette movement. Over the next seven years she became increasingly militant and known for her subversive activities. In 1909, she was caught throwing rocks at the carriage belonging to the Chancellor of the Exchequer, David Lloyd George. He had become a popular target of the suffragettes, having reversed his position from supporting the women's vote to opposing it. Davison was sentenced to a month's hard labour at Strangeways Prison in Manchester. In that year, Davison spent a total of six months in prison for obstruction and stone throwing. Her criminal activities continued, and in 1911 Davison became the first suffragette to set a post box alight.

Like many of the imprisoned suffragettes, Davison regularly embarked on hunger strikes. Not prepared to have women die in the prison cells, the prison authorities embarked on a policy of cat and mouse by which women who went on a hunger strike would be held until the last possible minute and then released onto the streets. This way, even if a woman was dangerously ill, there was no risk of her dying on prison grounds. Knowing the implications for the government should a woman die on prison property, Davison jumped off a prison balcony, crashing to the ground some 9 metres below. She suffered spinal injuries, and her reputation for recklessness increased.

BELOW: Davison was trampled after she leapt from the crowd to grab the horse's reins. She died in hospital four days later.

In February 1913, Davison was released from another stretch in prison. As usual, she immediately returned to her protests. She was one of a group of women who planted a bomb at a house belonging to Lloyd George—five rooms were destroyed. Emmeline Pankhurst was tried for the crime and sentenced to three years in prison; Davison was not caught. It now seemed that Davison would stop at nothing in her commitment to the cause.

In June 1913, Davison and a friend made a pact to attend the Epsom Derby. Choosing not to give too much away, Davison told her friends to check the papers the next day as she had something special planned.

Derby Day

The Epsom Derby was one of the most important days on the British racing calendar, and was known to draw enormous crowds. Royalty, society's elite and the working classes gathered together to see the horses take to the track. To win the Derby was considered one of the most prestigious achievements any jockey or owner could wish for. The track itself was a real test, with a long uphill ride to start, followed by a steep descent into Tattenham Corner, a dip just before the winning post and then a fast uphill finish in front of the royal box. It was a fast and gruelling dash over almost 2.5 kilometres.

At 3 p.m. the horses charged out of the gates. Davison had positioned herself as close to the railings as possible and was on the lookout for King George's horse, Anmer, which was being ridden by royal jockey Herbert 'Diamond' Jones. The jockey would be easy to spot, as he would be dressed in the royal silks. She stood near another suffragette, Mary Richardson, who later described Davison's mood at the time:

> She stood there, close to the white-painted rails where the course bends round at Tattenham Corner; she looked absorbed and yet far away from everyone else and seemed to have no interest in what was going on around her.

As the horses tore around the track, Anmer was holding his own alongside the favourite, Craganour, and an outside chance, Aboyeur. As they turned into the descent, Anmer fell back to the rear of the field. The crowd screamed and shouted as the horses, their flanks glistening with sweat, thundered by. As they charged around Tattenham Corner, the most dangerous part of the course, Davison calmly pulled out a piece of cloth sporting the suffragette colours—green, white and violet—and stepped out onto the track in front of the king's horse. She tried to grab the horse's bridle in an attempt to stop it mid-track, but within seconds she was trampled and hurled across the racecourse.

A report in London's *Daily Mirror* described the scene:

The horse struck the woman with its chest, knocking her down among the flying hoofs ... and she was desperately injured ... Blood rushed from her mouth and nose. Anmer turned a complete somersault and fell upon his jockey who was seriously injured.

Davison was crushed under the horse's body and kicked repeatedly by its hooves. Some reports said that as she raised her hands above her head someone in the crowd lifted a sign saying 'Vote for Women'. Others said that Davison herself shouted, 'Votes for Women!' before stepping onto the track.

Public Outrage

Davison was rushed to Epsom Cottage Hospital, where doctors operated on her skull in an attempt to save her life. As she lay there unconscious, the suffragettes formed a guard of honour around her bed. She died four days later, on 8 June. If Davison had hoped that by targeting the king's horse she might have met with some royal recognition for the suffragette cause, she was sadly mistaken. Queen Mary sent a telegram to her jockey, hoping that Jones had recovered after 'this sad accident caused through the abominable conduct of a brutal lunatic woman'. The Queen did, however, enquire several times about the state of Davison's health. Davison's actions caused a public outcry, with many viewing her actions as irresponsible: 'I hope you suffer torture until you die,' declared one outraged citizen in a letter sent to the hospital. The English public were, by and large, staunch royalists and saw the mission as an attack on the King.

The incident was caught on film and shown in picture houses throughout the country. Viewers were shocked to see the speed of the event, the grainy filmic jerkiness only adding to the shocking drama of the moment. Many people were unsure of whether Davison had intended to kill herself that day. She had made arrangements to see friends days later, and had bought a return train ticket, leading many people to think of it as a tragic accident. Some said that she was under the misapprehension that the race was over and was merely crossing the track to stand with a friend. However one eyewitness, John Ervine, seemed certain this wasn't Davison's intention:

I feel sure that [she] meant to stop the horse, and that she did not go on to the course in the belief that the race was over, for, as I say, only a few of the horses had gone by when I first saw her leave the railings, and others had not passed when she was knocked down. I could not see whether any other horses touched her, for the whole thing happened so quickly, and I was so horrified at seeing her pitched violently down by the horse that I did not think of anything. The affair distressed the crowd very much.

MORE CONTROVERSY AT THE TRACK

The Epsom Derby of 1913 will long be remembered for the death of Emily Davison, but the rest of the race was not without controversy. The leading horses and jockeys, unaware of the tragedy in their wake, became involved in a shoving match, much of it instigated by the jockey riding the favourite, Craganour. Craganour came in first, but the stewards disqualified the horse—for 'jostling' the horse behind—and awarded the 100-1 outsider, Aboyeur, first place. Despite the official explanation, punters speculated that the decision had gone against the favourite due to its owner being the son of the shipping line magnate whose premier ship, the *Titanic*, had sunk the previous year, killing more than 1500 people.

LEFT: Davison's funeral was held on 14 June 1913. Crowds gathered to watch the funeral procession.

TORTURED JOCKEY

Many people were affected by Davison's actions, perhaps none more so than jockey Herbert Jones, who surprised everyone by attending Emmeline Pankhurst's funeral in 1928. He recovered physically from the fall and carried on a successful career until retiring due to illness in 1923. However, in 1951 he committed suicide, after having spoken of being 'haunted by that woman's face' throughout his life.

A Soldier Fallen

An inquest held on 10 June decided that Davison's death was accidental, but the suffragette movement believed it was intentional. An essay by Davison, 'The Price of Liberty', written around 1912 and published after her death, was interpreted by many as a suicide note. In it she espoused her views on the noble nature of dying for the cause and spoke of how 'one big tragedy may save many others':

> *The glorious and inscrutable Spirit of Liberty has but one further penalty within its power, the surrender of Life itself. It is the supreme consummation of sacrifice, than which none can be higher or greater ... To lay down life for friends, that is glorious, selfless, inspiring!*

According to Christabel Pankhurst, 'Miss Davison has died for women'. In an article in *The Daily Sketch* she wrote:

> *[Davison] has died to call attention to their wrong, and win them the vote. The Government's refusal to grant the vote drove her to make her protest. Argument has not convinced [British Prime Minister] Mr Asquith of the seriousness of the position, but perhaps a woman's death will. Miss Davison's memory will live in women's hearts and in history for all time. There will be a public funeral in honour of this soldier fallen in a war of freedom.*

On 14 June 1913, central London came to a standstill as 6000 women in a sea of green, white and violet marched behind the funeral cortege that travelled from Buckingham Palace Road to St George's Church, Bloomsbury. Davison's body lay in state, surrounded by a thousand wreaths, before she was finally buried in the family grave. The suffragette movement proudly claimed their first martyr and ensured Emily Wilding Davison a place in history. As the WPSU expressed it:

SOCCER AND THE SUFFRAGETTES

In 1894, suffragette Nettie Honeyball placed an advertisement in the newspaper for women to join the British Ladies' Football Club. More than 30 women signed up. J. W. Julian, a player for the Tottenham Hotspur club, agreed to coach them twice a week. In an interview with *The Daily Sketch* in 1895, Honeyball explained her motivation:

I founded the association late last year, with the fixed resolve of proving to the world that women are not the 'ornamental and useless' creatures men have pictured. I must confess, my convictions on all matters where the sexes are so widely divided are all on the side of emancipation, and I look forward to the time when ladies may sit in Parliament and have a voice in the direction of affairs, especially those which concern them most.

With her clear and unflinching vision she realised that now as in days of old, to awake the conscience of people, a human life would be needed as sacrifice— human life freely given under circumstances of tragedy, the shock of which would travel round the world ... She heard the call, and made answer, 'I come.'

The suffragette battle cry of 'Deeds Not Words!' was inscribed on her headstone.

Aftermath

After Davison's death, there was much public discussion about why an intelligent woman would do such a thing. A year later World War I broke out, and Emmeline Pankhurst instructed all of the suffragettes to cease the campaign and to concentrate on the war efforts at home. In 1918, the work of women during the war was officially recognised, and the Representation of the Peoples Act 1918 allowed women over the age of 30 to vote.

BACKGROUND:	Gender equality
EVENT:	'Battle of the Sexes' tennis match
OPPONENTS:	Billie Jean King v Bobby Riggs
ARENA:	Houston Superdrome, Texas, US

Battle of the Sexes

HOUSTON, TEXAS, 1973

You felt this was a symbolic match that was going to be used against women and to humiliate them if Billie Jean lost ... And for her to take that on, to put herself under that pressure, is the true meaning of heroism.

— GLORIA STEINEM

OPPOSITE: Billie Jean King and Bobby Riggs shake hands after King beat Riggs in straight sets to win the 'Battle of the Sexes'.

At a time when women were striving for equality, the world of women's tennis was a microcosm of society itself. Men's tennis was seen as a far more prestigious game than the women's and consequently carried greater prize money. When Billie Jean King won the US Open in 1972, she received $15,000 less than her male counterpart, Ilie Nastase, and she refused to defend her title until women received equal prize money. That same year, ex-US-champion Bobby Riggs lay down the gauntlet by challenging Billie Jean King to a match that he claimed would prove that men were better players and so deserved more money. Having established herself as a campaigner for equality, King had no choice but to accept the challenge. Dubbed the 'Battle of the Sexes', the match was watched by the largest tennis audience of its day and has since been recognised as a pivotal moment in the history of the women's rights movement.

State of the Nation

By the 1960s and 1970s, feminism in America was undergoing a revival. Baby boomers were experiencing greater wealth and education than the previous generation and consequently started to demand greater opportunities. However, when women escaped the shackles of the kitchen and stepped into the workplace they found that their time and skills were considered to be worth less than their male co-workers'. By 1970, women's wages were 59 cents for every dollar earned by men and the idea of true equality of the sexes was unimaginable to the average US citizen. Meanwhile, the Watergate scandal was filling the news and President Nixon was close to resigning. Inflation was hitting everyone hard and the time for a diversion was ripe.

Billie Jean King

Born in California in 1943, Billie Jean King first arrived at Wimbledon in 1961 at the age of 17 under her maiden name, Billie Jean Moffat. Over the next two decades she went on to win 20 Wimbledon titles and four US Opens. In addition to her sporting success, she was a pioneer of women's rights and was bent on 'using sports for social change'. At a time when campaigning for equal rights was seen as childish and ridiculous, Billie Jean King led the way, applying her confident and aggressive manner both on and off the court. Her great rival was the Australian Margaret Court, who beat her in the finals of 1963 and 1970.

'You've Come a Long Way Baby'

In the early 1970s women tennis players were still getting paid much less than their male counterparts. Women's tennis was seen as inferior to the men's game and sponsors used the smaller crowds as an excuse for the poor prize money. Houston tennis promoter and founder of *World Tennis* magazine Gladys Heldman was a staunch supporter of women's tennis and in 1970 she persuaded a group of top female tennis players to break away from the traditional mixed-sex tournament to form a women's only tour. Billie Jean King and eight other players accepted one-dollar contracts from Heldman and formed their own circuit.

When the 'Houston Nine' threatened a boycott of a Los Angeles fixture that was offering an 8–1 advantage to men in prize money, the US Tennis Association threatened to suspend them all. When the women decided to hold out, King, Rosie Casals, Nancy Richey, Peaches Bartkowicz, Valerie Ziegenfuss, Julie Heldman, Kristy Pigeon, Judy Dalton and Kerry Melville were all suspended for a short time, but the stand signalled the start of a monumental change in women's tennis.

Next, Heldman managed to secure a US$7,500 sponsorship deal for a new brand of Philip Morris cigarettes called Virginia Slims, which would finance a women's tour. Nicknamed 'Women's Lob, featuring the Little Broads' and led with the Virginia Slims marketing slogan, 'You've come a long way, baby,' the tour marked the beginning of professional women's tennis.

'Without Gladys there wouldn't be women's professional tennis as we know it,' says King. 'She was a passionate advocate and driving force behind the start of the Virginia Slims Tour, and helped change the face of women's sports. Because of her vision women's tennis was changed forever.'

Phone Call from the President

The early 1970s saw rapid changes in the sport. In 1971 Billie Jean King received a congratulatory phone call from President Richard Nixon, as she became the first woman athlete to earn $100,000 in prize money in one year. However, the money still wasn't equal to that of the male players. King encouraged the female players to form a union and the Women's Tennis Association was formed in 1973 with King as president. One of her first actions was to advocate for equal money at the US Open. In 1972, King had received $15,000 less than Ilie Nastase and she threatened to boycott the 1973 US Open unless changes were made. Consequently in 1973, the US Open became the first major tournament to offer equal prize money.

'I want the women's lib leader!'

Billie Jean King was a very unlikely candidate for a Vegas-style extravaganza, but she was about to play in one of the most watched and remembered tennis matches of all time, and it wasn't even part of the professional circuit.

Bobby Riggs was a retired tennis player, ranked number 1 in the world in 1941, 1946 and 1947. In 1937 he swept Wimbledon, winning the singles, doubles and mixed doubles titles, and he later went on to win the US Open. However, at 55 he was known as a hustler, and outspoken in his chauvinistic attitude towards women. Revelling in the publicity, he laid down the gauntlet for King, saying:

TITLE IX

The largest single social change in US sport in the 1970s was the introduction of Title IX on 23 June 1972. It stated that 'No person in the United States shall, on the basis of sex, be excluded from participation in, be denied the benefits of, or be subjected to discrimination under any educational program or activity receiving federal financial assistance.' As a result of Title IX, the enrolment of women in athletics programs and professional schools increased dramatically.

FEMALE ATHLETES HAVE THEIR SAY

Luck has nothing to do with it, because I have spent many, many hours, countless hours, on the court working for my one moment in time, not knowing when it would come. – Serena Williams

The greatest obstacle to that swim, in my opinion, was fear. I was never fearful of anything, you know. I was a daring devil. – Gertrude Ederle, age 91, on her record-breaking swim of the English Channel at age 19 on 6 August 1926

It's not enough just to swing at the ball. You've got to loosen your girdle and let 'er fly. – Babe Didrikson Zaharias, a US athlete who excelled at golf, basketball, and track and field, and won two gold medals and a silver at the 1932 Los Angeles Summer Olympics.

'You insist that top women players provide a brand of tennis comparable to men's. I challenge you to prove it. I contend that you not only cannot beat a top male player, but that you can't beat me, a tired old man.' King at first refused, so Riggs challenged King's main rival, Australian Margaret Court.

On 13 May 1973, Mother's Day, Riggs beat Court in straight sets 6–2, 6–1. After the match he again challenged King. Riggs boasted that despite the fact that King was at the top of her game and only 29 years old, he would be able to beat her just as easily as he had beaten Court. He used the media to taunt King into accepting his offer, putting her in a position where it was almost impossible to refuse.

Despite her initial refusal, King began to realise that by not accepting the challenge she might halt the progress of women's tennis and even affect recent advances such as Title IX. The stakes were high, as sports journalist Frank Deford commented: 'If she lost [to Riggs], it truly would have hurt women's tennis ... and it would have hurt Billie Jean King ... I don't think she would have remained as substantive a character thereafter.'

The match was publicised as the ultimate decider in the age-old gender debate. As a self-promoter and likeable showman, Riggs saw it as an opportunity to make a lot of money. He wore a T-shirt proudly advertising 'men's liberation' and claimed to be the number 1 male chauvinist pig in America. However, despite the hype and the antics surrounding the event, King was careful to be taken seriously in the debates leading up to the match. This was fast becoming a game of great significance, and no-one knew that more than Billie Jean King herself: 'I couldn't even breathe for 2 months. As each day went by I got calmer and calmer and I let go about 20 minutes before the match.' It was impossible to overestimate what was riding on the game. 'I thought it would set us back 50 years if I didn't win that match,' she said. 'It would ruin the women's tour and affect all women's self-esteem.'

In 1985, aged 67, Bobby Riggs attempted to replicate the 1973 showdown, but this time in the doubles. Vitas Gerulaitis and Riggs took on Martina Navratilova and Pam Shriver. The women won.

LEFT: King returns the ball to Riggs in the first set of the match. She won the set 6-4.

Determined to get fair coverage, King noticed it was an all-male team of commentators and persuaded ABC to drop Jack Kramer from the telecast. A long-time sports commentator, Kramer was open in his disdain for female players. King wasn't going to put up with it. 'He doesn't believe in women's tennis,' King said. 'Why should he be part of this match? He doesn't believe in half of the match. I'm not playing. Either he goes—or I go.' Naturally, it was Kramer who went.

The Battle Commences

On 20 September 1973, Billie Jean King was carried out onto the court as if she were Cleopatra. She sat in a gold litter, which was raised aloft by four men dressed as her slaves, one of whom was boxer George Foreman. Bobby Riggs arrived in a rickshaw pulled by scantily clad models dubbed 'Bobby's bosom buddies'. This was a battle for equality and 50 million viewers across the globe couldn't wait to see what would happen.

In today's world the number 1 female tennis player would be expected to beat a 55-year-old opponent. But in 1973, it was thought that a woman would be unable to deal with the pressure, and there was every expectation King would cave in.

King served first and won the first game easily. In the third game Riggs had his longest winning streak of the night, winning seven straight points. This was to be his high point. King relaxed into the game and began driving Riggs to the far corners of the court. Her tactic of staying at the baseline and running the older tennis player into the ground began to work. In the first set, King hit 34 winners, and 26 of those went untouched by Riggs's racquet. Choking under the pressure, Riggs double-faulted on set point. It was 6–4 to King.

King's signature shot, the running crosscourt backhand, began to clobber Riggs with increasing regularity. His renowned lob shots were met with cracking overhead volleys. Riggs struggled to get the ball past her. King won a love game on her serve to close out the second set, winning 6–3.

In the third set, King broke Riggs in the opening game, then raced to a 4–2 lead. As he began to tire, she increased the pressure, sending down faster serves, charging the net and smashing volleys. At 4–2 in the third, hand cramps forced Riggs to take an injury break. At 5–3, King twice failed to put Riggs away at match point. Finally, a double-fault by Riggs gave King a third match point and, after 124 minutes, Riggs hit a high backhand volley into the net. King won the match 6–4, 6–3, 6–3.

After the game Riggs admitted, 'She was too good, too fast. She returned all my passing shots and made great plays off them.' She had hit 70 winners that he could not even get his racquet to. In the next day's *New York Times*, sports journalist Neil Amdur wrote, 'She beat Riggs to the ball, dominated the net and ran him around the baseline to the point of near exhaustion.' The London *Times* referred to it as 'the drop shot and volley heard around the world'.

It wasn't just King's physical skills that were admired. She had shown that female athletes can survive in pressure-filled situations—and that men can be susceptible to nerves, too. Frank Deford wrote in *Sports Illustrated*, 'She has prominently affected the way 50 per cent of society thinks and feels about itself in the vast area of physical exercise.' Her victory was felt deeply by the young players coming up through the tennis ranks. Martina Navratilova summed it up when she said, 'She was a crusader fighting a battle for all of us. She was carrying the flag; it was all right to be a jock.'

King took home US$100,000, the biggest prize purse ever for a single match. But it was never about the money. With the Title IX amendment the previous year, both men and women could now benefit from sporting scholarships. King's win earned women respect as athletes and demonstrated to girls that they could be taken seriously in the sporting arena. In 1975, legislation was passed in the US whereby schools offering sports for boys were obliged to do the same for girls. It was this generation of females that grew up with the defeat of Bobby Riggs fresh in their minds.

Billie Jean King later described the win as 'the most empowering moment in my life'. She and Bobby Riggs, having shared a piece of history, became firm friends, but it was only towards the end of his life that Riggs began to understand

WOMEN IN SPORT

▶ The first female Olympic athletes competed at the Olympic Games in 1900.

▶ In the 1930s women were discouraged from participating in sport for fear of affecting their fertility.

▶ In the 1940s men worried that a woman's sporting prowess would reduce her femininity. Athletes such as the women of the All Girls Professional Baseball League had to attend etiquette lessons to ensure they maintain their female attributes.

▶ It was not until 1971 that women were considered strong enough to play a full-court basketball game.

▶ In 1984 the Olympics held their first marathon for women. Joan Benoit Samuelson won the race, and dispelled the myths that women couldn't run the distance of 26 miles in a competitive time.

▶ Title IX ensured the success of athletes such as Mia Hamm, the world class US soccer star, who perfected the game in college. Hamm scored 158 goals in international competition—more than any other player in history. In 2004 Hamm was named by FIFA as one of the 125 greatest living soccer players, male or female.

FOR THE RECORD

Billie Jean King won 20 Wimbledon titles and 39 Grand Slam tennis titles.

She is the only woman to have won US singles titles on four different surfaces—clay, carpet, grass and hard court.

In 1971 she became the first female athlete in any sport to win over US$100,000 in a single season.

In 1974, as coach of the Philadelphia Freedoms tennis team, she became the first woman to coach a co-ed team in professional sports in the US.

In 1990 *Life* magazine named her 'one of the 100 most important Americans of the twentieth century'.

In 2003 she was one of the inaugural inductees into the USTA National Tennis Center's Court of Fame.

RIGHT: King holds the winner's trophy aloft after defeating Riggs 6-4, 6-3, 6-3.

how he had been instrumental in forging great changes in the fight for equality. As King herself said: 'It was about social change, it wasn't about tennis.'

The 'Battle of the Sexes' was a key moment in social history, an important step towards equality and respect. Billie Jean King continued with this fight tirelessly:

I keep striving for it every day. It helps move us forward. I don't see how anyone can argue that fact, that you should always have equal rights and opportunities for all people.

In the seventies we had to make it acceptable for people to accept girls and women as athletes. We had to make it okay for them to be active.

– BILLIE JEAN KING

BACKGROUND:	For recognition for transgender athletes
EVENT:	For a transgender player to compete professionally in the US Open
OPPONENTS:	Renée Richards v United States Tennis Association
ARENA:	1977 US Open, Queens, New York

Second Serve

QUEENS, NEW YORK, USA, 1977

I'm not a full-time major league tennis player. I'm here to make a point. It's a human rights issue. I want to show that someone who has a different lifestyle or medical condition has a right to stand up for what they are. **— RENÉE RICHARDS**

OPPOSITE: Renée Richards returns serve in her match against Carolyn Stoll at the Tennis Week Open in 1976. Soon after, she was denied permission to enter the US Open.

In 1976 transgender tennis player Renée Richards was denied entry into the US Women's Open when a chromosome test was pointedly introduced at the eleventh hour. One year later, having successfully sued the USTA, Richards walked on court for her first-round game against British player Virginia Wade. She lost the match, but scored an unprecedented win for transgender athletes everywhere.

State of the Nation

The United States had given up Panama. Jimmy Carter had pardoned Vietnam War draft evaders and Gary Gilmore became the first US citizen to be executed in the States since 1967. The US had just marked its bicentennial, celebrating 200 years of freedom, but many questioned if this was freedom for all or just for a chosen few.

Inner Battle

Renée Richards was born Richard Raskind on 19 August 1934. Raskind led a conventional life: a Yale University graduate, he became an officer in the navy and a high-profile ophthalmologist. By 1974, he was also a keen amateur tennis player, ranking third in the east and thirteenth nationally in the men's 35 and over division. Yet despite his success, Raskind was experiencing an inner battle far greater than anything he would ever experience on the tennis court.

Raskind had grown up feeling he was a girl trapped in a male body. Throughout his childhood he was tormented by a semi-split personality, as in his mind he alternated between Richard and Renée. During the 1960s, Raskind had taken female hormone treatment and had even travelled to Casablanca for gender reassignment surgery. However, when he was actually faced with the stark reality of the surgeon's knife and the loss of the only identity he had ever known, he balked at the last minute, unable to go through with the operation. As Richards later related:

> Up until that moment of truth in front of the clinic, I would have said confidently that I was a woman trapped in a man's body, but I had stood paralyzed not fifty feet from the remedy and had been unable to cross the remaining space. Somewhere inside me, the previously failing masculinity was rising up again and making a bid for life.

Trying to maintain a façade of 'normal' life, Raskind went on to marry and have a son before the battle once again became too much. In what must have been a heartbreaking yet emancipating decision, Raskind divorced his wife and in 1975 finally underwent gender reassignment.

Masquerading as a Woman

Now officially living his life as a woman, Renée Richards proceeded to get on with the life she had so long desired. At the age of 42, she was fit, agile and as keen as ever to take to the courts. Consequently, in July 1976 Richards entered her first women's tournament in La Jolla, California, seeing no reason to explain to officials that she had once been a man. However, her lanky figure and latent male characteristics caught the attention of a sports reporter who, on investigating her past, reported that she was a man dressed as a woman.

One month later Richards signed up for a women's tournament in South Orange, New Jersey. She reached the semi-finals and by this time was becoming quite a drawcard for organisers as curious crowds gathered to see this conundrum for themselves. But tournament officials felt she was breaking the rules, and the other female players felt she had an unfair physical advantage. Richards was six feet two inches (188 centimetres) tall and Amazon-like in appearance. When she was invited by a friend to take part in the Tennis Week Open, 25 female players withdrew in protest. Having held no previous aspirations in the tennis world, Richards was now determined to play in whatever tournament she chose and with the US Open slated for the following week, she signed up with the other players.

'I was happy starting a practice in ophthalmology in California,' she recalls. 'Then they told me I couldn't play, and all of a sudden I became the world's activist for the sexually disenfranchised.'

Sensing the building controversy around this player, the United States Tennis Association introduced a chromosome test: each entrant would be tested for XY chromosomes. The precedent had already been set by the International Olympic Committee at the 1968 Olympics in Mexico, when the chromosome test had become mandatory for competitors in women's events. During the 1960s it was suspected that many female athletes from Eastern Europe were being fed male hormones in order to win gold for their country. As undergoing gender reassignment does not affect a person's chromosomes, it was a foregone conclusion that Richards would fail.

Opening the Floodgates

The USTA was worried that if they allowed Richards to play, others would follow. She writes of their fear-mongering and their prejudices: 'If I was allowed to play, then the floodgates would be opened and through them would come tumbling an endless stream of made-over Neanderthals who would brutalise Chris Evert and Evonne Goolagong.'

She was also accused of using her reassignment as a way of making money off the women's circuit, but as Richards pointed out, 'How hungry for tennis success must you be to have your penis chopped off in pursuit of it?'

UNCHARTED WATERS

Gender-based disputes will always be a grey area, due to the individuality of each case. This was demonstrated in 1996 when Brazilian Olympic judo champion Edinanci Silva admitted that on reaching puberty she had both male and female organs. Despite this being a common condition known to the medical profession, her statement initially caused uproar. When she went on to explain that her male organs had been removed three years prior to competing, Silva was finally allowed to continue.

RIGHT: Richards reaches for a
backhand return while playing
Australia's Lesley Hunt in the
Women's Professional Tennis
Tournament in Boston in 1977.

RIGHT: Richards reaches for a backhand return while playing Australia's Lesley Hunt in the Women's Professional Tennis Tournament in Boston in 1977.

GENDER CONTROVERSY

Stanislawa Walasiewiczowna (Stella Walsh)

In the 1932 Los Angeles Olympics Stella Walsh, representing Poland, equalled the world record of 11.9 seconds and won gold in the 100-metre dash. Four years later, competing at the 1936 Olympics, Walsh was devastated when an arch-rival, Helen Stephens, beat her by 0.2 seconds, leaving Walsh to take out the silver. Walsh was so taken aback at being beaten that she accused Stephens of being a man. However, on examination the German doctors confirmed that Stephens was female. Walsh carried on with a successful career, and in 1975 she was inducted into the US Track and Field Hall of Fame. In 1980, Walsh was caught in the crossfire at a bank robbery and killed. The autopsy that followed revealed unexpected results. Walsh had male genitalia combined with both male and female chromosomes, a condition called mosaicism. Walsh had lived her life as a woman.

Ewa Klobukowska

In 1967 Polish sprinter Ewa Klobukowska was found to have 'ambiguous genitalia' and she was banned from the European Cup women's track and field competition. In 1968 the IAAF stripped her of the bronze and gold medals she had won in 1964. Klobukowska lived her life as a woman, and later went on to have a child.

Sue Sally Hale

Hale disguised herself as a man in order to play for the US Polo Association, which had a 'no women' ruling. Flattening her breasts and wearing a fake moustache, Hale masqueraded as Mr S. Jones. Eventually, when she had played for 20 years, Hale and her team mates pressured the US Polo Association into permitting women to play in tournaments. They threatened to break it to the press that a female had been playing polo since the early 1950s, and the Association quickly caved in. In 1972, Hale received her first membership card, describing it as 'the greatest moment in my sports life'.

No Advantage

One of the biggest criticisms levelled at Richards was that a male-to-female transsexual would be physically stronger than a female opponent. This isn't necessarily the case given that the increase of female hormones means a reduction of testosterone, which in turn leads to a lessening of muscle mass. At the time of the US Open there was little difference between Richards and Navratilova. Richards was taller, but Navratilova was the heavier of the two and there certainly didn't seem to be an unfair advantage in this particular case.

This was a time when gender reassignment was relatively unheard of and apart from Christine Jorgensen, a photographer who had changed from male to female, Richards was the lone voice. Rather than taking the pre-ordained test, Richards chose to seek legal action against the USTA.

Richards became a reluctant representative for marginalised people, her case being closely monitored by sporting factions throughout the world as well as at home. She found support from Billie Jean King, who filed an affidavit in court supporting Richards's right to play, and was backed by players such as Wendy Turnbull, Virginia Wade, Ilana Kloss and Martina Navratilova. However, despite the arguments, tournament director Mike Blanchard made it clear that there would be no backing down on the sex test, saying, 'There will be no exceptions.'

Finally, after a year-long battle, the New York Supreme Court ruled Dr Renée Richards was legally recognised as a female, and as such was eligible to play in the US Open. Now all that was left for Richards to do was to play.

In 1977, Richards walked on court to face her first-round opposition, British tennis player Virginia Wade. An unseeded player, Richards lost in straight sets, 6–1, 6–4. The scoreboard told of a loss, but it was an undisputed win for Richards and fellow transgender athletes.

It took until 1999, just before the Sydney Olympics, for mandatory sex testing to be discontinued. Then in May 2004 the IOC introduced new rules that allowed transgender athletes to compete as long as they met certain criteria: they were required to have completed genital surgery and two years of hormone treatment as well as having legal documentation proving their female status.

The floodgates feared by the USTA didn't open, but slowly transgender athletes are emerging and, like Richards, most are reluctant heroes. Michelle Dumares, the Canadian national champion in mountain biking, and Australian pro golfer Mianne Bagger have both made their marks in their respective sports. Both women would prefer to be known for their sporting ability rather than their transgender status, but for the time being that seems unlikely.

Ironically, Richards has described the Olympic International Committee's 2004 decision to allow transsexuals to compete as 'a particularly stupid decision'. Whatever her opinions in later life, there is no doubt that she paved the way for the transgender sporting community.

FOR THE RECORD

Renée Richards went on to successfully coach Martina Navratilova to two Wimbledon victories. Nineteen years later, Richards was invited to induct Navratilova into the International Tennis Hall of Fame and in 2000, Richards was herself inducted into the USTA Eastern Tennis Hall of Fame.

5

An Unsporting Advantage

BACKGROUND:	Against corruption in baseball
EVENT:	1919 World Series
OPPONENTS:	White Sox v Cincinnati Reds
ARENA:	Baseball fields of the United States

Curse of the Black Sox

BASEBALL WORLD SERIES, USA, 1919

This game, gentleman, has been the subject of a crime. The public, the club owners, even the small boys on the sandlots have been swindled. — **ASSISTANT STATE ATTORNEY EDWARD PRINDEVILLE, 29 JULY 1921**

PREVIOUS PAGE: Canadian sprinter Ben Johnson makes his break in the 100 metres in the 1988 Seoul Olympic Games. He set a world record and won gold, but was stripped of his record and medal when he tested positive for steroids.

OPPOSITE: 'Shoeless' Joe Jackson, one of the best players in the league, was banned from baseball because of his involvement in the 'Black Sox' game-fixing scandal.

THE YEAR WAS 1919

▶ The Versailles Treaty was signed, signalling an end to World War I.

▶ Mahatma Gandhi started peaceful protests against British rule in India.

▶ Albert Einstein's theory of relativity was confirmed in experimental observations of a solar eclipse.

▶ By the end of 1919, 30 million people worldwide had died from the outbreak of influenza commonly referred to as the Spanish flu.

▶ Ice hockey's Stanley Cup showdown between the Montreal Canadiens and the Seattle Metropolitans was cancelled due to the death of Canadiens player Joe Hall, a victim of the Spanish flu.

▶ Cricket matches began again following World War I, with the Australian Imperial Forces team touring England, winning 12 and losing only four of their 28 games.

▶ France's Suzanne Lenglen won the first of five consecutive women's singles Wimbledon titles.

In early twentieth-century America, baseball was a national pastime, interwoven with the very fabric of American society. Viewed as something pure and incorruptible, it experienced a huge leap in popularity in the aftermath of World War I. However, as attendance figures went up, so too did the amount of gambling associated with the game. The 1919 World Series witnessed the greatest scandal in baseball history, when eight players from the Chicago White Sox were accused of throwing the series against the Cincinnati Reds. The players were banished from the game forever and the American public was forced to acknowledge that baseball, like American society, was tainted with corruption.

State of the Nation

On 11 November 1918, the 'war to end all wars' was finally over. Eight and a half million people across the globe had been killed and everyone was desperate for a brighter future. The United States was seeing a shift in values as race riots, the suffragette movement, prohibition and urbanisation all threatened to tear conservative America apart. Seen as the quintessential American sport, baseball was used to celebrate nationalistic sentiment in a new era which was embracing a movement known as '100 per cent Americanism'. The American League was formed in 1901 to challenge the domination of baseball by the National League, and the rivalry of the leagues took the sport from strength to strength as they capitalised on every opportunity to promote it. The showpiece of every season was the World Series, which pitted that year's American League champions against the National League champions for the title of 'world' champions.

The All-American Game

When the war ended, the American League embarked on a campaign to link the image of baseball with the bravery and idealism of American soldiers. Baseball kits were sent to military bases overseas and soldiers about to head home were given a copy of a baseball handbook called *The Sporting News*. Returning players were given a hero's welcome, and some of them were even sponsored by the league to travel the country recounting tales of victory. War memorials were built to commemorate players who had died, and baseball was promoted as something that had upheld troop morale. In an inspired public relations campaign, it was as if the soldiers who had fought for American ideals on foreign battlefields were now assuming their new positions on the nationwide baseball diamonds. It was against this backdrop that emerging players such as Babe Ruth and Ty Cobb stunned fans with their talent. Crowd attendance had never been so high as Americans flocked to see their now favourite sport.

Shifting Odds

As the first post-war World Series approached, the American League's Chicago White Sox were not only 5–1 favourites, but were generally acknowledged as one of the greatest teams of all time. The owner of the club, Charles Comiskey, wasn't a popular man with the players, but he was the first person to train his fielders to adjust their positions according to a batter's hitting habits and was a huge contributor to the history of baseball. Like everyone at the club, he had high hopes of the Sox winning the series. They were up against the Cincinnati Reds of the National League, and American League champions had won eight of the previous nine World Series.

However, as the series began, it was noted that an unusual amount of money was being gambled and that the odds were dramatically shifting in favour of a Reds win. Rather than assuming foul play, commentators found various excuses for the shifting of the odds. The *New York Times* suggested than an arm injury which had sidelined star White Sox pitcher Clarence 'Red' Faber might explain the swing. It also conjectured that the amount of money being gambled was due to the surge of interest in the game in the aftermath of the war.

However, publications such as *The Sporting News* suggested that the level of gambling could be indicative of a deeper problem. They said what everyone already knew: that there were two types of gamblers—those who bet for fun and those who bet as a business. The game of baseball had radically changed. Gone were the old baseball parks and rickety bleachers—this was a professional game with money at stake.

The Fix

The series started at Redland Field in Cincinnati on 1 October 1919. Due to the high interest in the sport it had been decided to play a best-of-nine series rather than the usual seven games. It was a warm, sunny day and the grounds were packed. The White Sox's starting pitcher Eddie Cicotte threw a first-ball strike to the Reds' lead-off hitter Morrie Rath. With his next pitch he deliberately hit Rath in the back. Unbeknown to the excited crowd, this was the pre-arranged signal that the fix was on. To everyone's astonishment the White Sox went on to lose the first game 9–1. Immediately rumours started to circulate regarding the fixing of the match and the odds swung around to 8–5 in favour of the Reds winning the series. There were whispers that the big gamblers had managed to bribe some of the major players.

It was well known that the White Sox players were paid less than any others in the league and that self-serving club owner Comiskey was resented for his low rates and his lack of respect for the players. The 'reserve clause' in players' contracts meant that players couldn't switch teams without the permission of the owners. Consequently, they had no bargaining power. Players such as outfielder

'Shoeless' Joe Jackson and third baseman Buck Weaver were the best players in the league, yet Comiskey paid them only US$6000 a year compared with the $10,000 many other payers of far less talent were receiving. Even so, it was impossible for the American public to imagine any player risking the ramifications of being caught in any kind of corrupt dealings. People also speculated that to swing a series, the level of corruption would be far too high to keep hidden. Too many people would know and too many players would have to be involved.

With gambling odds stacked in the Reds' favour, the winnings rolled in as they won the second game 4–2. However, when it came to the third game the Reds were shut out 3–0, thanks to the efforts of first-year pitcher Dickie Kerr. This time rumours circulated that the Reds had been 'got to' by a different gambling syndicate. However, it later transpired that Kerr never was part of the fix. Eddie Cicotte returned as starting pitcher for Chicago in game 4, which Cincinnati won 2–0. It was noted that Cicotte made some stupid errors that seemed almost intentional.

The following Monday, Claude 'Lefty' Williams held the Reds to four hits but Reds pitcher Hod Eller did even better and Cincinnati won again, 5–0. Eller was pitching so well that he set a World Series record for that time, striking out six in a row in the second and third innings. This record was later disputed when it was found out that the game had been fixed. The Cincinnati fans loved their team's winning streak; they were now leading the series by four games to one.

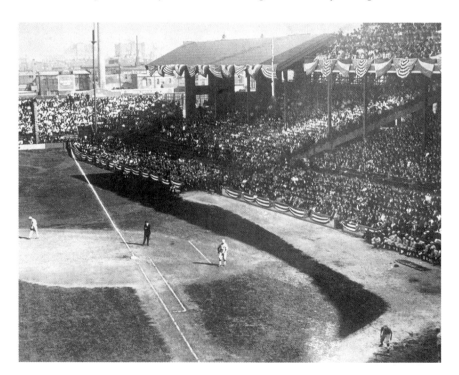

RIGHT: A shot taken during one of the rigged World Series games between the Chicago White Sox and the Cincinnati Reds in Chicago.

But games 6 and 7 saw White Sox wins, and Chicago fans knew they were back in with a chance. If the White Sox won the next game, it would be 4–4 and it would all hang in the balance for the ninth and deciding game.

Rumours later spread that Chicago gangsters approached Lefty Williams on the eve of the eighth game and threatened the White Sox left-hander and his wife. Whatever the truth of the matter, Williams gave up three runs in the first innings before being replaced, and the game saw the end to the series as Cincinnati won, 10–5. The World Series was over and, to the dismay of the city of Chicago, the legendary White Sox had lost.

Rumours Persist

After the series, the rumours continued and Charles Comiskey offered to pay a reward to anyone who had evidence of fixing, although he also insisted that 'these yarns are manufactured … and grow out of bitterness due to losing wagers.' Some sports reporters blamed the overconfidence of the White Sox for the loss.

The real story started to break early the following year, after some comments made by White Sox catcher Ray Schalk. Schalk predicted that when the next season started, seven White Sox players would be missing from the team. He had earlier complained to team manager Kid Gleason of how pitchers Cicotte and Williams had crossed him and ignored his signs, but he eventually recanted. The rumours, however, refused to die down and when the Cook County grand jury was convened in September 1920 to investigate other allegations of match fixing between the Chicago Cubs and the Philadelphia Phillies, it was decided to extend the investigation to cover the previous year's World Series.

'It ain't true, is it, Joe?'

On 27 September a major breakthrough took place when James Isaminger, a journalist for the *Philadelphia North American*, printed an interview with a small-time gambler called Bill Maharg. Maharg claimed that some of the Sox had thrown the first and second games of the World Series. Crumbling under the increasing pressure, Sox pitcher Eddie Cicotte stood before the grand jury the following day and confessed:

> *I don't know why I did it. I must have been crazy. [Charles] Risberg, [Arnold] Gandil, and [Fred] McMullin were at me for a week before the Series began. They wanted me to go crooked. I don't know. I needed the money. I had the wife and the kids. The wife and the kids don't know about this. I don't know what they'll think. I've lived a thousand years in the last twelve months. I would have not done that thing for a million dollars. Now I've lost everything, job, reputation, everything. My friends all bet on the Sox. I knew, but I couldn't tell them.*

FOR THE RECORD

In 'Shoeless' Joe Jackson's first full season in 1911, he hit .408, including 45 two-base hits and 19 triples in a total of 233 hits. Many consider him the greatest natural hitter in the history of baseball. Jackson batted .375 in the 1919 World Series and delighted fans by throwing out five base runners from his centrefield position and making 30 outs without committing any errors. However, there was no doubt that in the games against Cincinnati which the White Sox lost, his batting average decreased significantly. The loss of Jackson from the major leagues was seen as one of the greatest of baseball's tragedies.

I copied
['Shoeless' Joe]
Jackson's style
because
I thought he
was the greatest
hitter I had ever
seen, the greatest
natural hitter I
ever saw. He's the
guy who made me
a hitter.

– BABE RUTH

With Cicotte spilling the beans, the players expected the worst as star batter 'Shoeless' Joe Jackson was the next man to enter Judge McDonald's chambers to testify. Two hours later he walked out, telling the bailiffs that he'd got a lot off his chest. The *Chicago Herald & Examiner* reported that a youngster on the steps outside the courthouse said to him, 'It ain't true, is it, Joe?', to which Jackson replied, 'Yes, kid, I'm afraid it is.' (Jackson later denied that such an exchange ever occurred: 'The only one who spoke was a guy who yelled at his friend, "I told you he wore shoes."')

The boy's plea was repeated throughout the country, and has since become part of American folklore. The notion that the words had been uttered by a young boy resonated with fathers and sons everywhere. Baseball was a sport associated with the future of American youth, and the players involved were accused of betraying the dreams of young boys all across the country.

The investigation heard claims that there were another six team mates implicated in the fixing of the World Series. *The Sporting News*, once a supporter of the players, now went to town.

These are the White Sox who committed the astounding and contemptible crime of selling out the baseball world ... they will be remembered from now on only for the depths of depravity to which they could sink.

The Gambling Syndicate

As the story continued to emerge, it was revealed that the money at stake was $100,000, to be divided amongst the conspiring players. Such a sum would represent approximately one year's salary for the entire team. Joseph Sullivan, a small-time gambler and associate of first-baseman Gandil, was named as the man who raised the money. Gandil was approaching retirement and he had come to Sullivan with the idea for the fix, viewing it as his last chance to make good money. He must have been confident that his fellow team members would feel the same way, as he took the risk of sounding a number of them out to get them on side. When it became apparent that Sullivan couldn't afford to front up the cash he'd requested, Gandil involved other gamblers in the fix. A New York gambler and underworld figure named Arnold Rothstein was thought to have put up the majority of the money. He denied his part in it, although he admitted that ex-featherweight champion Abe Attell and former second-string pitcher 'Sleepy' Bill Burns had approached him with the proposition. Hal Chase, a former White Sox team member, was also implicated.

Gandil, Jackson, Cicotte, Williams, infielders McMullin and Risberg, outfielder Oscar Felsch and third-baseman Buck Weaver were all accused of conspiring to fix the series. The headline in *The Sporting News* was 'Fix These Faces In Your Memory', with the caption 'Eight Men Charged with Selling

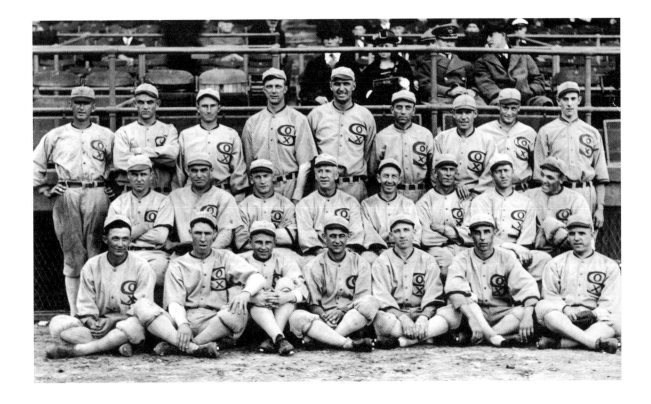

Out Baseball'. The nation was shocked by the scandal. On 22 October 1920, the grand jury issued its indictments, naming the eight Chicago players and five gamblers.

The case against them appeared watertight. The Illinois State Attorney had taken signed confessions from Jackson, Cicotte and Williams, and various gamblers had admitted their part in the fix. However, during an office handover to a newly elected Attorney, the Chicago underworld struck quickly and saw to it that all potentially incriminating papers were removed.

The case had to be rebuilt, and proceedings were considerably delayed.

The Great Baseball Trial

The trial eventually commenced on 27 June 1921. There were so many inconsistencies and oddities—including four of the prosecuting attorneys moving over to the defence—that it seemed the case could be as corrupt as the series itself. The gamblers originally indicted were excused from appearing before the court and little attempt was made to uncover the truth. Throughout the trial, the jurors were implored to think of the fans. In his summing up, prosecutor George Gorman reminded the jury of that fateful October day:

> *Thousands of men throughout the chilly hours of the night crouched in line waiting for the opening of the first World Series game. All morning they waited … never daring to leave their places for a moment. There they waited to see the great Cicotte pitch a ballgame. Gentleman, they went to see a ballgame. But all they saw was a con game!*

But it was to little effect. At the end of a month's trial, the judge instructed the jury 'that the State must prove that it was the intent of the Chicago White Sox players and others charged with conspiracy, through the throwing of the 1919 World Series, to defraud the public and others and not merely to throw baseball games'. After a mere two hours of deliberation on 2 August 1921, the jury acquitted all eight players, saying that they might have thrown a couple of games, but that in their minds that didn't constitute a criminal offence. It seemed that no-one wanted to contemplate the possibility that anything so thoroughly American could possibly be corrupt.

That night the accused and jury all went out for a celebratory meal, unaware that the players' real sentence was about to be handed down. The following day Judge Kenesaw Landis, the Commissioner of Baseball, gave his verdict:

> *Regardless of the verdict of juries, no player that throws a ball game, no player that undertakes or promises to throw a ball game, no player that sits in a conference with a bunch of crooked players and gamblers where the ways and means of throwing games are planned and discussed, and does not promptly tell his club about it, will ever play professional baseball.*

The players were banned from the professional league for life. Later, *The Sporting News* said that 'Baseball is determined to rise to a higher moral plane in all particulars.' By banning the players, the league was demonstrating values that transcended the judicial system or the fans who preferred to forgive and forget.

After the trial, two of the players attempted to establish their innocence. Jackson claimed, 'I am going to meet the greatest umpire of all—and He knows I'm innocent.' However, according to his grand jury testimony he was involved and, despite not attending the conspiracy meetings, he did accept money. Weaver attended many meetings, but apparently refused to take part. However, his silence was considered tantamount to participation.

Life after the Scandal

The White Sox club, later dubbed the 'Black Sox', managed to survive the fall-out. Rules about gambling were tightened up in many states, as were the penalties for match fixing. Most of the eight players involved continued to play ball, but their sporting lives never reached the same heights again.

BASEBALL CURSES

Curse of the Black Sox
Legend has it that the young boy who said 'It ain't true, is it, Joe?' to Jackson in 1920 declared that 'never again will the White Sox win another World Series'. The curse was finally broken 85 years later when the White Sox beat the Houston Astros in the 2005 Series.

Curse of the Bambino
In 1920, the Boston Red Sox sold legendary player Babe Ruth to their arch-enemies the New York Yankees. The Red Sox failed to win another World Series until 2004, by which time the Yankees had won an incredible 26 times.

Curse of the Billy Goat
It is said that the reason the Chicago Cubs have failed to win a World Series since 1945 is that tavern owner William Sianis put a curse on them after he was ejected from a game for attempting to bring his pet goat onto the grounds.

It transpired that the players had been hoodwinked by the gamblers, who had had no intention of paying them all of the promised money. It was a badly organised scheme and the real villain, Charles Comiskey, had not only escaped untouched, but even managed later to be inducted into the Baseball Hall of Fame. The American public has since looked back on the eight men more forgivingly as victims of an already corrupt system which favoured the needs of club owners over those of the players.

The appointment of Judge Kenesaw Landis, who became the first Commissioner of Major League Baseball in February 1920, was regarded as an inspired one. A huge proponent of baseball, Landis said that he took on the role 'for the sake of the youngsters'. He, too, saw baseball and the future of innocence as one and the same thing, and it was with a sigh of relief that fans saw baseball enter the 1920s determined to preserve its place as a bastion of traditional standards.

BACKGROUND:	Cricketing rivalry between England and Australia
EVENT:	The English struggle to contain the scoring of Don Bradman
OPPONENTS:	England v Australia
ARENA:	Melbourne Cricket Ground

The Bodyline Series

MELBOURNE CRICKET GROUND, AUSTRALIA, 1932

There are two sides out there. One is playing cricket.
The other is not. **— AUSTRALIAN CAPTAIN BILL WOODFULL
TO ENGLAND TOUR MANAGER P. F. 'PLUM' WARNER**

OPPOSITE: Don Bradman (right) heads out to bat in the second test against England in Melbourne in 1932 with Jack Fingleton (left).

THE YEAR WAS 1932

▶ Japanese troops occupied Tunhua, China.

▶ Adolf Hitler gained German citizenship. When congratulated he replied, 'You should congratulate Germany, not me!'

▶ Amelia Earhart became the first woman to fly solo across the Atlantic.

▶ An earthquake in Kansu, China, killed 70,000 people.

▶ The Sydney Harbour Bridge was opened.

▶ Fred Astaire and Ginger Rogers appeared together for the first time on screen in *Flying Down to Rio*.

▶ Lou Gehrig became the first baseball player to hit four consecutive home runs.

▶ Donald Bradman completed 10,000 runs in first class cricket, in 126 innings.

Bodyline bowling was regarded as a cricketing travesty that not only had the potential to end the game of cricket as we know it but seemed likely to sever friendly relations between England and Australia. Devised as a technique to curb the batting genius of Don Bradman, the aggressive style of bowling executed most effectively by bowler Harold Larwood resulted in Australian batsmen being hit by the ball 25 times throughout the 1932–33 Test series. England won the series, but the tactics used by captain Douglas Jardine will never be forgotten.

State of the Nation

Australia was struggling to recover from the ravages of the Depression. It had suffered huge losses of young men during World War I, and World War II was already seeming a possibility. Unemployment was high, wages were cut and taxes increased, fuelling resentment towards England for lending huge sums of money that the new country had no hope of repaying. The first Australian-born Governor-General, Sir Isaac Isaacs, was appointed, much to the annoyance of the British Crown. With people forced to live on the streets and in makeshift camps on the racecourses, Australian Prime Minister Joseph Lyons was desperate for any measures that might help the economy. For the time being it was essential that Australia and England maintained good diplomatic relations.

The Don and the Iron Duke

Australia had toured England in 1930 and won the five-Test series 2–1 against the mother country (the other two matches were drawn). Much of the Australians' success was put down to the presence of one batsman in particular. Don Bradman, a boy from the country, was emerging as the best cricketer the world had ever seen. He made his Test debut in 1928, and by 1930 he had amassed 974 runs with a batting average of 139.14. The English despised Bradman and would do anything to stop him. The Australians loved him, and any slight on 'the Don' was akin to a declaration of war. He was seen as a superstar, a phenomenal 'run machine' whose form defied attempts by experts to analyse what made him so good. However, it wasn't just the Australians who were examining their man; across the world the newly appointed English captain, Douglas Jardine, was sizing up the opposition.

Jardine was a product of the English class system. Educated at Winchester and Oxford, he trained as a lawyer and looked down on the British colonies as scum. Nicknamed 'the Iron Duke', he was cold, menacing and unapproachable. When first offered the opportunity to captain the side which was expected to be invited to play in Australia, Jardine complained of the heat and the flies, and it wasn't until his father reminded him of the honour that accompanied the position that he finally accepted.

Once he'd accepted the captaincy of England, Jardine was determined to do everything in his power to make sure the side won. In 1931 he met fellow cricketers at the Piccadilly Hotel in London and put forward a controversial idea which he believed had the potential to stop Bradman in his tracks. Jardine wasn't about to break any rules, but he was certainly prepared to play dirty. He proposed that his bowlers should bowl short-pitched deliveries aimed at leg stump. These deliveries would rear up quickly from the pitch towards the batsman, who would be forced to play defensively. The wicket would be surrounded by a group of fielders who would be expected to get regular chances of a catch from these defensive shots and deflections. Bowling to the leg stump as a way of cramping a batsman's style was a pre-existing strategy, known as 'leg theory'. Jardine used the term 'fast leg theory' to describe his idea.

Bowler Harold Larwood later confirmed what was proposed at the meeting: 'Mr Jardine asked me if I thought I could bowl on the leg stump making the ball come up into the body all the time so that Bradman had to play his shots to leg.' Larwood and bowlers Bill Voce and Arthur Carr all agreed to the tactic. The fourth bowler, Gubby Allen, who was Australian-born, would later refuse on the grounds of its being unsportsmanlike and un-British.

The fact was that since losing the Ashes in 1930, Jardine wasn't the only English player on a mission. Larwood, who was known as the Nottingham Express, was the fastest bowler in the world, and was still bitter over his last confrontation with Bradman, when the Australian batsman had finished his final innings by winning the game, the series and the Ashes. Since then, Larwood had improved his accuracy and stamina, with some of his fast balls coming in at 145 kilometres per hour. Having agreed to try Jardine's tactics, Larwood and Voce, who both played for Nottinghamshire, used county cricket to perfect the technique for the Australian tour. In the process they left their opponents battered and bruised as their team finished close to the top of the table. By October 1932, Jardine felt that his team was ready, and was looking forward to bringing the colonial upstarts back into line.

The First Test

Jardine was unpopular from the moment he arrived in Australia. When a journalist from the Sydney *Sun* newspaper asked Jardine to name his players for the opening match in Perth, Jardine answered, 'What damned rot! We didn't come here to provide scoops for yours or any other bally paper.' He certainly wasn't there to win friends.

Due to contractual matters, Don Bradman was unable to play in the First Test. Jardine was delighted, as the Don's absence left a huge hole in the Australian side. Despite the bodyline technique being designed with Bradman in mind, Jardine saw no reason not to use it on the other players. The technique was used

> **'BODYLINE' ORIGIN**
>
> The term 'bodyline' was first used by ex-Australian Test cricketer Jack Worrall of the *Australian* newspaper when he referred to 'half-pitched sluggers on the bodyline'.

ABOVE: Don Bradman (right) heads out to bat in the second test against England in Melbourne in 1932 with Jack Singleton (left).

in sudden bursts to unsettle the batsmen. As soon as they had bowled three overs and the ball had lost its shine, they would switch to bodyline. Larwood would clap his hands by way of a signal and the English would change so that three to five men were in short leg positions and two or three were in the deep fine leg and square leg.

Larwood took ten wickets and won the game for England. Throughout the tour, Larwood, Voce and Bill Bowes continued to attack the Australian batsmen. The Australian public was up in arms at what they considered dirty and dangerous tactics, and everyone looked to Bradman to teach the English a lesson.

Out for a Duck

Bradman returned for the second Test at the MCG on 30 December. A record-breaking crowd of 63,993 sweltered in the hot sun of the Australian summer. Bradman had decided that traditional batting was not the way to combat bodyline and had a more unorthodox approach in mind. When he strode on to the field there was rapturous applause. As he stepped out, he nodded to English cricketer Herbert Sutcliffe, who commented, 'Wonderful reception, Don.' To which Bradman replied, 'Yes, Herbert, but will it be so good when I'm coming back?' He didn't have to wait long to find out.

To the crowd's dismay, Bradman was out for a duck as he misjudged a short ball from Bowes. The ball hit the bottom edge of his bat as it came in at chest height. Ricocheting off the bat, it crashed down into the base of the leg stump. According to Bowes, 'Bradman walked off the field amid a silence that would have been a theatrical producer's triumph.'

Australia went on to be dismissed for 228, but England fared even worse, being dismissed for 169.

Fighting Fire with Fire

In their second innings, Australia made an inauspicious start. By the time Bradman stepped out at 12.54 pm, Australia were 27 for 2. Bradman's first stroke saw the ball racing towards the boundary and the crowd picked up, sensing that he meant business. Bradman would be facing Larwood and Voce and the Australian public couldn't wait. Bodyline commenced as Larwood thundered in on Bradman, who had 8 runs on the board.

By the time Bradman went in for tea he was on 77 and few partners were left. He was fighting fire with fire and the English were getting a basting. Bradman himself said:

The orthodox manner of playing the fast lifting ball is to move across to the off and out of the line of flight. The ball on middle and leg will go by and you're unlikely to get hit. The danger of being hit is if you stand precisely where you are, or if you back away a bit to the leg-side to try to play it on the off, because the ball is then following you. What I planned put me in much graver danger of being hit than if I had adopted an orthodox method. But there was no way I was going to get runs playing orthodox cricket.

As Bradman reached 98, Australia were on 9 for 186. With bodyline not working on the Don, Voce moved back to the usual approach. After 185 minutes, Bradman reached 101. The crowd stood up to salute their hero, the man who had now scored seven centuries in ten Tests and who was showing them that Australia could stand up to England's attempted domination. England were all out for 139, and Australia won the game.

A Blow to the Heart

By the third Test in Adelaide, there was increasing public fury over what was now being termed by Australian journalists the 'bodyline' technique. Mounted policemen stood by in case of trouble.

Two of the home side were injured early in the game. Then Larwood's first delivery was so fast that it knocked the bat out of Woodfull's hands, immediately enraging the crowd. Moments later Larwood bowled a short ball that bounced

We have seen sufficient of body-line bowling this season to realise that it does more to kill cricket than any other force ever brought into play ... it's premeditated brutality ... With a speed merchant like Larwood, the element of physical danger is so great that in the interests of cricket he should not use it.

– M. A. 'MONTY' NOBLE, FORMER AUSTRALIAN CAPTAIN

In 1965 Larwood left no doubt as to the reasons behind bodyline: 'Bodyline was devised to stifle Bradman's batting genius ... They said I was a killer with the ball without taking into account that Bradman with the bat was the greatest killer of all.' Larwood never regretted what he had done. He wrote of how he 'had a score to settle' with Bradman. 'Any scheme that would keep him in check appealed to me ... that's where it all started as far as I was concerned.'

up and struck Woodfull just above the heart, causing the captain to stagger pale-faced around the stumps. England's vice-captain Bob Wyatt later described 'an instant and violent explosion of rage from all over the ground'. As the crowd roared their disapproval, Jardine further inflamed the situation by congratulating Larwood and then giving the signal for the bodyline formation.

When Woodfull retired to the dressing room, he came face to face with England's manager, P. F. 'Plum' Warner. The usually gentle-mannered Woodfull vented his fury over the English tactics. After making his now-famous statement that of the two sides on the field, only one was playing cricket, he continued, 'The game is too good to be spoilt. It is time some people got out of it.' By Monday the press had somehow got hold of the comments and the bodyline debate was raging throughout every home and pub in the country.

The next afternoon, the popular keeper Oldfield went for a hook shot, which caused him to lose his line of vision and get hit on the head. As he fell to the ground, Larwood rushed up to apologise. The facts that Larwood was genuinely concerned and that it had not been a bodyline delivery were lost on the incensed crowd. For a moment it seemed the 30,000-strong crowd might riot. Bowler Gubby Allen helped the keeper off the field and play eventually restarted, but not before the police had formed a ring around the boundary to prevent a pitch invasion.

Enough is Enough

Despite pleas from the Australian team and many from the English camp, including Warner and Allen, Jardine refused to reconsider his controversial tactics. By the end of the fourth day the Australian Board of Cricket sent a cable to the MCC in London.

> *Bodyline bowling has assumed such proportions as to menace the best interests of the game, making protection of the body by the batsman the main consideration. This is causing intensely bitter feeling between the players, as well as injury. In our opinion it is unsportsmanlike. Unless stopped at once it is likely to upset the friendly relations ... between Australia and England.*

English authorities were enraged at the telegram, failing to understand what the fuss was about. English journalists were describing the technique as 'fast leg theory', making it sound like a well-known and harmless technique, and the English interpreted the telegram as the Australians simply being bad losers.

The reply from the MCC was straight to the point.

> *We, Marylebone Cricket Club, deplore your cable. We deprecate your opinion that there has been unsportsmanlike play ... We hope the situation is not now as serious as your cable would seem to indicate, but if it is such as to*

jeopardise the good relations between English and Australian cricketers and you consider it desirable to cancel remainder of programme we would consent, but with great reluctance.

The Prime Minister Steps In

England demanded that Australia withdraw their cable or they would refuse to play in the fourth Test. Australia was left with no option. Still a relatively new country, it could not afford to lose the support of the mother country and with World War II approaching, allegiances were crucial. However, relations were strained. The British saw the Australians as ungrateful and arrogant. The Australians, exhausted by the Depression, blamed England for their economic problems and were increasingly resentful of British ownership of Australian land and business. It was only when the Australian prime minister stepped in and explained the economic ramifications to the cricket board that the tour was saved. The board withdrew its allegations of unsportsmanlike behaviour.

England took the third and fourth Tests as Larwood removed Bradman three times in four innings. By the fifth Test, Larwood was struggling on the field. He had fractured two bones in his left foot and was in considerable pain. However, Jardine refused to allow him to retire until Bradman's wicket was taken. When Australia lost the fifth Test by eight wickets, England had won the series 4–1. Almost everyone was relieved that this controversial tour was over.

TEST MATCH AT CHANGI

In 1942, the Japanese invaded Singapore. Many of the allied forces stationed there were taken to Changi, a camp for prisoners of war that was located on the eastern tip of Singapore. Some of the captured soldiers were from the Royal Norfolk Regiment of Great Britain and the Australian Imperial Forces. One day, during a rare moment of down time, the Australians were playing a makeshift game of cricket when they were approached by two English officers. Australian Lieutenant Richard Conway recalled, 'Such is the charm of cricket, that presently we were talking like we'd all been friends all our lives.'

The next day the British suggested a Test match. Conway readily agreed and put a team together, ready to play on the next holiday announced by the Japanese. It was decided that the first Test match would take place in Sydney, as that was where it would have occurred had the war not intervened. When the Aussies turned up in their baggy shorts they saw to their amazement that the English had somehow got full kits together.

'All of us, Australians and Brits, had always dreamed since we were little boys of playing cricket for our countries,' said Conway, 'and this was it.' Suddenly they were no longer prisoners of war. 'It was a Test match between England and Australia and that was it. All of us forgot everything else.' The English won the first Test as well as the following Tests in 'Brisbane' and 'Melbourne'.

RIGHT: Don Bradman, circa 1935. Larwood's bowling in the bodyline series cut Bradman's batting average in half.

The Aftermath

On his return home Jardine was subjected to much criticism. English fast bowler Frank Foster said, 'Douglas Jardine, I am ashamed of England's win. I will face you on your return with these words on my lips.' To be accused of unfair play would have been a terrible insult to Jardine, who would have considered himself a man of honour.

The full significance of the English tactics took time to sink in with the establishment in London. But the following summer in a Test at Old Trafford, Learie Constantine and Manny Martindale from the West Indies gave England a taste of their own medicine, and E. W. Clark replied in kind. The wicket was slow and so the attack less effective, but people were still shocked. Finally, those in authority sat up and took notice.

At the end of the season the MCC passed a resolution that 'any form of bowling which is obviously a direct attack by the bowler upon the batsman would be an offence against the spirit of the game'. This was accepted by the county captains and ratified by the Imperial Cricket Conference. The MCC also demanded an apology from Larwood for his bowling in Australia, but Larwood refused, saying that he was only following the orders of his captain. Larwood was a miner and from a working class background and his stand was seen as a step towards breaking down the class distinction in England.

In 1935, the MCC gave umpires the power to intervene if a bowler was targeting the batsman with intent to do him harm. It took another 25 years to introduce a new law forbidding more than two men to field behind square leg.

Don Bradman remained the most outstanding player of the series, but as a result of Larwood's bowling in 1932–33, his batting average was cut in half. Ironically, it seems that Larwood's bodyline bowling had awoken a different style within Bradman, one that pushed him towards more originality, flair and recklessness. Bradman went on to be made Australian captain in 1936, but Word War II interrupted his brilliant career. He retired with an incredible Test batting average of 99.94. Without the bodyline series, Bradman would have finished his career with an average of 104.76.

The bodyline series has since been heralded as one of the major turning points in Australian–English relations, and is thought to have been a significant contributing factor in Australia establishing its own identity. As World War II approached and Australia chose to forge alliances with the United States, its reliance on the mother country lessened. The bodyline series is still considered one of the most controversial sporting affairs of all time.

BACKGROUND:	Over sportsmanship, money and conditions
EVENT:	Australia v New Zealand
OPPONENTS:	Greg Chappell and Brian McKechnie
ARENA:	Melbourne Cricket Ground

Underhanded Tactics

MELBOURNE, AUSTRALIA, 1981

One ball dints Australia's image as a sporting nation.

— HEADLINE IN THE *SYDNEY MORNING HERALD*

OPPOSITE: The moments after the infamous underhand bowling incident during the Australia v New Zealand World Series Cup one-day international in 1981. Trevor Chappell, who bowled the ball, is at far left.

During a one-day international against Australia, New Zealand needed six runs from the final ball to tie the match. When Australian captain Greg Chappell instructed his brother Trevor to foil the New Zealand batsman by bowling underarm, there was an immediate falling out between the two countries. New Zealanders were convinced they'd just witnessed the cricket crime of the century, and fans on both sides of the Tasman wondered if this was the end of sportsmanship in world-class cricket. It was the most controversial moment in Australian cricket history since the bodyline series, and it would forever blight Greg Chappell's reputation, despite his magnificent career record.

The State of the Nation

During the early twentieth century Australian cricketers had dominated New Zealand, but when the 1970s saw the introduction of one-day internationals as well as frequent Test matches between the two countries, a shift started to occur. As the New Zealanders improved their game and tasted success, the popularity of the sport and the intensity of the rivalry heightened. While England was the mother country and the traditional foe of both southern nations, the relationship between Australia and New Zealand quickly developed into something akin to sibling rivalry.

The 1980–81 cricket season featured the Benson and Hedges World Series Cup, a triangular one-day competition between Australia, New Zealand and India. The first match was held on 23 November 1980, and it saw New Zealand beat Australia by three wickets. India was eliminated in the course of the 16-match preliminary round, leaving Australia and New Zealand to battle it out in a best-of-five finals series for the 1980–81 World Series Cup.

The first final took place in Sydney on 29 January 1981. New Zealand bowler Richard Hadlee quickly claimed three Australian wickets to have the hosts in deep trouble at 4 for 18. Although they did not enter the game as favourites, New Zealand resoundingly won by 78 runs.

When the second match was played two days later at the Melbourne Cricket Ground, Australia found form, beating the Kiwis by seven wickets to level the series. Each country had won two of their five head-to-head matches in the preliminary round, with the fifth game abandoned due to rain, so the competition was fierce and the third final was highly anticipated.

'An unprecedented Decision'

It was Sunday, 1 February 1981 and nearly 53,000 spectators had gathered at the MCG, the biggest crowd there for a one-day international since 1971. As play commenced, a nail-biting drama unfolded. Australia scored 235 runs in their innings, and New Zealand was soon in hot pursuit. New Zealand's opening batsman Bruce Edgar managed to outlast a succession of batting partners as his team edged its way towards Australia's score. 'We ran lots of ones and twos,' he said. 'We got closer and closer.'

When it came to the beginning of the final over, New Zealand still required 15 runs to win. With the other four bowlers having already finished their allotted 10-over spells, captain Greg Chappell handed the ball to his younger brother. Initially, it looked like Trevor's medium-pace bowling might be just what the Kiwis needed to score the necessary runs—Richard Hadlee smashed the first ball of the over to the boundary for four. But on the next ball Trevor Chappell struck back, taking Hadlee's wicket. Ian Smith then scored twos off the third and fourth balls before being bowled out by the penultimate ball of the match.

With just one ball to go, six runs were needed to level the scores. As batsman Brian McKechnie walked out to the crease, Greg Chappell noted that he looked confident. If he managed to hit the ball clear over the boundary for a six, New Zealand would tie the match, and remain in the running to win the whole series.

A double All Black who played both rugby and cricket for his country, McKechnie was no stranger to pressure. Greg Chappell later said it had crossed his mind that if anyone was going to hit a six, it was McKechnie.

Trevor Chappell recalls how wicketkeeper Rod Marsh told him 'to try to bowl the same sort of delivery as I'd been bowling'. As Chappell was plotting his final ball and walking back to his mark, his older brother Greg came over and asked, 'How is your underarm bowling?'

'Oh, I don't know, why?' asked Trevor.

'Well, you're about to find out.'

Greg Chappell figured that if the ball was bowled underarm, there was no chance of New Zealand hitting it for six. His team was tired and had at least one more World Series final ahead of them as well as another Test match. If he could secure victory in this game, then a win in the fourth final would deliver them the World Series Cup and give the team an extra day's rest before the first Test against India. Greg communicated his decision to umpire Don Weser, who then passed the information on to the square-leg umpire.

Wicketkeeper Rod Marsh stood behind the stumps shaking his head, motioning Trevor Chappell not to do it. 'He was waving his arms in a sort of dead ball signal saying "No, don't do it",' said Chappell. 'I just nodded my head at Greg, as if to say "Don't tell me, tell him."' When McKechnie found out what was happening he could do nothing but prepare for the impending insult. Greg Chappell was making a decision unprecedented in world class cricket, and the ramifications would be huge.

DOUBLE ALL-BLACK

Brian McKechnie is one of the few players to have been involved in two controversial international incidents in different sports. In 1978 he calmly converted a disputed penalty in the last minute of the rugby union Test against Wales, winning the game for New Zealand 13-12.

ABOVE: Brian McKechnie (left) faces the controversial underarm delivery from Trevor Chappell (right).

The Commentary Begins

Meanwhile speculation was rife in the commentary box as ex-Australian captain Bill Lawry got wind of what was going on down on the field. 'It looks to me like they're going to bowl underarm off the last ball ... Rodney Marsh is saying "No, mate", but I'm sure he's going to bowl an underarm delivery...The umpires have been told, the batsmen have been told and this is possibly a little disappointing ... Let's make sure ... Would you ever have believed it?' No-one believed it. Trevor Chappell signalled to Rod Marsh what he was about to do and, despite Marsh shouting at him not to do it, Chappell followed his captain's orders.

Taking four paces forward, and staying inside the popping crease to avoid the no-ball, Chappell stepped up like a well-practised lawn bowler and rolled the ball towards McKechnie's leg stump. McKechnie blocked the ball and then tossed his bat skyward in disgust as pandemonium broke out throughout the stadium. New Zealand captain Geoff Howarth had played much of his cricket in England, where underarm bowling had already been outlawed, and he raced onto the field in disbelief thinking that the umpires were incorrect in allowing the ball. However, Greg Chappell was right and although underarm bowling was illegal in English cricket it was still permitted in Australia.

The game was over and Australia had won. The home crowd erupted, most of them booing, only a few applauding. Greg Chappell grabbed his hat and ran for the clubhouse. As he was leaving the field, a little girl jumped over the fence and pulled at his sleeve, saying, 'You cheated.' Chappell realised right then that a storm lay ahead. While a roar of disapproval filled the stadium, the Australian dressing room was deadly quiet. Greg later related that it had taken at least half an hour before any of his team mates could talk to him or look him in the eye.

It's Just Not Cricket

Cricket fans in New Zealand were outraged. The following day T-shirts appeared on the streets of Auckland emblazoned with the words 'Aussies Have an Underarm Problem—It Stinks'. A judge was reported to have asked ominously whether any Australians were appearing before him that day. New Zealand Prime Minister Robert Muldoon said that it was 'the most disgusting incident I can recall in the history of cricket, a game I thought was played by gentlemen'. He described it as an act of cowardice, and noted it was appropriate the Australian side wore yellow. Australian Prime Minister Malcolm Fraser was more restrained, referring to the incident as 'contrary to the traditions of the game'. Even cricketing legend Richie Benaud, an admirer of Greg Chappell, said it was 'the most gutless thing I have ever seen on a cricket field'.

Newspapers the world over discussed the incident as the underarm ball caused ripples throughout every cricketing nation. The next day Greg Chappell issued a public apology.

> *I have always played cricket within the rules of the game. I took a decision yesterday which, whilst within the laws of cricket, in the cool light of the day I recognise as not being within the spirit of the game. The decision was made whilst I was under pressure and in the heat of the moment. I regret the decision. It is something I would not do again.*

Trevor Chappell also deeply regretted the incident.

Greg Chappell later spoke about his decision, and how he had felt 'unfit to be captain'. He spoke about having to the bear the brunt of behind-the-scenes politics as well as trying to concentrate on his play. It was nearing the end of

CHAPPELL ALMOST OUT!

Earlier in the match there had been controversy when Greg Chappell appeared to have been caught in the outfield by Martin Snedden. Bowler Lance Reid described it as 'the most brilliant catch I've ever seen'. Unfortunately, the umpires hadn't seen the catch and were unable to confirm it. Chappell went on to score another 38 runs, eventually being out for 90, caught by Bruce Edgar off the bowling of Snedden.

There could not be a lonelier man in the cricket world than Greg Chappell.

– LONDON TIMES

the summer and he was tired of complaining about the playing conditions at the MCG. Mentally and physically exhausted, he felt that he would have done just about anything to get off the pitch. 'It was a protest to everyone, not least of all the administrators, but partly to my own players for some pretty ordinary performances.'

He later referred to it as a cry for help. 'The underarm had very little to do with winning that game of cricket because, in fact, we'd won the game.' He claimed that he had wanted to leave the field ten overs earlier, having already been out there six and a half hours, but had been encouraged to stay by vice-captain Marsh.

Many people blamed the circus-type nature of one-day cricket, fuelled by Kerry Packer's rcbcl World Series Cricket, and the subsequent adaptation of the game to suit a TV audience. There was a growing feeling that prize money was affecting the principles of the game. Greg took it hard when his older brother Ian Chappell weighed in: 'Fair dinkum, Greg, how much pride do you sacrifice to win $35,000?'

As both teams flew on the same plane to Sydney for the fourth final, the atmosphere was tense. By the next day the Australian Cricket Board had changed the rules and underarm bowling was made illegal. When the fourth match was played two days later, on 3 February 1981 at the Sydney Cricket Ground, there was none of the controversy and drama of the previous match. Australia dominated

RIGHT: Trevor Chappell and McKechnie walk away after the incident. The bat McKechnie flung to the ground in disgust lies on the ground behind them.

play, eventually winning by six wickets to win the series 3–1. Despite his apology for 'the underarm incident', when Greg Chappell strode onto the ground to bat he was greeted with boos from the crowd. However, 87 runs later, having played at his elegant best to guide Australia into a winning position, he left the field to a standing ovation.

Years Later

Brian McKechnie laughs at how he's always being told that he should have flicked the ball into the air and whacked it over the fence.

An hour or two after the game, when we'd all had a shower and were back at the hotel, we were joking about it, trying to work out how you could hit a six off an underarm. We tried a few years later to flick it up and hit it. You can flick it up if the ball is at the right pace, but the coordination of it is damn difficult. And then you'd have to hit it about 90 metres for it to be six at the MCG. I would defy anyone to do that. When we tried, it took about 30 or 40 goes to get to the level where you could actually hit the ball. But we could only hit it 40 metres.

McKechnie, like Chappell, wished that the incident had never occurred, but has learnt to live with it.

Greg Chappell continued to dominate domestic and international cricket until his retirement in 1984. He is widely acknowledged to have made a monumental contribution to Australian cricket and he is admired by players on both sides of the Tasman. Brian McKechnie sums up the sentiment felt by most cricketers: 'I don't hold any grudges against Greg Chappell, and my opinion that he was one of the finest batsmen of that era will never change.'

GREG CHAPPELL

Greg Chappell played 87 Test matches and captained Australia 48 times. During his last Test match in January 1984, he broke two major cricketing records. He surpassed Sir Donald Bradman (6996) as the highest run-getter in Australian Test history (7110) and set a new catching record (122).

At his retirement, Greg Chappell also held the Australian record for the most runs scored in a single Test match (380), and his total of four double centuries in Test cricket for Australia is second only to Bradman's. He is the only Test captain to have made a century in each innings of his first Test as captain, and to have scored a century before lunch in a Test match. When Chappell scored 182 in his last innings, he became the only Test cricketer to score a century in both his first and last Test innings.

BACKGROUND:	Against drugs in sport
EVENT:	100 metres men's final
OPPONENTS:	Ben Johnson v The Olympic drug-testing program
ARENA:	1988 Summer Olympics, Seoul

The Dirtiest Race in History

SEOUL, SOUTH KOREA, 1988

... not only is there no Santa Claus, but there's no Easter Bunny or Tooth Fairy either, in the world of sport ... I mean, the whole history of the Olympic Games is just full of corruption, cover-up, performance-enhancing drug use—it's not what the world thinks it is. **— VICTOR CONTE, FOUNDER AND PRESIDENT OF THE BAY AREA LABORATORY CO-OPERATIVE (BALCO)**

OPPOSITE: Canadian sprinter Ben Johnson holds one arm up triumphantly after winning the men's 100-metre final at the 1988 Seoul Olympics. That night a routine drug test detected steroids in Johnson's system.

THE YEAR WAS 1988

▶ The Iran-Iraq war ended, with the loss of an estimated one million lives.

▶ After eight years of fighting, the Russian Red Army began to withdraw from Afghanistan.

▶ In the Soviet Union, *perestroika*, a program of economic restructuring, was brought into force by Mikhail Gorbachev.

▶ Benazir Bhutto became the first woman to head the government of an Islamic-dominated state.

▶ U2's landmark record *The Joshua Tree* took home the Grammy for best album.

▶ The FA Cup was won by Wimbledon, who beat favourites Liverpool 1-0 at Wembley in one of the biggest upsets in soccer history.

▶ In tennis, Steffi Graf became only the third woman in history to win the Grand Slam.

▶ The USSR swept the board with their tally of medals at both the Summer and Winter Olympics.

▶ England lost the four-match cricket Test series to the West Indies in the 'Summer of Four Captains', as four different players led the team to defeat.

At the 1988 Olympic Games in Seoul, South Korea, Canadian sprinter Ben Johnson secured his position as the fastest man on earth. At what had been an eagerly anticipated 100 metres men's final, Johnson won the gold medal, shaving 0.10 seconds off the world record he had set in Rome the previous year. However, after the race Johnson shocked the world by testing positive for anabolic steroids. Within hours, he was stripped of his gold medal and the incident became a major turning point in the recognition of the impact that drugs were having on sport. Johnson was an elite athlete and his guilt cast a shadow of doubt across all Olympic achievements. In the years that followed, four of the top five sprinters who had been in the race with him were also tainted by controversy over the use of drugs, leading to the conclusion that Ben Johnson had been the only man unlucky enough to have been caught on the day. What should have been one of the most prestigious events of the 1988 Games has since been referred to as 'the dirtiest race in history'.

State of the Nation

Canada had not won an Olympic gold medal in track and field since 1932, and the Canadian government was putting pressure on its track and field coaches to come up with a winner. When Ben Johnson began to show world class running talents, the whole of Canada proudly got behind their potential national hero.

Lewis vs. Johnson

Ben Johnson had arrived in Canada from Jamaica in 1976, a gangly teenager who liked to run. For ten years he was trained and moulded by Canadian track and field coach Charlie Francis, until he emerged as one of Canada's top athletes. At the 1984 Summer Olympics in Los Angeles, Johnson reached the 100-metres final, where he won the bronze medal behind Carl Lewis and Sam Graddy with a time of 10.22 seconds.

Johnson had Carl Lewis firmly in his sights as the man to beat, but that year he lost to him on seven consecutive occasions. When he finally beat him on the eighth attempt, it seemed he had suddenly found exciting new form. Johnson proceeded to beat Lewis in four consecutive wins leading up to the 1987 World Championships in Rome, where he not only beat his rival, but also set a new world record of 9.83 seconds.

Lewis was deeply shaken by being beaten and tried to attribute Johnson's success to factors other than his superior running skills. He claimed Johnson had made a false start, then he blamed a stomach virus he himself had had. And then he began to allude to something far more sinister. 'There are a lot of people coming out of nowhere,' he said. 'I don't think they are doing it without drugs.' Lewis's comments were dismissed as the whingeing of a sore loser.

Now officially the fastest man on the planet, Johnson was offered lucrative sponsorship deals and began to enjoy celebrity status. Prior to Seoul, it was estimated that Johnson was already earning up to US$10 million in sponsorship deals. Company sponsors thought Johnson was a safe bet to win gold in Seoul. However, as the Olympics approached it seemed that things were beginning to unravel in the Johnson camp. Public disagreements with his coach, too many endorsements, and not enough training coupled with injury, all left Canadians wondering if their champion would be able to maintain the form he had exhibited previously in Rome.

A month before the Games, Johnson again competed against Lewis and the worst fears of his fellow Canadians were confirmed. Carl Lewis won in a time of 9.93 seconds and Johnson trailed in third place. Lewis was now full of confidence, boasting that 'the gold medal for the 100 metres is mine. I will never again lose to Johnson.'

The Fastest Race on Earth

When the Games started, Canadians were holding out little hope of Johnson winning gold, but as he took to the track, he looked fit and confident. In fact, he looked better than he ever had before.

The race began and as the eight 'thoroughbreds' of sport powered down the track, the voice of the commentator rose in excitement.

Away, Johnson got away well, Williams got away quickly, so did Mitchell. Lewis was slow, so was Christie. Johnson in front at the half-way; five metres, Lewis might not get up. Johnson's going to win it! Johnson wins by a metre from Lewis, Christie is third!

In 46 strides Johnson reached a top speed of almost 50 kilometres per hour and won the 100-metres by breaking his own world record and setting a new time of 9.79 seconds. He led for the entire race, his powerful start proving that a race could be won in the first seconds. Johnson hadn't just matched his performance in Rome, he had exceeded it, and this time he had beaten Lewis by a far greater margin.

It is worth putting his achievement in context. Between 1968 to 1983 the 100 metres record was shaved by four hundredths of a second; in just one year Johnson took 16 hundredths of a second off the record. Carl Lewis was devastated by Johnson's win and was again seen as a bad loser. 'That race was shocking,' he complained. 'I don't know how he does it ... but he does something.'

Canada had won the gold and the whole world had witnessed the beauty of what seemed like the ultimate running machine in action. In a televised interview after the race, the Canadian Prime Minister Brian Mulroney phoned Johnson,

When Carl Lewis was winning everything, I never said a word against him. And when the next guy comes along and beats me, I won't complain about that either.

– BEN JOHNSON

LEFT: Johnson (second from left) winning the 100 metres. Of the top five in that race, only Calvin Smith, who came fourth, remained free of drug allegations.

claiming that it was 'a marvelous evening for Canada'. Across the country, parties were held to celebrate Johnson's triumph.

The Test Results

That night, the laboratory was processing routine tests on the athletes when one of the hundreds of samples tested positive. Each sample was identified only by a number, and laboratory technicians couldn't believe it when they tracked the positive sample back to its source. The next day, Lewis's comments seemed strangely prophetic when it was announced by shocked IOC officials that the sample belonged to Ben Johnson. The 'fastest man on earth' had tested positive for the anabolic steroid stanozolol, a substance that assists in the building of lean muscle mass. At 3.30 am, Carol Anne Letheren, chef de mission of the Canadian delegation, stripped Johnson of the gold medal, which he had already presented to his mother. Johnson was forced to leave the Olympic Village under a cloud of shame.

Johnson fiercely denied that he was using steroids, but the tests proved otherwise. Carl Lewis was awarded the gold medal, which people believed he rightly deserved. Coach Charlie Francis said he was convinced the drug tests had been manipulated. Johnson's doctor refused to talk to the press.

A Tainted History

Drugs and sport have been intertwined since sport began. As far back as the first Olympics in Greece, athletes were ingesting extracts from plants. In Roman times, horses were given drugs to give them optimum speed during the chariot races. Steroids became part of international competition when Hitler's regime fed them to German soldiers to increase their levels of aggression. Amphetamine-based drugs were also developed during World War II to fight battle fatigue.

When the Russian weightlifters arrived at the 1952 Olympics, speculation ran rife that these new, finely-tuned bodies owed something to the use of drugs. By the 1960s—an era known for its liberated drug culture—amphetamines were eagerly embraced as the perfect drug by the cycling community, whose sport revolved around sprinting and endurance. When British cyclist Tommy Simpson died during a televised stage of the 1969 Tour de France, it led to the first demands for drugs to be banned.

By the 1970s, East Germany had emerged as a sporting powerhouse where state-run labs created a new generation of undetectable drugs and unsurpassable athletes. Despite having refused to take part in the Olympics for 23 years, the East Germans began to realise the propaganda value in beating West Germany in the medal count. The government instigated a secret operation in which young athletes were forced to take drugs, believing that they were vitamins. Soon East Germany was winning more medals per capita than any other country in the

LEFT: Johnson was suspended from competition for two years after the Seoul Olympics. He attempted a comeback in 1991, but was caught using banned drugs again in 1993 and banned for life by the IAAF.

history of the Games. By 1976 they beat the United States 40 gold to 34, making them second only to the Soviets.

The Dubin Enquiry

By the early 1980s performance-enhancing drugs were nothing new, but they had never previously been an issue in such a high-profile sport. The fact that this was the most watched race in the world, run by the fastest men in sport, meant that a question mark now hung over every athlete's performance, and the reputation of the Olympic Games was called into question.

The Canadian government set up a Commission of Enquiry into the Use of Drugs and Banned Practices Intended to Increase Athletic Performance. At what became known as the Dubin Enquiry, coach Charlie Francis eventually testified that Johnson was one of many athletes taking illegal substances. He blamed increasing pressure from the Canadian government for the athletes to win, accompanied by a reduction in budgets and training facilities.

Francis testified that Johnson had been taking steroids since 1981, when Francis had discussed the issue with his top athletes, Johnson, Desai Williams and Tony Sharpe. Together they had decided that steroids were 'worth approximately a meter' and in a race like the 100 metres where a fraction of a second made the difference, steroids seemed the only solution.

When Johnson was tested, they had miscalculated the amount of steroids that would be left in his body at the time of testing. The questioning of the doctor supplying Johnson with the steroid eventually led to the uncovering of an extensive drug distribution network among elite athletes.

Johnson also appeared before the commission and gave an emotional testimony, saying he alone was to blame. He claimed he had initially denied taking drugs because 'I was just in a mess. I was ashamed for my family and

FOR THE RECORD

Olympics	Tests Conducted	Positive Results
1968 Mexico City	667	1
1972 Munich	2079	7
1976 Montreal	786	11
1980 Moscow	645	0
1984 Los Angeles	1507	12
1988 Seoul	1598	10
1992 Barcelona	1848	5
1996 Atlanta	1923	2
2000 Sydney	2700	6

friends and kids who looked up to me as a Canadian athlete and want to be in my position.' He spoke out against drugs and pledged his support in cleaning up the sport.

Return of the Hero

After a two-year suspension, Johnson returned to the track and a forgiving Canada came out in support of their fallen hero. Over 17,000 people—the largest crowd ever to attend an indoor Canadian track and field event—turned up to see him run a 50 metres men's final. Johnson ran well, but came second and seemed disappointed. He wore a small piece of black cloth on his vest in memory of his father, who had died the previous year. He was desperate to redeem himself to his family and his fans, and to prove to the world that he was genuinely the best, with or without drugs.

However, the pressure for an elite athlete such as Johnson to succeed again proved too much and five years after the Olympics in Seoul he failed another test, which resulted in a ban for life. This time there were no attempts to hide the truth, and when interviewed in 1996 he spoke openly of the Olympic debacle.

> *Yes, I was taking steroids, but so were others on the starting line that day. They know it. I know it. That's all that counts. If people are naive enough to believe that athletes don't take drugs, that is their problem.*

In the years that followed, other athletes from the Seoul final were also involved in drug controversy. In 1999 Linford Christie, who won the gold in 1992, received a two-year ban after testing positive for nandrolone. It was also revealed that Carl Lewis had failed three tests at the 1988 Olympic trials, but that the American Olympic body had accepted his protests that he had thought he was taking a herbal supplement.

Calvin Smith—who had originally came fourth, but was upgraded to bronze medallist when Johnson was stripped of his gold—was the only one of the top five in the race to remain free of drug allegations. Many other athletes who had made the same tough decision to remain drug-free echoed the disillusionment he felt. 'I should have been the gold medallist,' he claimed. 'During the last five years of my career I knew I was being denied the chance to show I was the best clean runner.'

The Holy Grail of Sport

Since the scandal of 1988, testing for drugs has become ever more prevalent, but with every new test comes the introduction of a new drug on the market or a new way to conceal it. The year 2007 saw the explosion of the BALCO case in the US, in which a San Francisco pharmaceutical company was investigated for the long-

OFF THE RECORD

In 2003 *Sports Illustrated* received some documents provided by Dr Wade Exum, director of drug control administration for the US Olympic Committee from 1991 to 2000. The papers revealed that at least a hundred American athletes had failed drug tests but had been allowed to compete in the 1992 and 1998 Olympics.

term supply of drugs to top athletes in baseball's Major League and the National Basketball League, as well as American football and track and field.

Victor Conte, the founder of BALCO, said that the use of drugs was a necessity to level the playing field: 'It's not cheating if everybody is doing it. And if you've got the knowledge that that's what everyone is doing, and those are the real rules of the game, then you're not cheating.'

Conte also admitted that he worked on a drug program with US track and field star Tim Montgomery with the aim of breaking the 100-metres world record, a feat Montgomery accomplished at the 2002 IAAF Grand Prix Final in Paris with a time of 9.78 seconds. 'I knew that this was the most coveted of all records ... and gold medals. So we kind of had a collective dream, and I was the mastermind, so to speak,' said Conte.

Montgomery was stripped of his world title. So too was Marion Jones, winner of five Olympic medals at the Sydney 2000 Olympics, the world's fastest woman, another client of BALCO's and a one-time partner to Montgomery.

In Conte's mind, these records still stand:

When you say legitimate, I believe if it was achieved using the exact same playing field as the previous record, and the previous record, and the previous record, then it is legitimate because you're competing with the same terms and conditions ... I mean, otherwise you'd have to wipe out all the world records.

And in an interview on US television show 20/20 Conte said, 'In short, the Olympic Games are a fraud.'

Perhaps that is why Ben Johnson no longer has any interest. 'I don't watch the sport any more,' he said. 'It's a waste of time. Nobody impresses me.'

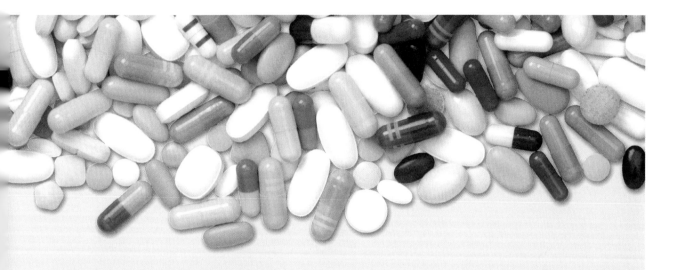

DRUGS AND SPORT TIMELINE

1807 Briton Abraham Wood admits to using opium to stay awake for 24 hours in an endurance walking race.

1886 Cyclist Arthur Linton overdoses on trimethyl—the first recorded drug-related sporting death.

1870s–90s Nitroglycerine and cocaine-based doping agents are used by riders in American six-day cycle races.

1904 American marathon runner Thomas Hicks narrowly escapes death after mixing brandy and strychnine at the St Louis Olympics, but is still awarded the gold medal.

1920s Sporadic reports of cocaine, chloroform and other drug use in the Tour de France hit the press.

1928 The International Amateur Athletic Federation instigates a ban on doping, but without putting testing procedures in place.

1936 The first appearance of benzedrine or 'speed' in sport is recorded at the Berlin Olympics.

1942 Italian cyclist Fausto Coppi is reported to have taken seven packets of amphetamines to enable him to beat the world one-hour track cycling record.

1952 Amphetamine use is widespread amongst speed skaters at the Oslo Winter Olympics.

1954 Soviet weightlifters at the World Championships smash world records and win gold medals in all weight categories—with the help, it is later alleged, of testosterone injections.

1960 On the first day of competition at the Rome Olympics, cyclist Knud Jensen collapses and fractures his skull, his post-mortem later revealing traces of amphetamine and nicotinyl nitrate.

1962–3 Everton's title-winning soccer season is blighted after investigations reveal that victory had been achieved with the help of benzedrine.

1966 Soccer's governing body FIFA and cycling's UCI ban doping. One year later, the International Olympic Committee follows suit.

1967 England's Tom Simpson dies during the Mont Ventoux stage of the Tour de France. It is later discovered he had mixed amphetamines and alcohol.

1968 Drugs testing commenced at the Mexico Olympics.

1969 British cyclist Tommy Simpson dies during a televised stage of the Tour de France, leading to the first demands for drugs to be banned.

1976 East German swimmers take 11 of the 13 gold medals. Details later emerge of a state-sponsored doping policy.

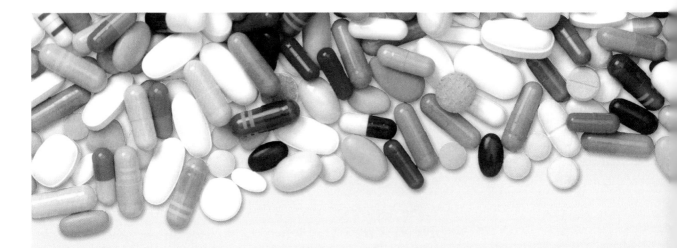

1977 East German shot-putter Ilona Slupianek is banned for 12 months by the IAAF after testing positive for anabolic steroids.

1978 After fleeing to West Germany from the East, sprinter Renate Neufeld reveals she was given anabolic steroids by her trainers and pressured to use them by the Stasi in preparation for the 1980 Olympics.

1987 Deaths occur in cycling and orienteering as a result of the use of EPO (erythropoietin), which increases the blood's oxygen-carrying capacity.

1992 German sprinters Katrin Krabbe, Silke Möller and Grit Breuer escape a competition ban on a technicality after submitting identical urine samples.

1994 Eleven Chinese athletes, including seven swimmers, test positive for dihydrotestosterone at the Asian Games.

1996 Irish swimmer Michelle Smith collects four gold medals at the Atlanta Olympics, but is later banned for four years after doctoring her test samples.

1998 The whole Festina team is banned from competition in the Tour de France after a team car is discovered packed with banned performance-enhancing substances.

East German athlete Carola Nitschke becomes the first athlete to voluntarily return her medals and request that her name be struck off the records. She had been given anabolic steroids and testosterone injections since the age of 13.

1999 The World Anti-Doping Agency is created.

2001 Four major soccer players test positive for nandrolone.

2002 The use of a Vicks inhaler leads British skier Alain Baxter to be stripped of the bronze slalom medal he had won at the Salt Lake City Winter Olympics.

2003 A newly developed anabolic steroid, tetrahydrogestrinone (THG), causes controversy in the worlds of athletics and American football.

2004 Twenty-four athletes are expelled for drug-related violations at the Athens Olympics.

2006 The Operación Puerto doping trial against Spanish doctor Eufemiano Fuentes and several alleged accomplices begins. He is accused of administering performance-enhancing drugs to around 200 professional athletes, including stars of football, tennis and cycling.

2006—7 The Tour de France is shaken by numerous doping scandals and allegations. Rumours abound of the use of EPO by former champions Lance Armstrong and Bjarne Riis.

2007 Multiple Olympic and World Championship track gold medallist Marion Jones is stripped of all titles won since September 2000 after admitting to the use of tetrahydrogestrinone (THG).

2009 Eight months after the Beijing Olympics, six athletes test positive for CERA, an advanced version of EPO.

BIBLIOGRAPHY

CHAPTER 1: THE FIRST ELEVEN

BOOKS

200 Years of Australian Cricket 1804–2004 (Afterword by Gideon Haigh), Pan Macmillan Australian, Sydney, 2004

Cricket History: Prime Minister's XI versus ATSIC Chairman's XI; Adelaide Oval, Friday 21 March 2003, ATSIC, ACT, 2003

Rex Harcourt and John Mulvaney, *Cricket Walkabout: The Aboriginal Cricketers of the 1860s*, Golden Point Press, Victoria, 2005

Qantas Aboriginal Cricket Tour of England 1988, Qantas, Aboriginal Cricket Association, 1988

Bernard Whimpress, *Passport to Nowhere: Aborigines in Australian Cricket 1850–1939*, Walla Walla Press, Sydney, 1999

NEWSPAPERS

'Eleven Aboriginal Black Australians v Eleven Gentlemen of Surrey Club', *Times*, London, 26 May 1868

INTERNET

The 1868 cricket tour:

www.abc.net.au/rn/talks/8.30/sportsf/stories/s347703.htm

www.atmitchell.com/journeys/social/cricket/first/firstTour.cfm (includes score book)

www.cricinfo.com/db/ARCHIVE/1860S/1868/ABORIGINES_IN_ENG/

Background to 1868:

www.cultureandrecreation.gov.au/articles/goldrush

www.cultureandrecreation.gov.au/articles/royalvisits/

European Network for Indigenous Australian Rights: www.eniar.org/news/cricket2.html

CHAPTER 2: THE GREAT WHITE HOPE: JIM JEFFRIES V THE BLACK MENACE

BOOKS

Hugh Fullerton and James J. Jeffries, *Two-fisted Jeff*, Consolidated Book Publishing, Chicago, 1929

Jack Johnson, *Jack Johnson: In the Ring and Out*, National Sports Publishing Company, Chicago, 1927

Graeme Kent, *The Great White Hopes: The Quest to Defeat Jack Johnson*, Sutton, London, 2005

Patrick B. Miller and David Kenneth Wiggins (eds), *Black Athletes and Race Relations in Twentieth Century America*, Routledge, New York, 2004

Randy Roberts and Papa Jack, *Jack Johnson and Era of White Hopes*, Free Press, New York, 1983

INTERNET

Background on Jack Johnson: http://en.wikipedia.org/wiki/Jack_Johnson_(boxer)

Jack Johnson's biography: www.boxrec.com/media/index.php?title=Human:1187

Background on Jim Jeffries: en.wikipedia.org/wiki/James_J._Jeffries

Jim Jeffries's bouts and stats: www.boxrec.com/list_bouts.php?human_
      id=9022&cat=boxer

Jim Jeffries's biography: www.boxrec.com/media/index.php?title=Human:9022

'Unforgivable Blackness': the comprehensive site of Ken Burns's 2005 film about
      Jack Johnson: www.pbs.org/unforgivableblackness/index.html

The quest for a presidential pardon for Jack Johnson: www.nytimes.
      com/2005/01/18/sports/othersports/18sandomir.html?_
      r=2&oref=login&oref=slogin

List of heavyweight champions: en.wikipedia.org/wiki/List_of_heavyweight_
      boxing_champions

www.encyclopedia.com/doc/1G1-14969862.html EBONY magazine:

Biography of Tex Rickard:

www.ibhof.com/rickard.htm

www.ibhof.com/ibhfhvy3.htm

CHAPTER 3: A DEMONSTRATION OF ARYAN SUPREMACY

BOOKS

Jesse Owens with Paul Neimark, *I Have Changed*, William Morrow, New York, 1972

Jeremy Schaap, *Triumph: The Untold Story of Jesse Owens and Hitler's Olympics*,
      Houghton Mifflin Books, New York, 2007

INTERNET

The Berlin Olympics:

http://espn.go.com/sportscentury/features/00016393.html

www.olympic.org/uk/games/past/index_uk.asp?OLGT=1&OLGY=1936

Jesse Owens: www.infoplease.com/spot/summer-olympics-jesse-owens.html

CHAPTER 4: THE RELUCTANT NAZI WARRIOR

BOOKS

Gavin Evans, *Kings of the Ring: The History of Heavyweight Boxing*, Weidenfeld &
      Nicolson, UK, 2007

Jack Hails, *Classic Moments of Boxing*, Moorland Publishing, 1986

John D. McCallum, *The Encyclopedia of World Champion Boxing Champions Since 1882*,
      Chilton Book Company, Radnor, US, 1975

INTERNET

Louis v Schmeling footage 1936 (from PBS documentary 'The Fight'): www.youtube.
      com/watch?v=dtVK7uqI4cU

Louis v Schmeling footage 1938 (from PBS documentary 'The Fight'): www.youtube.
      com/watch?v=VwPY5CzOGzw

Website of PBS documentary 'The Fight': www.pbs.org/wgbh/amex/fight/index.html

Wikipedia on Max Schmeling: en.wikipedia.org/wiki/Max_Schmeling

Wikipedia on Joe Louis: en.wikipedia.org/wiki/Joe_Louis

Max Schmeling's career bouts and stats: www.boxrec.com/list_bouts.php?human_
    id=009041&cat=boxer

'The Championship Fight that Went Beyond Boxing', *New York Times*, 1988:
    http://www.nytimes.com/1988/06/19/sports/the-championship-fight-that-
    went-beyond-boxing.html

Arlington National Cemetery obituary of Joe Louis: www.arlingtoncemetery.net/
    joelouis.htm

'The Brown Bomber': info.detnews.com/history/story/index.
    cfm?id=52&category=sports

'Max Schmeling: The Story of a Hero': www.auschwitz.dk/schmeling.htm

List of heavyweight boxing champions: en.wikipedia.org/wiki/List_of_heavyweight_
    boxing_champions

Nazi concentration camps: en.wikipedia.org/wiki/List_of_concentration_camps_of_
    Nazi_Germany

The Holocaust: en.wikipedia.org/wiki/The_Holocaust

NEWSPAPER

'Schmeling Still Battles to Grasp the Past', *New York Times*, 19 June 1988

CHAPTER 5: A SALUTE TO BLACK POWER

BOOKS

Christopher Brasher, *Mexico 1968: A Diary of the XIXth Olympiad*, Stanley Paul,
    London, 1968

James Coote, *Olympic Report 1968: Mexico and Grenoble*, Robert Hale, London, 1968

Harry Edwards, *Revolt of the Black Athlete*, The Free Press, New York, 1969

Helen Jefferson Lenskyj, *Inside the Olympic Industry: Power, Politics and Activism*, SUNY
    Press, Albany, 2000

Alfred Erich Senn, *Power, Politics, and the Olympic Games*, Human Kinetics Publishers,
    Champaign, 1999

Tommie Smith and David Steele, *Silent Gesture: The Autobiography of Tommie Smith*,
    Temple University Press, Philadelphia, PA, 2007

NEWSPAPERS

'2 Accept Medals Wearing Black Gloves', *New York Times*, 17 October 1968

'"Black Power" on Victory Stand', *Los Angeles Times*, 17 October 1968

'US Apologizes for Athletes' "Discourtesy"', *Los Angeles Times*, 18 October 1968

'Black Power Wins 200-Metres', *Australian*, 18 October 1968

'US Sends Black Power Runners Home', *Australian*, 19 October 1968

'Olympic Protest Heroes Praise Norman's Courage', *Sydney Morning Herald*,
    10 October 2006

INTERNET

Background on Tommie Smith:
www.tommiesmith.com/about_tommie/bio.html

www.usatf.org/HallOfFame/TF/showBio.asp?HOFIDs=157

Background on John Carlos:

www.usatf.org/HallOfFame/TF/showBio.asp?HOFIDs=195

en.wikipedia.org/wiki/John_Carlos

www.johncarlos.com/

Background on Peter Norman:

www.athletics.com.au/community/news/vale_peter_norman

web.archive.org/web/20010701060753/www.dallasnews.com/sports_day/olympics/1
        80747_29olyblackistone.html

www.smh.com.au/articles/2006/10/03/1159641325056.html

Mexico Olympic Games:

www.olympic.org/uk/games/past/index_uk.asp?OLGT=1&OLGY=1968

www.olympic.org/uk/games/past/table_uk.asp?OLGT=1&OLGY=1968

CHAPTER 6: MUNICH MASSACRE

BOOKS

Christopher Brasher, *Munich 72*, Stanley Paul, London, 1972

James Coote and John Goodbody, *Olympics 1972*, Robert Hale & Co, London, 1972

Richard Espy, *Politics of the Olympic Games*, University of California Press, 1979

David Guiney, *Dunlop Book of the Olympics*, Eastland Press, UK, 1975

David Wallechinsky, *Complete Book of the Olympics*, Hardie Grant Books, Australia, 2000

NEWSPAPERS

'Hostages in Munich Rescued', *Jerusalem Post*, 6 September 1972

'How Hostages Died Remains Unclear', *Jerusalem Post*, 7 September 1972

'Olympic Games Are Suspended', *Australian*, 6 September 1972

'Death Toll Now 17', *Australian*, 7 September 1972

'Tears Flow as Dead Israelis Come Home', *Australian*, 8 September 1972

'Germany Tells ... Why They Fired First at Munich', *Australian*, 9 September 1972

INTERNET

Background on the massacre of Israeli Athletes:

http://en.wikipedia.org/wiki/Munich_massacre

www.time.com/time/archive/collections/0,21428,c_munich,00.shtml

www.palestinefacts.org/pf_1967to1991_munich.php

Background on the 1972 Munich Olympic Games: www.olympic.org/uk/games/
        past/index_uk.asp?OLGT=1&OLGY=1972

1972 timeline: en.wikipedia.org/wiki/1972

Time magazine's major article on the massacre: www.time.com/time/magazine/
        article/0,9171,906384,00.html

A site set up as a memorial for the murdered Israeli hostages: www.geocities.com/
        munichseptember1972/default.html

IMDB site for *One Day in September*: www.imdb.com/title/tt0230591/

Another Jewish account of the tragedy: www.jewishvirtuallibrary.org/jsource/
        Terrorism/munich.html

CHAPTER 7: RUMBLE IN THE JUNGLE

BOOKS

Muhammad Ali and Richard Durham, *Soul of a Butterfly: Reflections on Life's Journey*, Simon & Schuster, New York, 2005

Muhammad Ali and Thomas Hauser, *The Greatest: My Own Story*, Random House, New York, 1975

Stephen Brunt, *Facing Ali: The Opposition Weighs In*, Knopf, Canada, 2002

Gavin Evans, *Kings of the Ring: The History of Heavyweight Boxing*, Weidenfeld & Nicolson, UK, 2005

George Foreman with Joe Engel, *By George*, Villard, New York, 1995

Randy Gordon, *Muhammad Ali: The Eyewitness Story of a Boxing Legend*, Carlton, London, 2000

Ken Gorman, *40 Boxers Describe My Greatest Fight*, Mainstream Publishing, Edinburgh, 1996

Mike Marqusee, *Redemption Song: Muhammad Ali and the Spirit of the Sixties*, Verso, London, 1999

CHAPTER 8: BLOODY SUNDAY: THE CROKE PARK MASSACRE

BOOKS

Tim Carey, *Croke Park: A History*, Collins Press, Cork, 2004

Padraic O' Farrell, *Who's Who in the Irish War of Independence 1916–1921*, Mercier Press, Dublin and Cork, 1980

NEWSPAPERS

'The Outbreak in Dublin', *Chicago Daily Tribune*, 22 November 1920

'Irish, English Set to Tackle History', *Boston Globe*, 24 February 2007

CONFERENCE PAPERS

John Ainsworth, 'The Black and Tans and Auxiliaries in Ireland, 1920–1921: Their Origins, Roles and Legacy'. Paper presented to the Annual Conference of the Queensland History Teachers' Association in Brisbane, Saturday 12 May 2001

INTERNET

Official site of the Gaelic Athletics Association: www.gaa.ie/

CHAPTER 9: BLOOD IN THE WATER

BOOKS

Anna Ambrosy, *Brave Nation: A Short Political and Social History of Twentieth Century Hungary*, Hungarian Life Publishing, Melbourne, 2001

Richard Espy, *Politics of the Olympic Games*, University of California Press, Los Angeles, 1979

Charles Gati, *Failed Illusions: Moscow, Washington, Budapest and the 1956 Hungarian Revolt*, Woodrow Wilson Center Press, Washington, 2006

Allen Guttmann, *Olympics: A History of the Modern Games*, University of Illinois Press, Illinois, 1992

Paul Ignotus, *Hungary*, Ernest Benn Ltd, London, 1972

Alfred Erich Senn, *Power, Politics, and the Olympic Games*, Human Kinetics Publishers, Champaign, 1999

NEWSPAPERS

'Martial Law Declared in Hungary; Major Uprising Against Soviet', *Sydney Morning Herald*, 25 October 1956

'Soviet Government Expresses Regret to Hungary', *Age*, 1 November 1956

'Fighting in Streets as Soviet Tanks Enter Budapest,' *Age*, 5 November 1956

'Russians in Rough Game', *Melbourne Herald*, 6 December 1956

'Hungarians on the Bus to Freedom', *Melbourne Herald*, 7 December 1956

'Reds Booed After Fight', *Daily Telegraph*, 7 December 1956

'Player Punched in Rough Water Polo', *Age*, 7 December 1956

'Hungarian Punched by Russian: Angry Games Scene', *Sydney Morning Herald*, 7 December 1956

'Half Hungary's Olympic Team Won't Go Home', *Daily Telegraph*, 8 December 1956

'Emotional Scenes as Hungarians Leave: Nine Miss the Plane', *Sydney Morning Herald*, 8 December 1956

'Hungarians Who Stay Weep for Those Who Return,' *Sunday Telegraph*, 9 December 1956

'Ervin Zador: Blood on the Water', *Independent*, 2 December 2006

'Raw Emotion and Spilled Blood of '56', *New York Times*, 21 July 1996

INTERNET

Melbourne Olympic Games and final medal tally for Hungary and Russia: http://corporate.olympics.com.au/games.cfm?GamesID=7 www.olympic.org/uk/games/past/index_uk.asp?OLGT=1&OLGY=1956

Official scores: http://olympic-museum.de/o-reports/report1956.htm

Wikipedia article on the match: http://en.wikipedia.org/wiki/Blood_In_The_Water_match

Match dates and results of the 1956 Olympic water polo competition: http://en.wikipedia.org/wiki/Water_polo_at_the_1956_Summer_Olympics

The Hungarian revolution: www.britannica.com/eb/article-34819/Hungary

List of Olympic water polo medallists: http://en.wikipedia.org/wiki/Water_polo_at_the_Summer_Olympics

IOC site for the Melbourne Olympics: www.olympic.org/uk/games/past/index_uk.asp?OLGT=1&OLGY=1956

On the documentary *Freedom's Fury*: www.imdb.com/title/tt0322332/

CHAPTER 10: THE BAREFOOT IDEALIST

BOOKS

Paul Rambali, *Barefoot Runner: The Life of Champion Abebe Bikila*, Serpent's Tail, London, 2006

NEWSPAPERS

'Barefoot Runner—The Life of Marathon Champion Abebe Bikila', *Independent*, 4 December 2006

INTERNET

The Abebe Bikila story:

www.ethiopians.com/abebe_bikila.htm

www.olympic.org/uk/athletes/profiles/bio_uk.asp?PAR_I_ID=18263

www.time.com/time/europe/hero2006/bikila.html

www.tadias.com/2008/07/26/remembering-olympic-hero-abebe-bikila

www.runnerstribe.com/AbebeBikila

CHAPTER 11: PING PONG DIPLOMACY

BOOKS

Jonathan Aitken, *Nixon: A Life*, Regnery Publishing, Washington, 1994

Robert Dallek, *Nixon and Kissinger*, HarperCollins, New York, 2007

Philip Short, *Mao: A Life*, Holt Paperbacks, 2001

INTERNET

Tim Boggan, *History of US Table Tennis, Volume V, Part 1: Ping Pong Oddity* (online publication): www.usatt.org/articles/ppoddity04.shtml

CHAPTER 12: THE POISONED PAWN

BOOKS

David Edmonds and John Eidinow, *Bobby Fischer Goes to War*, Faber and Faber, London, 2004

Richard Roberts with Harold C. Schonberg, Al Horowitz and Samuel Reshevsky, *Fischer/Spassky: The New York Times Report on the Chess Match of the Century*, Quadrangle Books, New York, 1972

NEWSPAPERS

'Fischer Crushes Spassky, Takes Lead in Title Match', *New York Times*, 24 July 1972

'Fischer Captures Chess Title as Spassky Resigns by Phone', *New York Times*, 2 September 1972

'Fischer Takes Title as Spassky Quits', *London Daily Telegraph*, 2 September 1972

'Fischer Wins World Title', *Australian*, 2 September 1972

CHAPTER 13: THE GREAT GOLD ROBBERY

BOOKS

British Olympic Association, *Official Report of the Olympic Games 1972*, Sportsworld, London, 1972

James Coote and John Goodbody, *Olympics 72*, Robert Hale & Co, London, 1972

Cleve Deenshaw and Deanna Binder, *Celebrate the Spirit: The Olympic Games*, ABC Books, Sydney, 1996

Richard Espy, *Politics of the Olympic Games*, University of California Press, Berkeley, 1979

Allen Guttmann, *Olympics: A History of the Modern Games*, University of Illinois Press, Champaign, 1992

Melvyn P. Leffler and David S. Pai, *Origins of the Cold War: An International History*, Routledge, London, 1994

Miroslav Nincic, *Anatomy of Hostility: The US–Soviet Rivalry in Perspective*, Harcourt Brace Jovanovich, San Diego, 1989

Jeffrey O. Segrave and Donald Chu, *Olympic Games in Transition*, Human Kinetics Publishers, Champaign, 1988

NEWSPAPERS

'Grimmest Olympics Nearing a Merciful End: A Disputed US Loss', *Washington Post*, 10 September 1972

'Olympic Group Disallows US Basketball Protest: Americans Question Why Clock was Turned Back', *Washington Post*, 11 September 1972

'Basketball Door Left Barely Ajar', *Washington Post*, 12 September 1972

'Russia Ends US Basketball Reign', *Los Angeles Times*, 10 September 1972

'The Great Gold Robbery', *Los Angeles Times*, 11 September 1972

'Soviet Quintet Wins 51–50, Ending US Supremacy', *New York Times*, 10 September 1972

'US Protest Rejected', *Australian*, 11 September 1972

INTERNET

Background on US versus Russia Olympic basketball:

http://espn.go.com/classic/s/Classic_1972_usa_ussr_gold_medal_hoop.html

http://en.wikipedia.org/wiki/Basketball_at_the_Summer_Olympics

Background on 1972 Munich Olympic games: www.olympic.org/uk/games/past/index_uk.asp?OLGT=1&OLGY=1972

1972 timeline: http://en.wikipedia.org/wiki/1972

CHAPTER 14: MIRACLE ON ICE

BOOKS

Lester Brune and Richard Dean , *Chronology of the Cold War 1917–1992*, Taylor Francis, New York, 2006

Larry R. Gerlach (ed), *The Winter Olympics: From Chamonix to Salt Lake City*, University of Utah Press, Salt Lake City, 2004

Bud Greenspan, *Frozen in Time: The Greatest Moments at the Winter Olympics*, Stoddart, Toronto, 1997

Report of the Olympic Games 1980: XXIInd Olympiad, Moscow, 19 July – 3 August 1980; XIIIth Winter Olympics, Lake Placid, 13–24 February 1980, Australian Olympic Federation, Ferntree Gully, 1980

David Wallechinsky, *The Complete Book of the Winter Olympics*, Overlook Press, New York, 1998

NEWSPAPERS

'Bittersweet Memories of Lake Placid Will Endure', *Washington Post*, 24 February 1980

INTERNET

An account of the 'Miracle on Ice': http://espn.go.com/classic/s/miracle_ice_1980.html

Last 15 seconds of the game on YouTube: www.youtube.com/watch?v=CGACsSW4Iqw

An oral history of the US 1980 hockey team: www.doingoralhistory.org/project_archive/2002/papers/PDF/A_derios.pdf

Soviet ice hockey squads: www.azhockey.com/squads/squadsussr.html

CHAPTER 15: 'THE TOUR': 1981 SPRINGBOKS V ALL BLACKS

BOOKS

Graeme Barrow, *All Blacks versus Springboks: A Century of Rugby Rivalry*, Reed, Auckland, 1992

Barry Gustafson, *His Way: A Biography of Robert Muldoon*, Auckland University Press, Auckland, 2000

Grant Harding and David Williams, *Toughest of Them All: New Zealand and South Africa—The Struggle for Rugby Supremacy*, Penguin, Auckland, 2000

Ross Meurant, *The Red Squad Story*, Harlan, Auckland, 1982

Graham Mourie, *Captain: An Autobiography*, Moa Publications, Auckland, 1982

Robert Muldoon, *Number 38/Robert Muldoon*, Reed Methuen, Auckland, 1986

Spiro Zavos, *The Real Muldoon*, Fourth Estate Books, Wellington, 1978

Spiro Zavos, *Winters of Revenge: The Bitter Rivalry Between the All Blacks and the Springboks*, Viking, Auckland, 1997

NEWSPAPERS

'Games Head Warns Still Time to Say "No Tour"', *New Zealand Herald*, 17 July 1981

'Bok Arrival Will Halt Shipping', *New Zealand Herald*, 17 July 1981

'Police Assembling 1000-Strong in Biggest NZ Mobilisation', *New Zealand Herald*, 1 August 1981

'Violence Will Be "Answered", Police Warn Tour Protestors', *New Zealand Herald*, 7 August 1981

'Wire Goes Up at Eden Park', *New Zealand Herald*, 15 August 1981

'Police Braced for Action as Talks Fail', *New Zealand Herald*, 5 September 1981

'Violent Clashes as Police Lines Hold Back Protestors', *New Zealand Herald*, 7 September 1981

'Evacuation of Park Was Considered', *New Zealand Herald*, 14 September 1981

'Police Tested by Thousands', *New Zealand Herald*, 17 August 1981

'Springbok Team in Rotorua', *New Zealand Herald*, 31 August 1981

'Final Whistle for Boks to Airport Cheers, Jeers', *New Zealand Herald*, 14 September 1981

INTERNET

Background, and accounts of the events of the Tour:

www.nzhistory.net.nz/culture/1981-springbok-tour

www.nzhistory.net.nz/media/video/the-third-test-auckland

www.anc.org.za/un/reddy/sam-ram.html

CHAPTER 16: THE HAND OF GOD

BOOKS

Jimmy Burns, *Hand of God: The Life of Maradona*, Bloomsbury Publishing, London, 1996

Terry Crouch, *The World Cup: The Complete History*, Cameron House, Wingfield, 2006

Keir Radnedge (ed), *The Ultimate Encyclopaedia of Soccer* (with Foreword by Gary Lineker), Teach Yourself Books, UK, 1998

Diego Maradona, *El Diego: The Autobiography of the World's Greatest Footballer*, Yellow Jersey Press, London, 2004

INTERNET

Article regarding the two goals scored by Maradona: http://ussoccerplayers.typepad.com/ussoccerplayers/feet-of-god.html

Demonstration of *Gambetta*: 'Crespo does a Gambetta': www.youtube.com/watch?v=z_R4bCYFnKE

'The "Hand of God" Is a Way of Life': www.chrishunt.biz/features22.html

CHAPTER 17: CHRISTMAS TRUCE FOOTBALL MATCH

BOOKS

Peter Fitzsimons, *Great Australian Sports Champions*, Harper Sports, Pymble, 2006

John Keegan, The First World War, Pimlico, London, 1999

Wilfred Owen, 'Anthem for Doomed Youth' in Louis Untermeyer (ed), *Collins Albatross Book of Verse: English and American Poetry from the Thirteenth Century to the Present Day*, Collins, London, 1960

Stanley Weintraub, *Silent Night: The Story of the World War I Christmas Truce*, Plume, New York, 2002

INTERNET

The Christmas truce:

www.guardian.co.uk/uk/2004/dec/19/christmas.lornamartin

www.spiritoffootball.com/2002/blog/2002/04/03/the-christmas-truce

www.firstworldwar.com/features/christmastruce.htm

www.nytimes.com/2005/12/25/weekinreview/25word.ready.html

CHAPTER 18: GAME OF DEATH: GERMANY V UKRAINE

BOOKS

Andy Dougan, *Dynamo: Defending the Honour of Kiev*, Fourth Estate Ltd, London, 2001

INTERNET

Accounts of the game:

http://www.pierretristam.com/pdfs/wc6.pdf

www.ukemonde.com/sports/matchofdeath.html

www.kiev-life.com/kyiv/match-of-death

The National Centre for History Education: www.hyperhistory.org/index.php?option=displaypage&Itemid=714&op=page

CHAPTER 19: THE FUTBOL WARS

BOOKS

Alison Acker, *Honduras: The Making of a Banana Republic*, Between the Lines, Toronto, 1988

Thomas P. Anderson, *The War of the Dispossessed: Honduras and El Salvador 1969*, University of Nebraska Press, Lincoln, 1981

Robert Armstrong and Janet Shenk, *El Salvador: The Face of Revolution*, Pluto Press, London, 1982

William Durham, *Scarcity and Survival in Central America*, Stanford University Press, Palo Alto, 1979

El Salvador: A Dossier, CISCAC Publications, Sydney, 1981

Mary Martz, *Central American Soccer War*, Centre for International Studies, Ohio, 1978

James A. Morris, *Honduras: Caudillo Politics and Military Rulers*, Westview Press, Boulder, 1984

Alistair White, *El Salvador*, Ernest Benn Ltd, London, 1973

NEWSPAPERS

'Poetic Licence: The Soccer War Revisited', *Daily Times*, Pakistan, 13 June 2002

'El Salvador Is Off to War with Mustangs', *Australian*, 16 July 1969

'Honduran Planes Destroy Refinery in El Salvador', *Daily Telegraph*, London, 16 July 1969

'Salvador Defies OAS Ceasefire Order', *Australian*, 18 July 1969

'"Soccer War" Truce After Honduras Hits Back', *Daily Telegraph*, London, 18 July 1969

'Fighting on Three Fronts in "Soccer War"', *Daily Telegraph*, London, 19 July 1969

'Ceasefire "Broken" in Latin War', *Australian*, 21 July 1969

'Salvador Goes On Invading', *Australian*, 23 July 1969

INTERNET

General background:

http://en.wikipedia.org/wiki/Football_War

http://libcom.org/library/soccer-war-1969-el-salvador-honduras-kapuscinski

www.globalsecurity.org/military/world/war/elsalvador.htm

Statistics re Honduras versus El Salvador in World Cup soccer: www.fifa.com/worldfootball/statisticsandrecords/headtohead/team1=HON/team2=SLV/index.html

CHAPTER 20: THE KICK WITHOUT A BALL

BOOKS

Paul Mojzes, *Yugoslavian Inferno: Ethnoreligious Warfare in the Balkans*, Continuum, New York, 1995

JOURNALS

Allen L. Sack and Zeljan Suster, 'Soccer and Croatian Nationalism: A Prelude to War' (2000) *Journal of Sport and Social Issues*, Vol. 25, No. 3, 305

INTERNET

An account of the events: www.soccerphile.com/soccerphile/news/balkans-soccer/football-war.html

Ten-minute video of the riot: www.youtube.com/watch?v=uXr1Z-MiApo

CHAPTER 21: DEEDS NOT WORDS: EMILY DAVISON AND DERBY DAY

BOOKS

Fran Abrams, *Freedom's Cause: Lives of the Suffragettes*, Profile Books, London, 2003

Melanie Phillips, *The Ascent of Woman: A History of the Suffragette Movement and the Ideas Behind It*, Little, Brown Book Group, London, 2004

Andrew Rosen, *Rise Up Women!*, Routledge, London, 1974

NEWSPAPERS

'A Memorable Derby', *Times*, London, 5 June 1913

'The Derby and the Suffragette', *Guardian Unlimited*, 13 May 1913

'The Suffragette Face', *Daily Mirror*, 5 June 1913

CHAPTER 22: BATTLE OF THE SEXES

BOOKS

Billie Jean King and Frank Deford, *Billie Jean*, Viking Adult, New York, 1982

Selena Roberts, *A Necessary Spectacle: Billie Jean King, Bobby Riggs, and the Tennis Match That Leveled the Game*, Crown, New York, 2005

NEWSPAPERS

'Gladys Heldman, 81, a Leader in Promoting Women's Tennis', *New York Times*, 25 June 2003

INTERNET

www.billiejeanking.com/

Larry Schwartz, 'Billie Jean Won for All Women': http://espn.go.com/sportscentury/features/00016060.html

CHAPTER 23: SECOND SERVE

BOOKS

Renée Richards, *Second Serve*, Madison Books, Lanham, 1984

Renée Richards, *No Way Renée: The Second Half of My Notorious Life*, Simon & Schuster, New York, 2007

INTERNET

Renée Richards reflects on fame: http://www.reuters.com/article/domesticNews/idUSN1619986120070218

Renée Richards's story: www.nytimes.com/packages/html/sports/year_in_sports/08.27.html

CHAPTER 24: CURSE OF THE BLACK SOX

BOOKS

Richard Crepeau, *Baseball: America's Diamond Mind*, University of Nebraska Press, Lincoln, 1980

Fred Lieb, *Baseball as I Have Known It*, Coward, McCann & Geoghegan, New York, 1977

Leverett T. Smith, *The American Dream and the National Game*, Bowling Green University Popular Press, Bowling Green, 1975

J. G. Taylor Spink, *Judge Landis and Twenty-Five Years of Baseball*, Amereon, New York, 1947

NEWSPAPERS

'Eight White Sox Are Indicted on Charge of Fixing 1919 World Series', *New York Times*, 29 October 1920

'White Sox Players Are All Acquitted by Chicago Jury', *New York Times*, 3 August 1921

INTERNET

Background:

www.chicagohs.org/history/blacksox.html

www.1919blacksox.com/index2.htm

www.iht.com/articles/2005/10/19/sports/base.php

www.baseball-almanac.com/ws/yr1919ws.shtml

www.law.umkc.edu/faculty/projects/ftrials/blacksox/blacksox.html

CHAPTER 25: THE BODYLINE SERIES

BOOKS

Sir Donald Bradman, *Farewell to Cricket*, Hodder & Stoughton, London, 1950

David Firth, *Bodyline Autopsy*, ABC Books, Sydney, 2002

Harold Larwood and Kevin Perkins, *The Larwood Story*, WH Allan, London, 1965

Michael Page, *Bradman: The Illustrated Biography*, Macmillan, Australia, 1983

Roland Perry, *The Don*, Ironbark, Sydney, 1996

INTERNET

Background:

http://www.bbc.co.uk/dna/h2g2/A38208035

CHAPTER 26: UNDERHANDED TACTICS

BOOKS

Geoff Armstrong and Mark Gately, *People's Game: Australia in International One-Day Cricket*, Ironbark, Sydney, 2004

Richie Benaud, *World Series Cricket Cup*, Lansdowne Press, Sydney, 1981

Ian Brayshaw, *Chappell Era*, ABC Books, Sydney, 1984

David Lemmon, *Book of One-Day Internationals*, Hutchinson, London, 1983

Rod Marsh, *The Gloves of Irony*, Lansdowne Press, Sydney, 1982

Lynn McConnell, *McKechnie: Double All Black—An Autobiography*, Craigs, Invercargill, 1983

Adrian McGregor, *Greg Chappell*, Collins, Sydney, 1985

Ken Piesse, *Cricket's Greatest Scandals*, Penguin, 2001

Nigel Smith, *Kiwis Declare: Players Tell the Story of New Zealand Cricket*, Random House, Auckland, 1994

NEWSPAPERS

'Underarm Ball Sparks a Storm of Protest', *Australian*, 2 June 1981

'Trevor Chappell Reflects: "Why I Bowled Underarm"', *Sydney Morning Herald*, 26 March 1986

'Howzat? Not Cricket, Says MCG Crowd', *Age*, 2 June 1981

'Greg Chappell Rebuked—Repents', *Age*, 3 June 1981

INTERNET

History of One-Day Internationals—Australia v New Zealand: http://stats.
cricinfo.com/guru?sdb=filter;team=AUS&class=oditeam

History of Test matches—Australia v New Zealand: http://stats.cricinfo.com/guru?s
db=filter;team=AUS&class=testteam

History of Twenty20 international matches—Australia v New Zealand: http://stats.
cricinfo.com/guru?sdb=filter;team=AUS&class=t20iteam

Trevor Chappell's stats: http://content-aus.cricinfo.com/australia/content/
player/4561.html

CHAPTER 27: THE DIRTIEST RACE IN HISTORY

BOOKS

David Mottram, *Drugs in Sport*, Routledge, New York, 2005

Dick Pound, *Inside the Olympics*, Wiley, Canada, 2004

Michael Shannon, *Drugs in Australia: Drugs in Sport*, Binara Publishing, Carlton, 2002

Pat Sheil, *Olympic Babylon*, Pan Macmillan, Sydney, 1998

NEWSPAPERS

'The Most Corrupt Race Ever', *Observer*, 1 August 2004

'Drugs in Sport: A Brief History', *Observer*, 8 February 2004

INTERNET

http://www.cbc.ca/sports/indepth/drugs/

ACKNOWLEDGMENTS

Thank you to my Editor, Tricia Dearborn, whose expertise I greatly appreciated. Thank you to Ariana Klepac for all her work in developing the concept and helping to shape and inspire the book. Thank you to my in-house editor, Paul O' Beirne, for making the whole process so pleasurable. Thanks also to Nicole Saunders, Peter Barker, Chris Jones and Amanda Smith for their invaluable research. And to fellow writer, Carolyn Sally Jones, for her ongoing creative support. Special thanks finally to my grandmother who is a wonderful armchair referee for the Welsh rugby team.

IMAGE CREDITS

AAP images: page 256

AP images: pages 155, 197, 201, 205

Corbis: pages 23, 28, 48, 51, 55, 57, 62, 65, 70, 72, 82–83, 86–87, 89, 91, 92, 100, 105, 116, 146, 161, 181, 217, 225, 229, 235, 238, 240–241, 243

Getty images: back cover, front cover (right), pages 6, 10–11, 27, 37, 38, 41, 45, 75, 78, 97, 103, 108–109, 113, 118–119, 123, 128, 132, 135, 139, 140, 143, 146, 151, 165, 170–171, 175, 184–185, 202, 212–213, 215, 220–221, 232, 246, 249, 253, 260, 274–275, 277

iStock: pages 281–282

National Library of Australia: pages 17, 18–19

Newspix: pages 263, 266, 268

Photolibrary: front cover (left), pages 33, 271

Picture Desk / Art Archive: page 188

Pixsell: pages 178–179, 209, 210

State Library of New South Wales: page 13

INDEX

Published in 2009 by Pier 9, an imprint of Murdoch Books Pty Limited

Murdoch Books Australia
Pier 8/9
23 Hickson Road
Millers Point NSW 2000
Phone: +61 (0) 2 8220 2000
Fax: +61 (0) 2 8220 2558
www.murdochbooks.com.au

Murdoch Books UK Limited
Erico House, 6th Floor
93–99 Upper Richmond Road
Putney, London SW15 2TG
Phone: +44 (0) 20 8785 5995
Fax: +44 (0) 20 8785 5985
www.murdochbooks.co.uk

Book concept: Ariana Klepac and Jan Stradling
Publisher: Diana Hill
Editor: Tricia Dearborn
Designer: Simon Rattray

Text and design copyright © Murdoch Books Pty Limited 2009

National Library of Australia Cataloguing-in-Publication Data
Author: Stradling, Jan.
Title: More Than a Game / Jan Stradling.
ISBN: 9781741961355 (pbk.)
Notes: Includes index.
                Bibliography.
Subjects: Sports.
                Sports—Social aspects.
                Sports—Sociological aspects.

Dewey Number: 796

A catalogue record for this book is available from the British Library.

Printed on FSC-accredited paper in 2009. PRINTED IN CHINA.